A Catholic
Book of Hours
and Other Devotions

Other Loyola Press books
by William G. Storey

A Book of Advent and Christmas Prayers

A Book of Lenten Prayers

A Book of Marian Prayers
A Compilation of Marian Devotions from the
Second to the Twenty-First Century

The Complete Rosary
A Guide to Praying the Mysteries

Novenas
Prayers of Intercession and Devotion

A Prayer Book of Catholic Devotions
Praying the Seasons and Feasts of the Church Year

Prayers of Christian Consolation

A Beginner's Book of Prayer
An Introduction to Traditional Catholic Prayers

A Prayer Book for Eucharistic Adoration

The Little Office of Jesus and Mary

A Catholic
Book of Hours
and Other Devotions

Composed, edited, and translated by
William G. Storey
Professor Emeritus of Liturgy
University of Notre Dame

LOYOLA PRESS.
A JESUIT MINISTRY
Chicago

LOYOLAPRESS.
A JESUIT MINISTRY

3441 N. Ashland Avenue
Chicago, Illinois 60657
(800) 621-1008
www.loyolapress.com

© 2007 William G. Storey
All rights reserved

Unless otherwise noted, all the Scripture quotations are taken from the New Revised Standard Version of the Bible © 1989, Division of Christian Education of the National Council of Churches of Christ in the USA and are used by permission. All rights reserved. NRSV.

Twelve passages from Scripture are taken from the New American Bible with the revised psalms. Nashville: Thomas Nelson, 1987. NAB.

One passage is taken from The Good News Bible, Today's English Version. New York: The American Bible Society, 1992. TEV.

Unless otherwise noted all the psalms are taken from *Psalms for Prayer and Worship: A Complete Liturgical Psalter* by John Holbert et al. Nashville: Abingdon Press, 1992.

Twenty hymns from James Quinn, SJ, *Prayer for All Seasons*, 1994. Used by permission of Selah Publishing Co., Inc. North American agent. www.selahpub.com. Used by permission. License no. pending.

The Gospel canticles of Mary, Zachary, and Simeon, the Te Deum, the Gloria in Excelsis, the Gloria Patri, and the Lord's Prayer from *Praying Together: English Language Liturgical Consultation.* Nashville: Abingdon Press, 1988. ELLC.

Acknowledgments continued on page 384.

Interior design by Donna Antkowiak

Library of Congress Cataloging-in-Publication Data

A Catholic book of hours and other devotions / composed, edited, and translated by William G. Storey.
    p. cm.
  Includes bibliographical references.
  ISBN-13: 978-0-8294-2584-0
  ISBN-10: 0-8294-2584-5
  1. Catholic Church—Prayers and devotions. I. Storey, William George, 1923–
BX2149.2.C38 2007
242—dc22
                              2007012320

Printed in China
20 21 22 23 24 25 26 27 28 29 RRD/China 14 13 12 11 10 9 8 7 6 5

Contents

II: Devotions

Introduction

The Church presents the central teachings of Jesus in many ways, but never more fully than in its liturgy and popular devotions. The way the Church prays is the way it believes. Those who want to be Catholics in both head and heart need to activate in prayer each day the central themes of our religion. This is a book for men and women who desire to do this. It is a Book of Hours and of devotional prayer that expresses the very heart and soul of Catholic Christianity.

This book is divided into two parts. The first part is a Book of Hours that provides a framework of prayer in five "hours" spaced throughout the day. Two versions of the hours are provided: one we call "Hours of Jesus," which can be said on any day of the week, and a more extensive presentation of the five hours for each day separately. The second part of this book is a compilation of prayers expressing devotion to the Eucharist, Jesus, Mary, and the Holy Spirit.

A common heritage in popular Catholic devotion unites the two parts of this book. The Books of Hours have been staples of popular devotion for centuries. They arose in the Middle Ages as small portable prayer books that focused attention on the central medieval devotions: our Lady and her essential role in the Incarnation and our salvation, the faithful departed so in need of our prayers, the call to repentance and change of life in a turbulent world of sin, and the intercessory role of the saints in our life of spiritual warfare. These books were popular versions of the Divine

Office, which required numerous ministers, volumes, and forms of music for its celebration each day. Popular Books of Hours centered people's prayers on the great truths of the faith and could be prayed by individuals and small groups alike. Sections of these books could even be committed to memory.

Books of Hours have the same attractions today. These set forms of prayer are marked by their devotional character and their internal invariability. They contain some of the best of the long Catholic tradition of prayer, and they represent a depth of teaching and authentic religious feeling that binds us to all our fellow believers. Such prayer books are "orthodox," meaning they contain "correct praise." They show us how to pray well, correctly, in tune with the tradition, without deviating from the norms of belief and holiness—a reliable way of praying that leads us deeper into the fullness of the Church's liturgy, while avoiding expressions of purely individual attitudes and feelings.

Liturgy and Popular Devotion

The sacred liturgy is the chief and indispensable way of celebrating the divine mysteries of our religion. It takes precedence over all other kinds of Catholic prayer. However, popular devotions such as those in this book are compatible with and supplement the official liturgy. They deepen our personal prayer life and assist us in understanding the liturgy. They help us come to the liturgy with a heightened awareness of its beauty, content, and spiritual power to transform us in the likeness of Christ.

In fact, liturgy is continuously overflowing into devotions, and devotions are often adopted as parts of the liturgy. The liturgy and the spirit of prayer are too rich and lively to be confined to the official books. Sometimes a liturgical text is actually an expression of a once-popular devotion that matured to the point of entering the official liturgy. The Feasts of the Holy Trinity, of the Blessed Sacrament (Corpus Christi), of the Sacred Heart of Jesus, and of the Rosary are examples of popular devotions that entered the liturgy as special feasts. The liturgy never stops trying to appropriate and enjoy more fully what has been handed down from generation to generation. It is always developing fresh forms of prayer that express and articulate the Good News.

Thus, alongside the liturgy itself there is a treasured inheritance of popular devotions that is indispensable to the Christian life. Regular use of these devotions will result in a solid, personal conviction about the value of such prayer and its connection to the liturgy. Experience, conviction, and a deeper interior life will, in time and with the blessing of God, produce fresh forms of prayer and liturgy suitable to the third millennium.

The Congregation for Divine Worship and the Discipline of the Sacraments articulates the importance of popular devotions: "The history of the Western Church is marked by the flowering among the Christian people of multiple and varied expressions of simple and fervent faith in God, of love for Christ the Redeemer, of invocations of the Holy Spirit, of devotions to the Blessed Virgin Mary, of the veneration of the saints, of commitment to conversion and to fraternal charity."[1]

The Congregation continues:

Although not part of the Liturgy, they are considered to be in harmony with the spirit, the norms, and the rhythms of the Liturgy. Such pious exercises are inspired to some degree by the Liturgy and lead the Christian people to the

Liturgy. . . . Many of these exercises are part of the cultic patrimony of particular churches or religious families. . . . Popular piety has rightly been regarded as a "treasure of the people of God" and manifests a thirst for God known only to the poor and the humble, rendering them capable of a generosity and of sacrifice to the point of heroism in testifying to the faith while displaying an acute sense of the profound attributes of God. . . . It also generates interior attitudes otherwise rarely seen to the same degree: patience, an awareness of the Cross in everyday life, detachment, openness to others, and devotion. . . .

Popular piety is also characterized by a great variety and richness of bodily gestures and symbolic expressions: kissing or touching of images, relics and sacred objects; pilgrimages, processions, . . . kneeling and prostrating; wearing of medals and badges. These are direct and simple ways of giving external expression to the heart and to one's commitment to live the Christian life.[2]

The Books of Hours and other devotions presented here use psalms, canticles, and readings from the Bible, traditional prayers from many sources, and the pious patterns of prayer from many different centuries and backgrounds. This approach is in keeping with the instruction of the Church: "While drawn up in terms less exacting than those employed for the prayers of the Liturgy, devotional prayers and formulae should be inspired by Sacred Scripture, the Liturgy, the Fathers of the Church and the Magisterium, and concord with the Church's faith."[3]

The Home Altar

Another characteristic of popular devotion is the home altar. Long before Christians built churches for public prayer, they worshipped daily in their homes. In order to orient their prayer (to orient means literally "to turn toward the East"), they painted or hung a cross on the east wall of their main room. This practice was in keeping with ancient Jewish tradition ("Look to the east, Jerusalem," Baruch 4:36); Christians turned in that direction when they prayed morning and evening and at other times. This expression of their undying belief in the coming again of Jesus was united to their conviction that the cross, "the sign of the Son of Man," would appear in the eastern heavens on his return (see Matthew 24:30).

Building on that ancient custom, devout Catholics often have a home altar, shrine, or prayer corner containing a crucifix, religious pictures (icons), a Bible, holy water, lights, and flowers as part of the essential furniture of a Christian home. Often erected on a shelf or table in the living or dining room, the family assembles there before or after meals at day's beginning and at day's ending. Many Catholics keep a perpetual candle burning on the home altar to remind themselves of Christ's promise: "Where two or three are gathered in my name, I am there among them" (Matthew 18:20).

How to Use This Prayer Book

Though many people who pray with this prayer book will probably do so in private and by themselves, it may also be used with family, friends, in prayer groups, and at church meetings.

Some people may be able to fit in all five times of prayer each day, while others will have to adopt an abbreviated schedule, praying perhaps the morning and evening prayers (the cardinal hours), or just Mattins, the Night Prayer (Compline), or the Noonday Hour. In any case, even one hour will provide a taste, at least, of the mystery of the day.

Before beginning any of these devotions, recall that God is present everywhere and hears us always, in our words and our thoughts. Also recall that by holy baptism we are the shrines of the Holy Spirit, who calls out without ceasing: "Abba, dear Father!" (see Mark 14:36; Romans 8:15; Galatians 4:6).

Mindful of these central theological principles, we pause for a few moments of silence before starting our prayer. The pauses that are suggested elsewhere in the text are equally helpful. In private recitation we may stop briefly whenever we feel called to dwell on phrases that particularly move our minds and hearts.

Each sacred text should be recited with the attention and devotion it deserves. We are addressing the Maker of the universe and cannot afford to be casual about it! The prophets, priests, and saints who put these texts at our disposal urge us to pray both with the lips and with the heart.

People who pray alone may sit, stand, or kneel as they see fit, but they must remember that they do so in the presence of the whole court of heaven.

People who pray in families or other groups may adopt certain postures—especially for the hours—that facilitate common prayer: standing for hymns, psalms, and canticles; sitting for readings and meditation; kneeling for intercessions and the final prayers. Change of posture is often helpful to recollection and attention.

Gestures—the sign of the cross, bowing at references to the Holy Trinity, hands extended during the Lord's Prayer, a kiss of peace at the end of the devotions, and others—are very helpful to both common and private prayer.

Group Prayer

Prayer in families or other small groups is facilitated by designating both a leader of prayer and a reader for the Scripture lessons when they are present.

The leader should
❖ call the group to silent prayer and initiate the vocal prayer;
❖ alternate the stanzas of the hymns, psalms, and canticles with the group;
❖ call for silent or spontaneous prayer where it is indicated after psalms, readings, or at the close of the intercessions;
❖ begin the first few words of the antiphon (refrain) before a psalm or canticle and lead its repetition at the close or even between every stanza;
❖ lead the petitions of a litany or of intercessions;
❖ pray the closing prayers;
❖ encourage the group to respond to the prayers and to voice their petitions during the pause for intercessory prayer.

The reader reads the Scripture lessons aloud.

A note on the name of God: Some of the biblical canticles used in this book contain the unutterable name of God in the Hebrew (its letters in English are

YHWH). The name derives from the verb *to be* and indicates the God who was and is and will be present to the human race, and in a particular way to the people of the covenant. In this prayer book, this unutterable name is represented by the word LORD.

A note on symbols: Throughout the text the cross [†] indicates that those praying should make the sign of the cross. The tilde [~] followed by text in small capital letters indicates a response by a group or a person other than the leader of prayer. For example: ~AMEN or ~HOSANNA IN THE HIGHEST!

These forms of prayer might be unfamiliar to some people, but a bit of patience and attention will show how helpful they are to devotional growth. Devotions are a special gift of the Holy Spirit that lead us deeper and deeper into the mystery of Christ and the communion of his Blessed Mother and of all the saints in glory.

I
A Book of Hours

The Hours of Jesus-Messiah

This Little Office of Jesus is a devotion of five "hours" for each day that may be used at any time of the year. It is modeled on the Books of Hours, which have been so popular for lay Catholics from the twelfth century to the present. The five hours in this office are focused on the principal events in the life of Jesus: his incarnation, baptism, public ministry, passion and death, resurrection, ascension, and great return.

This devotion may be said in its entirety in one day or broken up by section to be used when time allows.

Mattins   **The Word Made Flesh**

"Deservedly did the Prophets announce, that He'd been born; the Heavens and the Angels, that He'd been born. He lay in a manger, and yet the world rested in his hands. As an infant, He was wordless, and yet He was the Word Itself. Him whom the heavens couldn't huddle, the lap of a single woman could easily cuddle. She was toting about on her hip Him Who carries her about the universe. Her breasts were

running, but they were enriching the Bread of
Life."

St. Augustine of Hippo Regius (354–430),
Sermons to the People[4]

"Through this union of the divine nature with
the human nature, God was made human and
humanity was made God."

St. Catherine of Siena (1347–1380),
The Dialogue[5]

LEADER: O Lord, † open my lips,
ALL: ~AND MY MOUTH WILL DECLARE YOUR
PRAISE.
LEADER: Glory to God in the highest,
ALL: ~AND PEACE TO GOD'S PEOPLE ON EARTH.

PSALM 100   A CALL TO PRAYER

ANTIPHON Come, LET US ADORE JESUS THE
MESSIAH,
WHO WAS BORN OF THE VIRGIN MARY.

Make a joyful noise to the Lord, all the lands!
Serve the Lord with gladness!
Come into God's presence with singing!

~COME, LET US ADORE JESUS THE MESSIAH,
WHO WAS BORN OF THE VIRGIN MARY.

Know that the Lord, who made us, is God.
We are the Lord's;
the sheep of God's pasture.

~Come, let us adore Jesus the Messiah,
who was born of the Virgin Mary.

Enter God's gates with thanksgiving,
and God's courts with praise!
Give thanks and bless God's name!

~Come, let us adore Jesus the Messiah,
who was born of the Virgin Mary.

For the Lord is good;
God's steadfast love endures for ever,
God's faithfulness to all generations.

~Come, let us adore Jesus the Messiah,
who was born of the Virgin Mary.

Glory to the Father, and to the Son,
and to the Holy Spirit:
as it was in the beginning, is now,
and will be for ever. Amen.

~Come, let us adore Jesus the Messiah,
who was born of the Virgin Mary.

Hymn

O glorious Lady, throned in rest,
Amidst the starry host above,
Who gave sweet nurture from your breast
To God, with pure maternal love;

O gate, through which has passed the King,
O hall, whence Light shone through the gloom:
The ransomed nations praise and sing
Life given from the Virgin's womb.

Lord Jesus, Virgin-born, to you
Eternal praise and laud are due
With whom the Father we adore
And Spirit blest for evermore. Amen.[6]

PSALM 2:1–11   THE LORD'S ANOINTED

ANTIPHON The Lord's decree: "YOU ARE MY SON,
TODAY I HAVE BEGOTTEN YOU."

Why do the nations conspire,
and the people plot in vain?
The kings of the earth rise up,
and the rulers take counsel together
against God and God's anointed, saying,
"Let us burst their bonds,
and cast their cords from us."

The One who sits in the heavens laughs,
and holds them in derision.
Then God will speak to them in anger,
and terrify them in fury, saying,
"I have set my king on Zion, my holy hill."

I will tell the decree of the Lord
who said to me: "You are my son,
today I have begotten you.
Ask of me, and I will make the nations your
        heritage,
and the ends of the earth your possession.
You shall break them with a rod of iron,
and dash them in pieces like a potter's vessel."

Now, therefore, O kings, be wise;
be warned, O rulers of the earth.
Serve the Lord with fear and trembling;
humble yourselves before the Lord.

ANTIPHON THE LORD'S DECREE: "YOU ARE MY SON,
TODAY I HAVE BEGOTTEN YOU."

PSALM PRAYER

LEADER: Let us pray *(pause for quiet prayer):*

God and Father,
we praise you for our original dignity
and for our restoration in Christ.
Your Son stooped to our lowly condition
in order to present us to you
as adopted children and heirs of the kingdom.
Blest be the name of Jesus, now and for ever!
ALL: ~AMEN.

READING   **THE SON OF GOD**   **ROMANS 1:1–4**
Paul, a servant of Jesus Christ, called to be an
apostle, set apart for the gospel of God, which
he promised beforehand through his prophets
in the holy scriptures, the gospel concerning his
Son, who was descended from David according
to the flesh and was declared to be Son of God
with power according to the spirit of holiness by
resurrection from the dead, Jesus Christ our Lord.

MEDITATION

RESPONSE

LEADER: The Word became flesh, alleluia!

ALL: ~AND LIVED AMONG US, ALLELUIA!

CANTICLE OF THE CHURCH

We praise you, O God,
we acclaim you as Lord;
all creation worships you,
the Father everlasting.

To you all angels, all the powers of heaven,
the cherubim and seraphim, sing in endless praise:
Holy, holy, holy Lord, God of power and might,
heaven and earth are full of your glory.

The glorious company of apostles praise you.
The noble fellowship of prophets praise you.
The white-robed army of martyrs praise you.

Throughout the world the holy Church acclaims
you:
Father, of majesty unbounded,
your true and only Son, worthy of all praise,
the Holy Spirit, advocate and guide.

You, Christ, are the king of glory,
the eternal Son of the Father.
When you took our flesh to set us free
you humbly chose the Virgin's womb.

You overcame the sting of death
and opened the kingdom of heaven to all believers.
You are seated at God's right hand in glory.
We believe that you will come to be our judge.

Come then, Lord, and help your people,
bought with the price of your own blood,
and bring us with your saints
to glory everlasting.

St. Nicetas of Remesiana (ca. 335–ca. 414),

Te Deum laudamus[7]

CLOSING PRAYER

O God, eternal majesty, whose ineffable Word
the immaculate Virgin received through the
   message of an Angel
and so became the dwelling-place of divinity,
filled with the light of the Holy Spirit,
grant, we pray, that by her example
we may in humility hold fast to your will.
Through our Lord Jesus Christ, your Son,
who lives and reigns with you in the unity of the
   Holy Spirit,
one God, for ever and ever.
ALL: ~AMEN.[8]

May Christ, Son of God and Son of Mary,
† bless us and keep us.
ALL: ~AMEN.

Morning Prayer   The Baptism of Jesus

"Christ descends into the Jordan's waters and we
descend with him; he steps forth from the waters
and we with him. The old Adam is buried in the
waters and Jordan's waters are made holy for the
sake of baptism. When the Baptist hesitated about
baptizing him, Jesus said, 'Let it be so now to
fulfill all righteousness.' So spoke a candle to the
Sun, a voice to the very Word of God."

St. Gregory Nazianzen, *Oratio in Sancta Lumina*[9]

O God, † come to my assistance.
~O LORD, MAKE HASTE TO HELP ME.
Jesus saw the heavens torn apart
~AND THE SPIRIT DESCENDING LIKE A DOVE IN
    BODILY FORM.

HYMN
I bind unto myself today
The strong name of the Trinity,
By invocation of the same
The Three in One and One in Three.

I bind this day to me forever
By power of faith, Christ's incarnation;
His baptism in the Jordan river,
His death on the Cross for our salvation;
His bursting from the spicèd tomb,
His riding up the heavenly way,
His coming at the day of doom
I bind unto myself today.

I bind unto myself the name,
The strong name of the Trinity,
By invocation of the same,
The Three in One and One in Three.
Of whom all nature has creation,
Eternal Father, Spirit, Word:
Praise to the Lord of my salvation,
Salvation is of Christ the Lord.[10]

Psalm 29   God's Majestic Voice

ANTIPHON The voice of the LORD IS FULL OF
    MAJESTY!

Ascribe to the Lord, O heavenly beings,
ascribe to the Lord glory and strength.
Ascribe to the Lord a glorious name;
worship the Lord in holy splendor.

The voice of the Lord is upon the waters;
the God of glory thunders,
the Lord, upon many waters.
The voice of the Lord is powerful,
the voice of the Lord is full of majesty.

The voice of the Lord breaks the cedars,
the Lord breaks the cedars of Lebanon.
The Lord makes Lebanon skip like a calf,
and Sirion like a wild young ox.

The voice of the Lord flashes forth flames of fire.
The voice of the Lord shakes the wilderness,
shakes the wilderness of Kadesh.

The voice of the Lord makes the oaks to whirl,
and strips the forests bare;
and in God's temple all cry, "Glory!"

The Lord sits enthroned over the flood;
the Lord sits enthroned as Ruler forever.
May the Lord give strength to God's people!
May the Lord bless the people with peace!

Antiphon The voice of the Lord is full of
majesty!

Psalm Prayer

Let us pray *(pause for quiet prayer):*

God of might and majesty,
in your incarnate Son you speak the truth
that the world awaits.
May his divine voice call us to worship
the splendor of your holy Name
and humble us before your might
until we all shout "Glory" in your temple.
Blest be the name of Jesus, now and for ever!
~Amen.

Reading **The Baptism of Jesus** **Mark 1:9–15**
Jesus came from Nazareth of Galilee and was
baptized by John in the Jordan. And just as he was
coming up out of the water, he saw the heavens
torn apart and the Spirit descending like a dove
on him. And a voice came from heaven, "You are
my Son, the Beloved; with you I am well pleased."

And the Spirit immediately drove him out into the wilderness. He was in the wilderness forty days, tempted by Satan; and he was with the wild beasts; and the angels waited on him.

MEDITATION

RESPONSE

Prepare the way of the Lord,
~MAKE HIS PATHS STRAIGHT.

THE CANTICLE OF ZACHARY   **LUKE 1:68–79**[11]

ANTIPHON You have raised up for us A MIGHTY
        SAVIOR, ALLELUIA!

Blessed † are you, Lord, the God of Israel,
you have come to your people and set them free.
You have raised up for us a mighty Savior,
born of the house of your servant David.

Through your holy prophets, you promised of old
    to save us from our enemies,
    from the hands of all who hate us,
    to show mercy to our forebears,
    and to remember your holy covenant.

This was the oath you swore to our father
        Abraham:
    to set us free from the hands of our enemies,
    free to worship you without fear,
    holy and righteous before you,
    all the days of our life.

And you, child, shall be called the prophet of the
     Most High,
for you will go before the Lord to prepare the way,
to give God's people knowledge of salvation
by the forgiveness of their sins.

In the tender compassion of our God
the dawn from on high shall break upon us,
to shine on those who dwell in darkness
     and the shadow of death,
and to guide our feet into the way of peace.

Glory to the Holy and Undivided Trinity:
now and always and for ever and ever. Amen.

ANTIPHON YOU HAVE RAISED UP FOR US A MIGHTY
     SAVIOR, ALLELUIA!

LITANY

By the mystery of Christ's baptism in the Jordan
     river:
~WE PRAISE YOU, O GOD.

By his consecration as Prophet, Priest, and King:
~WE PRAISE YOU, O GOD.

By the revelation of the Holy Trinity: Father, Son,
     and Holy Spirit:
~WE PRAISE YOU, O GOD.

By the sanctification of water for our baptismal
     rebirth:
~WE PRAISE YOU, O GOD.

By our death to sin and our call to holiness:
~WE PRAISE YOU, O GOD.

(Pause for special intentions.)

By the prayers of the great Mother of God,
Mary most holy, and of all the saints in glory:
~WE PRAISE YOU, O GOD.

THE LORD'S PRAYER
Lord, have mercy.
~CHRIST, HAVE MERCY. LORD, HAVE MERCY.

Our Father in heaven,
~HALLOWED BE YOUR NAME,
YOUR KINGDOM COME,
YOUR WILL BE DONE,
ON EARTH AS IN HEAVEN.
GIVE US TODAY OUR DAILY BREAD.
FORGIVE US OUR SINS
AS WE FORGIVE THOSE WHO SIN AGAINST US.
SAVE US FROM THE TIME OF TRIAL
AND DELIVER US FROM EVIL.
FOR THE KINGDOM AND THE POWER AND THE
GLORY ARE YOURS
NOW AND FOREVER. AMEN.[12]

CLOSING PRAYER
Gracious Father,
by your voice from heaven,
the dove in bodily form,
and your Son immersed in the Jordan,

you revealed the mystery of the Holy Trinity
and the power of baptism in that holy Name.
May we who share in Christ's humanity
come to share in his divinity,
to your honor and glory,
now and for ever.
~Amen.

May the blessing of almighty God,
the Father, † the Son, and the Holy Spirit,
descend upon us and remain with us for ever.
~Amen.

Noonday   Jesus' Public Ministry

"We fell miserably, God descended mercifully, we fell pridefully, God descended graciously."

St. Augustine of Hippo Regius,
Sermo 2, De Tempore 13[13]

Our help † is in the name of the Lord,
~The Creator of heaven and earth.

Blessed is anyone
~Who takes no offense at me.

Hymn

Hail to the Lord's anointed!
Great David's greater Son;
Hail, in the time appointed,
His reign on earth begun!
He comes to break oppression,
To set the captives free,
To take away transgression,
And rule in equity.

He comes in succor speedy
To those who suffer wrong;
To help the poor and needy,
And bid the weak be strong;
To give them songs for sighing,
Their darkness turn to light,
Whose souls, condemned and dying,
Were precious in his sight.

He shall come down like showers
Upon the fruitful earth,
And love, joy, hope, like flowers
Spring in his path to birth;
Before him on the mountains,
Shall Peace, the herald, go;
And righteousness, in fountains
From hill to valley flow.

O'er every foe victorious,
He on his throne shall rest,
From age to age more glorious,
All-blessing and all-blest;
The tide of time shall never
His covenant remove;
His name shall stand for ever;
That name to us is Love.[14]

PSALM 19   CHRIST, THE SUN OF RIGHTEOUSNESS

ANTIPHON Christ is the bridegroom leaving his
    chamber,
THE STRONG MAN RUNNING HIS COURSE WITH JOY.

The heavens are telling the glory of God;
and the firmament proclaims God's handiwork.
Day to day pours forth speech,
and night to night declares knowledge.

There is no speech, nor are there words;
their voice is not heard;
yet their voice goes out through all the earth,
and their words to the end of the world.

In them God has sent a tent for the sun,
which comes forth like a bridegroom leaving his
      chamber,
and runs its course with joy like a strong man.
Its rising is from the end of the heavens,
and its circuit to the end of them,
and nothing is hid from its heat.

ANTIPHON CHRIST IS THE BRIDEGROOM LEAVING
      HIS CHAMBER,
THE STRONG MAN RUNNING HIS COURSE WITH JOY.

PSALM PRAYER

Let us pray *(pause for quiet prayer):*

Lord Christ, our Sun of righteousness,
obedient to the will and designs of your Father,
you came among us like a bridegroom
emerging from his bridal chamber
and like a strong man rejoicing to run his course.
Inspire your servants and friends
to understand and acclaim your holy Gospel
so that you may shine on the whole world
and so fulfill all righteousness.
Blest be Jesus, true God and true Man!
~AMEN.

READING **JESUS, TEACHER AND HEALER** **MATTHEW 4:23–25**

Jesus went throughout Galilee, teaching in their
synagogues and proclaiming the good news
of the kingdom and curing every disease and

every sickness among the people. So his fame
spread throughout all Syria, and they brought to
him all the sick, those who were afflicted with
various diseases and pains, demoniacs, epileptics,
and paralytics, and he cured them. And great
crowds followed him from Galilee, the Decapolis,
Jerusalem, Judea, and from beyond the Jordan.

MEDITATION

RESPONSE
Blessed is the One who comes in the name of the
    Lord,
~HOSANNA IN THE HIGHEST!

THE CANTICLE OF
JEREMIAH THE PROPHET   JEREMIAH 7:2–7[15]

ANTIPHON Bring forth fruits WORTHY OF
    REPENTANCE.

Change the way you are living
and the things you are doing,
and I will let you go on living here.

Stop believing those deceitful words,
"We are safe! This is the LORD's Temple,
this is the LORD's temple, this is the LORD's
    temple!"

Change the way you are living
and stop doing the things you are doing.
Be fair in your treatment of one another.

Stop taking advantage of aliens, orphans, and
   widows.
Stop killing innocent people in this land.
Stop worshiping other gods, for that will destroy
   you.

If you change, I will let you go on living here
in the land which I gave your ancestors
as a permanent possession.

Glory to the Holy and Undivided Trinity:
now and always and for ever and ever. Amen.

ANTIPHON BRING FORTH FRUITS WORTHY OF
   REPENTANCE.

LITANY
For the glory of the Gospel in every place, we
   pray:
~LORD, HEAR OUR PRAYER.

For the grace of sound preaching in every age, we
   pray:
~LORD, HEAR OUR PRAYER.

For the gift of healing for our souls and bodies, we
   pray:
~LORD, HEAR OUR PRAYER.

For good news for the poor and afflicted, we pray:
~LORD, HEAR OUR PRAYER.

For the spiritual and corporal works of mercy, we
   pray:
~LORD, HEAR OUR PRAYER.

For those who have fallen asleep in Christ, we
    pray:
~LORD, HEAR OUR PRAYER.

(Pause for special intentions.)

For the intercession of the great Mother of God,
    Mary most holy, and of all the saints in glory,
    we pray:
~LORD, HEAR OUR PRAYER.

CLOSING PRAYER
Lord Jesus, Son of the living God,
as you traveled throughout Galilee and Judea
declaring the Good News of the kingdom,
you cured every kind of disease and sickness,
giving sight to the blind, sanity to the possessed,
forgiveness to repentant sinners,
and even new life to the dead.
By your power and great mercy,
continue your mission on this earth
and make your Church a foretaste
of the full and everlasting reign of God.
Blest be the name of Jesus, now and for ever!
~AMEN.

Let us bless the Lord.
~THANKS BE TO GOD.

"'One of the soldiers pierced Jesus' side with a spear, and at once blood and water came out' (John 19:34). John says *pierced* or *opened* to show that the sacraments are available through the open doors of his heart from which they flow. The blood that flows from his heart washes away all our sins. The water that flows with the blood signifies baptism that remits all sin. His open side recalls the creation of Eve taken from Adam's side; Christ, the second Adam, bowed his head on the cross, fell asleep in death and brought forth his bride, the Church, from his side. Nothing is as purifying as this blood! Nothing is as health-giving as this wound!"

St. Augustine of Hippo Regius,
Commentary on John, 120[16]

O God, ✝ come to my assistance.
~O LORD, MAKE HASTE TO HELP ME.

We adore you, O Christ, and we bless you,
~FOR BY YOUR HOLY CROSS YOU HAVE REDEEMED
   THE WORLD.

HYMN
There is a green hill far away,
Outside a city wall,
Where our dear Lord was crucified
Who died to save us all.

We may not know, we cannot tell,
What pains he had to bear,
But we believe it was for us
He hung and suffered there.

He died that we might be forgiven,
He died to make us good,
That we might go at last to heaven,
Saved by his precious blood.

There was no other good enough
To pay the price of sin,
He only could unlock the gate
Of heaven and let us in.

O dearly, dearly has he loved!
And we must love him too,
And trust in his redeeming blood,
And try his works to do.[17]

PSALM 54　　THE GODLESS PLOT JESUS' DEATH

ANTIPHON　God is my savior, GOD ALONE.

Save me, O God, by your name,
and vindicate me by your might.
Hear my prayer, O God;
listen to the words of my mouth.

For the insolent have risen against me,
the ruthless seek my life;
they do not set God before them.

But surely, God is my helper;
the Lord is the upholder of my life.

God will repay my enemies for their evil.
In your faithfulness, put an end to them.

With a freewill offering I will sacrifice to you;
I will give thanks to your name, O Lord, for it is
    good.
For God has delivered me from every trouble,
and my eye has looked in triumph on my enemies.

ANTIPHON GOD IS MY SAVIOR, GOD ALONE.

PSALM PRAYER

Let us pray *(pause for quiet prayer)*:

Lord Jesus, suffering servant of God,
you submitted to the inscrutable will of God
and laid down your life for us.
By your precious death and burial,
lift us out of our sins
and give us the grace to embrace your Gospel
that teaches us to revere God's endless love for us.
Your reign is a reign for all ages.
~AMEN.

READING **JESUS DIES ON THE CROSS** **MARK 15:33–34B, 37–39**

When it was noon, darkness came over the whole
land until three in the afternoon. At three o'clock
Jesus cried out with a loud voice, "My God, my
God, why have you forsaken me?" Then Jesus gave
a loud cry and breathed his last. And the curtain
of the temple was torn in two, from top to bottom.
Now when the centurion, who stood facing him,

saw that in this way he breathed his last, he said, "Truly this man was God's Son!"

MEDITATION

RESPONSE

Jesus suffered under Pontius Pilate;

~HE WAS CRUCIFIED, DIED, AND WAS BURIED.

THE CANTICLE OF THE VIRGIN MARY   LUKE 1:46–55

ANTIPHON Thanks be to God, WHO HAS GIVEN US
THE VICTORY
THROUGH THE CROSS OF CHRIST OUR SAVIOR,
ALLELUIA!

My soul † proclaims the greatness of the Lord,
my spirit rejoices in God my Savior,
for you, Lord, have looked with favor on your
lowly servant.

From this day all generations will call me blessed:
you, the Almighty, have done great things for
me
and holy is your name.
You have mercy on those who fear you,
from generation to generation.

You have shown strength with your arm
and scattered the proud in their conceit,
casting down the mighty from their thrones
and lifting up the lowly.
You have filled the hungry with good things
and sent the rich away empty.

You have come to the aid of your servant Israel,
to remember the promise of mercy,
the promise made to our forebears,
to Abraham and his children forever.

Glory to the Holy and Undivided Trinity:
now and always and for ever and ever. Amen.

Antiphon Thanks be to God, who has given
us the victory
through the cross of Christ our Savior,
alleluia!

LITANY OF THE SACRED PASSION
Jesus was handed over to Pilate for judgment:
~O Savior, save us!

Jesus was flogged by a band of pitiless soldiers:
~O Savior, save us!

Jesus was mocked and vilified by the whole
cohort:
~O Savior, save us!

Jesus was burdened with the cross of shame:
~O Savior, save us!

Jesus was fastened to the cross by spikes
through his hands and feet:
~O Savior, save us!

Jesus was ridiculed, scoffed at, and mocked
for three long hours on the cross:
~O Savior, save us!

Jesus was accompanied on the cross by his mother,
Mary Magdalene, and his beloved disciple:
~O Savior, save us!

Jesus was taken down from the cross
and laid in noble Joseph's tomb:
~O Savior, save us!

(Pause for special intentions.)

By the tears and prayers of the Mother of Sorrows
and her companions:
~O Savior, save us!

THE LORD'S PRAYER
Lord, have mercy.
~Christ, have mercy. Lord, have mercy.

Our Father in heaven,
~hallowed be your name,
your kingdom come,
your will be done,
on earth as in heaven.
Give us today our daily bread.
Forgive us our sins
as we forgive those who sin against us.
Save us from the time of trial
and deliver us from evil.
For the kingdom and the power and the
glory are yours
now and forever. Amen.

CLOSING PRAYER

Lord Jesus Christ, Son of the living God,
set your passion, your cross, and your death
between your judgment and our souls,
now and at the hour of our death.
In your great goodness,
grant mercy and grace to the living
and forgiveness and rest to the dead,
to the church and to the nations,
peace and concord,
and to us sinners,
life and glory without end.
~AMEN.[18]

By his five precious wounds,
may Christ our Lord ✝ protect us and keep us.
~AMEN.

"Our Redeemer's visible presence has passed over into the sacraments."

St. Leo the Great, *Sermon on the Lord's Ascension*

Light and peace ✝ in Jesus Christ our Lord.
~THANKS BE TO GOD.

Christ is risen, alleluia!
~HE IS RISEN INDEED, ALLELUIA!

HYMN

The head that once was crowned with thorns
Is crowned with glory now;
A royal diadem adorns
The mighty Victor's brow.

The highest place that heaven affords
Is his, is his by right,
The King of Kings and Lord of Lords
And heaven's eternal Light;

The joy of all who dwell above,
The joy of all below,
To whom he manifests his love,
And grants his name to know.

The Cross he bore is life and health,
Though shame and death to him;
His people's hope, his people's wealth,
Their everlasting theme.[19]

PSALM 67   THE GLORIOUS CROSS

ANTIPHON Christ has risen from the dead,
CONQUERING DEATH BY HIS DEATH,
AND BRINGING LIFE TO THOSE IN THE GRAVE!

O God, be gracious to us and bless us
and make your face shine upon us,
that your ways may be known upon earth,
your saving power among all nations.

Let the peoples praise you, O God,
let all the peoples praise you!

Let the nations be glad and sing for joy,
for you judge the nations with equity
and guide the nations upon earth.

Let the peoples praise you, O God,
let all the peoples praise you!

The earth has yielded its increase;
God, our God, has blessed us.
May God bless us;
let all the ends of the earth fear God!

Let the peoples praise you, O God,
let all the peoples praise you!

ANTIPHON CHRIST HAS RISEN FROM THE DEAD,
CONQUERING DEATH BY HIS DEATH,
AND BRINGING LIFE TO THOSE IN THE GRAVE!

PSALM PRAYER
Let us pray *(pause for quiet prayer)*:

Holy, mighty, and immortal God,
you raised your dear Son out of death
as the first fruits of our salvation.
By the power of his glorious resurrection,
raise our hearts to things that are above
that we may live with him and all his saints,
for ever and ever.
~Amen.

READING   **NEW BIRTH**   **1 PETER 1:3–5**

Blessed be the God and Father of our Lord Jesus
Christ! By his great mercy he has given us a new
birth into a living hope through the resurrection
of Jesus Christ from the dead, and into an
inheritance that is imperishable, undefiled, and
unfading, kept in heaven for you, who are being
protected by the power of God through faith for a
salvation ready to be revealed in the last time.

MEDITATION

RESPONSE

Christ has risen from the tomb, alleluia!
~WHO FOR OUR SAKE HUNG ON THE CROSS,
    ALLELUIA!

THE CANTICLE OF REVELATION   **REVELATION 1:4–7**

ANTIPHON O death, where is your victory?
O DEATH, WHERE IS YOUR STING?

Grace and peace from him who is
and who was and who is to come,

and from the seven spirits
who are before his throne,
and from Jesus Christ, the faithful witness,
the firstborn from the dead,
and the ruler of the kings of the earth.

To him who loves us and freed us
from our sins by his blood,
and made us to be a kingdom,
priests serving his God and Father,
to him be glory and dominion
forever and ever. Amen.

Look! He is coming with the clouds;
every eye will see him,
even those who pierced him;
and on his account
all the tribes of the earth will wail. Amen.

Glory to the Holy and Undivided Trinity:
now and always and for ever and ever. Amen.

ANTIPHON O DEATH, WHERE IS YOUR VICTORY?
O DEATH, WHERE IS YOUR STING?

LITANY

We adore your five precious wounds
    displayed on the cross for our salvation:
~LORD, HAVE MERCY.

We adore you descending among the dead
    to enlighten and release them:
~LORD, HAVE MERCY.

We adore your appearances to Mary Magdalene,
   the apostle of the apostles:
~LORD, HAVE MERCY.

We adore you for appearing to your chosen
      witnesses
   and speaking about the kingdom of God for
      forty days:
~LORD, HAVE MERCY.

We adore you ascending to your Father and our
      Father,
   to your God and our God:
~LORD, HAVE MERCY.

We adore you coming in glory to judge the living
   and the dead:
~LORD, HAVE MERCY.

(Pause for special intentions.)

We adore you in union with the great Mother
      of God, Mary most holy,
   and with all the saints in glory:
~LORD, HAVE MERCY.

CLOSING PRAYER
Heavenly Father,
you raised Jesus your Son from the dead
and made him sit at your right hand.
Rescue us from our sins,
bring us to new life in Christ,
raise us up with Christ,

and give us a place with him in heaven,
in the same Christ Jesus our Lord.
ALL: ~AMEN.

By his dazzling resurrection,
may Christ **†** conduct us to our heavenly home.
ALL: ~AMEN.

CONCLUDING ANTHEM TO THE MOTHER OF GOD
We turn to you for protection,
HOLY MOTHER OF GOD.
LISTEN TO OUR PRAYERS
AND HELP US IN OUR NEEDS.
SAVE US FROM EVERY DANGER,
GLORIOUS AND BLESSED VIRGIN.[20]

OR THIS ANTHEM FOR EASTERTIDE
Rejoice, O Virgin Mary, alleluia!
FOR THE SON YOU BORE, ALLELUIA!
HAS ARISEN AS HE PROMISED, ALLELUIA!
PRAY FOR US TO GOD OUR FATHER, ALLELUIA![21]

(The Kiss of Peace may be exchanged after Night Prayer.)

The Christian Week

This week of devotions is inspired by the Books of Hours that arose in the Middle Ages. Books of Hours were collections of devotions that supplemented the great Office, or "Work of God" as it was called, that was prayed in monasteries. By the thirteenth century these devotions were gathered into small pocket books for the laity and had the advantage of being almost invariable each day, fairly brief compared to the monastic Office, and often in the vernacular language. They became best sellers in the Middle Ages, both in illuminated gift editions for the rich and famous, and in simple, inexpensive formats for almost any literate Christian.

A particular inspiration for the prayers that follow is John Plummer's edition of *The Hours of Catherine of Cleves* (New York: George Braziller, 1966). Similar to the famous Cleves book, each day of the week in these hours is focused on a theme: the Resurrection of our Lord on Sunday, the Holy Spirit on Monday, the Holy Souls on Tuesday, All Saints on Wednesday, the Blessed Sacrament on Thursday, the Holy Cross on Friday, and the Blessed Virgin Mary on Saturday. These traditional themes derive from both ancient and medieval sources.

From the earliest times, Sunday was devoted to the resurrection of our Lord and Friday to his passion and death. Setting aside Saturday for Mary began in the ninth century, perhaps because she persevered in faith all through the long hours Jesus spent in the tomb during the Saturday of Holy Week.

The Thursday devotion to the Blessed Sacrament came from the Thursday of Holy Week itself, and from the famous thirteenth-century feast of Corpus Christi, whose liturgical texts were composed by St. Thomas Aquinas, the prince of theologians.

Nearly all the Books of Hours contained devotions to the Holy Spirit and to all the saints while the Office of the Dead came from an even more ancient Roman source and was often celebrated on Mondays or Tuesdays.

In more modern times the twelve months of the year were dedicated to many of these same devotions: May to the Blessed Virgin Mary, June to the Sacred Heart of Jesus, July to the Precious Blood of Jesus, November to the Holy Souls, and so on. Such monthly dedications were not imposed by authority but were encouraged and promoted by it, especially in popular church calendars.

Sunday, the Lord's Day

He Has Risen as He Promised!

One of the earliest accomplishments of the apostolic age was the choice of the first day of the week, the Lord's Day, to celebrate the Lord's Supper. Long before there was an Easter Sunday proper or a Pentecost Sunday to conclude the great fifty days of Eastertide, Sunday had become the weekly celebration of the glorious resurrection of our Lord God and Savior, Jesus Christ.

"What you call Sunday, we call the Lord's Day."

St. Augustine of Hippo Regius (354–430)

Mattins

LEADER: O Lord, † open my lips,

ALL: ~AND MY MOUTH WILL DECLARE YOUR PRAISE.

LEADER: This is the day which the Lord has made;

ALL: ~LET US REJOICE AND BE GLAD IN IT.

PSALM 100   A CALL TO PRAYER

ANTIPHON Enter God's courts WITH PRAISE!

Make a joyful noise to the Lord, all the lands!
Serve the Lord with gladness!
Come into God's presence with singing!

~ENTER GOD'S COURTS WITH PRAISE!

Know that the Lord, who made us, is God.
We are the Lord's;
we are the people of God,
the sheep of God's pasture.

~ENTER GOD'S COURTS WITH PRAISE!

Enter God's gates with thanksgiving,
and God's courts with praise!
Give thanks and bless God's name!

~ENTER GOD'S COURTS WITH PRAISE!

For the Lord is good;
God's steadfast love endures forever,
God's faithfulness to all generations.

~ENTER GOD'S COURTS WITH PRAISE!

Glory to the Father, and to the Son,
and to the Holy Spirit:
as it was in the beginning, is now,
and will be for ever. Amen.

~ENTER GOD'S COURTS WITH PRAISE!

HYMN

O Day of resurrection!
Let us beam with festive joy!
Today indeed is the Lord's own Passover.
For from death to life, from earth to heaven
Christ has led us
As we shout the victory hymn!

~CHRIST HAS RISEN FROM THE DEAD!

Let our hearts be spotless
As we gaze upon our dazzling Christ.
See his rising—a brilliant flash of light divine!
Let us listen,
Clearly hear him greeting us:

As we shout the victory hymn!
~CHRIST HAS RISEN FROM THE DEAD!

Let all heaven burst with joy!
Let all earth resound with gladness!
Let all creation dance in celebration!
For Christ has risen:
Christ, our lasting joy!
~CHRIST HAS RISEN FROM THE DEAD![22]

St. John of Damascus (ca. 675–ca. 749)

PSALM 99:1–5   CHRIST LIVES AND REIGNS!

ANTIPHON HOLY IS THE LORD CHRIST!

The Lord reigns; let the peoples tremble!
The Lord sits enthroned upon the cherubim;
let the earth quake!

The Lord is great in Zion;
and is exalted over all the peoples.
Let them praise your great and wondrous name.
Holy is the Lord!

Mighty Ruler, lover of justice,
you have established equity;
you have executed justice
and righteousness in Jacob.

Extol the Lord our God;
worship at the Lord's footstool.
Holy is the Lord!

ANTIPHON HOLY IS THE LORD CHRIST!

PSALM PRAYER

LEADER: Let us pray *(pause for quiet prayer)*:

Lord Jesus Christ,
faithful witness and firstborn from the dead,
ruler of the kings of the earth:
wash away our sins in your blood
and make us a line of royal priests
to praise and serve your God and Father;
to him be honor and glory for ever and ever.
ALL: ~AMEN.

GOSPEL OF THE RESURRECTION   MARK 16:1–7

When the sabbath was over, Mary Magdalene, and
Mary the mother of James, and Salome bought
spices, so that they might go and anoint him. And
very early on the first day of the week, when the
sun had risen, they went to the tomb. They had
been saying to one another, "Who will roll away
the stone for us from the entrance to the tomb?"
When they looked up, they saw that the stone,
which was very large, had already been rolled
back. As they entered the tomb, they saw a young
man, dressed in a white robe, sitting on the right
side; and they were alarmed. But he said to them,
"Do not be alarmed; you are looking for Jesus of
Nazareth, who was crucified. He has been raised;
he is not here. Look, there is the place they laid
him. But go, tell his disciples and Peter that he is
going ahead of you to Galilee; there you will see
him, just as he told you. So they went out and fled

from the tomb, for terror and amazement had seized them; and they said nothing to anyone, for they were afraid.[23]

Response
Leader: Christ is risen from the dead, alleluia!
All: ~He is risen indeed, alleluia!

Canticle of the Church
We praise you, O God,
we acclaim you as Lord;
all creation worships you,
the Father everlasting.

To you all angels, all the powers of heaven,
the cherubim and seraphim, sing in endless praise:
　Holy, holy, holy Lord, God of power and might,
　heaven and earth are full of your glory.

The glorious company of apostles praise you.
The noble fellowship of prophets praise you.
The white-robed army of martyrs praise you.

Throughout the world the holy church acclaims
　　you:
　Father of majesty unbounded,
　your true and only Son, worthy of all praise,
　the Holy Spirit, advocate and guide.

You, Christ, are the king of glory,
the eternal Son of the Father.
When you took our flesh to set us free
you humbly chose the Virgin's womb.

You overcame the sting of death,
and opened the kingdom of heaven to all believers.
You are seated at God's right hand in glory.
We believe that you will come to be our judge.

Come then, Lord, and help your people,
bought with the price of your own blood,
and bring us with your saints
to glory everlasting.[24]

CLOSING PRAYER
Heavenly Father, Lord of life and death,
when Christ our Paschal Lamb was sacrificed,
he overcame death by his own dying
and restored us to life by his own rising.
In virtue of his life-giving Passover,
pour your Holy Spirit into our hearts,
fill us with awe and reverence for you,
and with love and compassion for our neighbor.
We ask this through the same Christ our Lord.
ALL: ~AMEN.

May the Son of God, risen from the dead,
✝ bless us and keep us.
ALL: ~AMEN.

Morning Prayer
O God, ✝ come to my assistance.
~O LORD, MAKE HASTE TO HELP ME.
Lead the festal procession with branches, alleluia!
~UP TO THE HORNS OF THE ALTAR, ALLELUIA!

HYMN

Truly, he comes to us: darkness is ended;
now night is over, his light is ascended:
ultimate sunrise, that floods all creation,
bringing his secret from death's desolation.

Night has made way for the great proclamation,
morning has broken, with songs of elation;
Christ comes in light from the depths of his
      prison,
Death is abandoned, and Jesus is risen.

Stripped of the grave-clothes, the body now
      glorious,
rises immortal, for ever victorious;
come to fulfill all the prophets have spoken;
promise of life that will never be broken.

Weeping is over, and death is defeated,
life is recovered and joy is completed;
guards, at the sepulcher, scatter before him,
Jesus is risen, and angels adore him.

Highest, Most Holy, once lost and forsaken:
now, from the sleep of the dead you awaken;
Angels appear at the tomb with the story:
"He is not here but is risen in glory."

Give God the glory and glad adoration,
from whom and *through* whom and *in* whom,
      creation
looks for the joy which, in Christ, we inherit:
praising the Father, the Son and the Spirit![25]

ANTIPHON Alleluia, ALLELUIA, ALLELUIA!

Clap your hands, all peoples!
Shout to God with loud songs of joy!
For the Lord, the Most High, is to be feared,
a great Ruler over all the earth,

who subdues peoples under us,
and nations under our feet,
who chose our heritage for us,
the pride of Jacob whom God loves.

God has gone up with a shout,
the Lord with the sound of a trumpet.
Sing praises to God, sing praises!
Sing praises to our Ruler, sing praises!

For God is the Ruler of all the earth;
sing praises with a psalm!
God reigns over the nations;
God sits on a holy throne.

The princes of the people gather
as the people of the God of Abraham.
For the shields of the earth belong to God,
who is highly exalted.

ANTIPHON ALLELUIA, ALLELUIA, ALLELUIA!

PSALM PRAYER

Let us pray *(pause for quiet prayer)*:

By your power, O Mighty One,
you raised Christ with a trumpet blast

and exalted him with songs of joy.
By his glorious resurrection,
lift our hearts on high
to praise and thank you, now and for ever.
We ask this through Christ, our risen Lord.
~AMEN.

READING   CHRIST IN GLORY   **COLOSSIANS 3:1–4**

Brothers and sisters, if you have been raised with Christ, seek the things that are above, where Christ is, seated at the right hand of God. Set your minds on things that are above, not on things that are on earth, for you have died, and your life is hidden with Christ in God. When Christ who is your life is revealed, then you also will be revealed with him in glory.

RESPONSE
We adore your cross, O Lord, alleluia!
~AND WE GLORIFY YOUR HOLY RESURRECTION, ALLELUIA!

CHRIST, OUR PASCHAL LAMB   **1 CORINTHIANS 5:7–8; ROMANS 6:9–11; 1 CORINTHIANS 15:20–22**

ANTIPHON   Thanks be to God, WHO GIVES US THE VICTORY THROUGH OUR LORD JESUS CHRIST, ALLELUIA!

Christ, our paschal lamb, has been sacrificed.
Therefore, let us celebrate the festival,

not with the old yeast, the yeast of malice and evil,
but with the unleavened bread of sincerity and
truth. Alleluia!

Christ, being raised from the dead, will never die
again;
death no longer has dominion over him.
The death he died, he died to sin, once for all;
but the life he lives, he lives to God.
So also you must consider yourselves dead to sin
and alive to God in Christ Jesus. Alleluia!

Christ has been raised from the dead,
the firstfruits of those who have died.
For since death came through a human being,
the resurrection of the dead has also come
through a human being;
for as all die in Adam,
so all will be made alive in Christ. Alleluia!

ANTIPHON THANKS BE TO GOD, WHO GIVES US THE
VICTORY THROUGH OUR LORD JESUS CHRIST,
ALLELUIA!

LITANY OF THANKSGIVING
Thanks be to God for the mighty resurrection
of his only Son, our Savior.
~THANKS BE TO GOD.
Thanks be to God for the forty days Jesus spent
with his apostles.
~THANKS BE TO GOD.

Thanks be to God for the many convincing proofs
Jesus gave of his risen life.
~THANKS BE TO GOD.

Thanks be to God for his constant speaking
about the kingdom of God.
~THANKS BE TO GOD.

Thanks be to God for the Lord's final commission
to his apostles to baptize all nations.
~THANKS BE TO GOD.

Thanks be to God for his wondrous ascension
into heaven.
~THANKS BE TO GOD.

(Pause for special intentions.)

Thanks be to God for the abiding faith of Mary
and the other women from Galilee.
~THANKS BE TO GOD.

THE LORD'S PRAYER
Lord, have mercy.
~CHRIST, HAVE MERCY. LORD, HAVE MERCY.

Our Father in heaven,
   ~HALLOWED BE YOUR NAME,
   YOUR KINGDOM COME,
   YOUR WILL BE DONE,
      ON EARTH AS IN HEAVEN.
GIVE US TODAY OUR DAILY BREAD.
FORGIVE US OUR SINS
   AS WE FORGIVE THOSE WHO SIN AGAINST US.

Save us from the time of trial
      and deliver us from evil.
For the kingdom and the power and the
      glory are yours
   now and forever. Amen.

Closing Prayer
Most High God,
you raised your dear Son from the grave
and enthroned him in glory at your right hand.
By the power of his holy cross,
raise our hearts and minds to you,
and bring us into everlasting bliss;
through the same Christ Jesus our Lord.
~Amen.

Let us bless the Lord, alleluia, alleluia!
~Thanks be to God, alleluia, alleluia!

May our radiant Christ
† lead us from earth to heaven,
from death to life.
~Amen.

Noonday Hour
O God, † come to my assistance.
~O Lord, make haste to help me.
I shall not die, but I shall live
~And recount the deeds of the Lord.

HYMN

Easter glory fills the sky!
Christ now lives, no more to die!
Darkness has been put to flight
By the living Lord of life!

See the stone is rolled away
From the tomb where once he lay!
He has risen as he said,
Glorious Firstborn from the dead!

Mary, Mother, greet your Son,
Radiant from his triumph won!
By his cross you shared his pain,
So forever share his reign!

Christ, the Victor over death,
Breathes on us the Spirit's breath!
Paradise is our reward,
Endless Easter with our Lord![26]

PSALM 118:1, 13–17, 21–24   ALLELUIA!

ANTIPHON This is the day which the Lord has made;
LET US REJOICE AND BE GLAD IN IT.

O give thanks to the Lord, who is good;
whose steadfast love endures forever!
I was pushed hard, so I was falling,
but the Lord helped me.

The Lord is my strength and my power;
the Lord has become my salvation.

There are joyous songs of victory
in the tents of the righteous:
"The right hand of the Lord does valiantly,
the right hand of the Lord is exalted,
the right hand of the Lord does valiantly!"

I shall not die, but I shall live
and recount the deeds of the Lord.
I thank you that you have answered me
and have become my salvation.

The stone which the builders rejected
has become the cornerstone.
This is the Lord's doing;
it is marvelous in our eyes.

ANTIPHON THIS IS THE DAY WHICH THE LORD HAS
MADE;
LET US REJOICE AND BE GLAD IN IT.

PSALM PRAYER
Let us pray *(pause for quiet prayer):*

Abba, Father,
by the grace of the risen Christ,
who slept that we might keep watch
and who died that we might live,
may we reign with him in glory,
in the life that knows no end;
through the same Christ our Lord.
~AMEN.

The women left the tomb quickly with fear and great joy, and ran to tell his disciples. Suddenly Jesus met them and said, "Greetings!" And they came to him, took hold of his feet, and worshiped him. Then Jesus said to them, "Do not be afraid; go and tell my brothers to go to Galilee; there they will see me."

RESPONSE

For fear of the angel the guards shook, alleluia!
~AND BECAME LIKE DEAD MEN, ALLELUIA!

CLOSING PRAYER

Holy, mighty, and immortal God,
in raising Jesus from the dead
you restored the whole world
to its pristine condition
and liberated us from sin and error.
May we rejoice and dance for joy
in the Eastertide of our existence
and live for ever in your embrace.
We ask this through our risen Savior.
~AMEN.

Christ is risen, alleluia, alleluia!
~HE IS RISEN, INDEED, ALLELUIA, ALLELUIA!

Evening Prayer

Light and peace † in Jesus Christ our Lord.
~THANKS BE TO GOD.

Think of yourselves as dead to sin, alleluia!
~And alive to God in Christ Jesus, alleluia!

Hymn

That Easter day with joy was bright;
The sun shone out with fairer light,
When, to their longing eyes restored,
The apostles saw their risen Lord.
Alleluia!

O Jesus, king of gentleness,
With constant love our hearts possess;
To you our lips will ever raise
The tribute of our grateful praise.
Alleluia!

O Christ, you are the Lord of all
In this our Easter festival,
For you will be our strength and shield
From every weapon death can wield.
Alleluia!

All praise, O risen Lord, we give
To you, once dead, but now alive!
To God the Father equal praise,
And God the Holy Ghost, we raise!
Alleluia![27]

Psalm 114   A Passover Song

Antiphon All of us who have been baptized
into Christ Jesus were baptized into his
       death.

When Israel went forth from Egypt,
the house of Jacob from a people
  of strange language,
Judah became God's sanctuary,
Israel God's dominion.

The sea looked and fled,
Jordan turned back.
The mountains skipped like rams,
the hills like lambs.

O sea, why do you flee?
O Jordan, why do you turn back?
O mountains, why do you skip like rams?
O hills, like lambs?

Tremble, O earth, at the presence of the Lord,
at the presence of the God of Jacob,
who turns the rock into a pool of water,
the flint into a spring of water.

ANTIPHON ALL OF US WHO HAVE BEEN BAPTIZED
INTO CHRIST JESUS WERE BAPTIZED INTO HIS
  DEATH.

PSALM PRAYER

Let us pray *(pause for quiet prayer):*

Rescuing God,
you delivered your chosen people
from the slavery of Egypt
and led them into a land flowing
with milk and honey.
Save now your people of the new covenant

from the slavery of sin
and make your Church a land of promise
for the whole human race.
We ask this through Christ, our blessed Savior.
~AMEN.

READING   **LIFE IN CHRIST**   **ROMANS 6:5–8**
Sisters and brothers, if we have been united with
Christ in a death like his, we will certainly be
united with him in a resurrection like his. We
know that our old self was crucified with him so
that the body of sin might be destroyed, and we
might no longer be enslaved to sin. For whoever
has died is freed from sin. But if we have died with
Christ, we believe that we will also live with him.

RESPONSE
Christ was raised from death, alleluia!
~BY THE POWER OF THE FATHER, ALLELUIA!

THE CANTICLE OF THE VIRGIN MARY   **LUKE 1:46–55**

ANTIPHON
Rejoice, O Queen of Heaven, alleluia!
FOR THE SON YOU BORE, ALLELUIA!
HAS ARISEN AS HE PROMISED, ALLELUIA!
PRAY FOR US TO GOD THE FATHER, ALLELUIA!

My soul † proclaims the greatness of the Lord,
my spirit rejoices in God my Savior,
for you, Lord, have looked with favor
    on your lowly servant.

~PRAY FOR US TO GOD THE FATHER, ALLELUIA!

From this day all generations will call me blessed:
    you, the Almighty, have done great things for me
    and holy is your name.
    You have mercy on those who fear you,
    from generation to generation.

~PRAY FOR US TO GOD THE FATHER, ALLELUIA!

You have shown strength with your arm
and scattered the proud in their conceit,
casting down the mighty from their thrones
and lifting up the lowly.
You have filled the hungry with good things
and sent the rich away empty.

~PRAY FOR US TO GOD THE FATHER, ALLELUIA!

You have come to the aid of your servant Israel,
to remember the promise of mercy,
the promise made to our forebears,
to Abraham and his children forever.

~PRAY FOR US TO GOD THE FATHER, ALLELUIA!

Glory to the Holy and Undivided Trinity:
now and always and for ever and ever. Amen.

~PRAY FOR US TO GOD THE FATHER, ALLELUIA!

ANTIPHON

REJOICE, O QUEEN OF HEAVEN, ALLELUIA!
FOR THE SON YOU BORE, ALLELUIA!
HAS ARISEN AS HE PROMISED, ALLELUIA!
PRAY FOR US TO GOD THE FATHER, ALLELUIA![28]

LITANY

Lord Jesus, Savior of the world and Ruler
   of the new creation:
~HEAR US, RISEN LORD.
Lord Jesus, who established the new
   and eternal covenant in your blood:
~HEAR US, RISEN LORD.
Lord Jesus, who set us free from the law of sin and
    death:
~HEAR US, RISEN LORD.
Lord Jesus, pleading for us at God's right hand:
~HEAR US, RISEN LORD.
Lord Jesus, the hope of those who die in you:
~HEAR US, RISEN LORD.

(Pause for special intentions.)

Lord Jesus, by the prayers of the great Mother of
    God,
Mary most holy, and of the whole company of
    heaven:
~HEAR US, RISEN LORD.

THE LORD'S PRAYER

Lord, have mercy.
~CHRIST, HAVE MERCY. LORD, HAVE MERCY.
Our Father in heaven,
    ~HALLOWED BE YOUR NAME,
    YOUR KINGDOM COME,
    YOUR WILL BE DONE,
      ON EARTH AS IN HEAVEN.

GIVE US TODAY OUR DAILY BREAD.
FORGIVE US OUR SINS
 AS WE FORGIVE THOSE WHO SIN AGAINST US.
SAVE US FROM THE TIME OF TRIAL
 AND DELIVER US FROM EVIL.
FOR THE KINGDOM AND THE POWER AND THE
  GLORY ARE YOURS
 NOW AND FOREVER. AMEN.

CLOSING PRAYER

Lord Christ, victorious Redeemer,
a new song is sung throughout the world
because of your triumph over death and hell.
Extend your gentle rule over all nations
and prepare us for your awesome coming
to judge the world in glory and might.
You live and reign, now and for ever.
~AMEN.

Let us bless the Lord, alleluia, alleluia!
~THANKS BE TO GOD, ALLELUIA, ALLELUIA!

May Christ who reigns from the tree of the cross,
† bless us and keep us.
~AMEN.

Night Prayer

Our help † is in the name of the Lord,
~THE MAKER OF HEAVEN AND EARTH.
I lie down and sleep, alleluia!

~I WAKE AGAIN, FOR THE LORD SUSTAINS ME,
   ALLELUIA!

HYMN

Love's redeeming work is done;
Fought the fight, the battle won:
Lo, our Sun's eclipse is o'er!
Lo, he sets in blood no more.

Vain the stone, the watch, the seal,
Christ has burst the gates of hell;
Death in vain forbids his rise;
Christ has opened Paradise.

Lives again our glorious King;
Where, O death, is now thy sting?
Dying once, he all doth save;
Where thy victory, O grave?

                              Charles Wesley (1707–1788)

PSALM 22:23–32   CHRIST REIGNS AND RULES

ANTIPHON Christ was raised from the dead
BY THE GLORY OF THE FATHER!

I will tell of your name to my kindred;
in the midst of the congregation I will praise you;

All who fear the Lord, shout praise!
All you offspring of Jacob, glorify God!
Stand in awe, all you offspring of Israel!

For God did not despise or abhor,
the affliction of the afflicted,

nor hide from me,
but heard when I cried out.

From you comes my praise
    in the great congregation;
my vows I will pay before those
    who worship the Lord.
The poor shall eat and be satisfied;
those who seek the Lord shall praise the Lord!
May your hearts live forever!

All the ends of the earth shall remember
and turn to the Lord;
and all the families of the nations
shall worship before the Lord.
For dominion belongs to the Lord,
who rules over the nations.

All who are prosperous in the land
shall eat and bow down to the Lord.
All who go down to the dust
    shall bow before the Lord,
for they cannot keep themselves alive.

Posterity shall serve the Lord;
each generation shall tell of the Lord,
and proclaim deliverance to a people yet unborn:
surely the Lord has done it.

ANTIPHON CHRIST WAS RAISED FROM THE DEAD
BY THE GLORY OF THE FATHER!

Psalm Prayer

Let us pray *(pause for quiet prayer):*

Lord God Almighty,
you manifested your power and glory
when Jesus, your beloved Son,
dealt death a deathblow
and brought life to those in the grave.
May all the earth remember and turn to you,
paying their vows with profound thanksgiving.
We ask this through the same Christ our Lord.
~Amen.

| Reading | **The Great Commission** | **Matthew 28:16–20** |

The eleven disciples went to Galilee, to the mountain to which Jesus had directed them. When they saw him, they worshiped him; but some doubted. And Jesus came and said to them, "All authority in heaven and on earth has been given to me. Go therefore and make disciples of all nations, baptizing them in the name of the Father and of the Son and of the Holy Spirit, and teaching them to obey everything that I have commanded you. And remember, I am with you always, to the end of the age."

Response

Holy, holy, holy Lord, God of power and might,
~Heaven and earth are full of your glory.

The Canticle of Simeon the Prophet

ANTIPHON Remember, I AM WITH YOU ALWAYS, TO THE END OF THE AGE.

Now, Lord, † let your servant go in peace:
your word has been fulfilled.

My own eyes have seen your salvation
which you have prepared in the sight
    of every people:

a light to reveal you to the nations
and the glory of your people Israel.

Glory to the Father, and to the Son,
and to the Holy Spirit:

as it was in the beginning, is now,
and will be for ever. Amen.

ANTIPHON REMEMBER, I AM WITH YOU ALWAYS, TO THE END OF THE AGE.

CLOSING PRAYER

Saving God,
when your Son cried out to you
from the cross of pain and humiliation,
you lifted him out of the sleep of death
and exalted him to your right hand.
By the grace of his resurrection,
uphold your people, shield us from our enemies,
and bring us home with him

60 A Book of Hours

to the resurrection of the body and life everlasting;
through Christ Jesus, our blessed Lord.
~AMEN.

By the precious and life-giving cross,
may our risen Lord † guard us and keep us.
~AMEN.

Monday   Hours of the Holy Spirit

At the end of his earthly existence Jesus would not leave us orphans. His final gift to us was more than a church or a Bible; it was the Third Person of the Blessed Trinity, the Holy Spirit of God residing in the hearts of believers. According to St. John, Jesus spent a good part of the Last Supper (chapters 13–17) talking about the gift of the Holy Spirit and the Spirit's role in the life of the Church. In the final chapter of Luke's Gospel and in the first and second chapters of the Acts of the Apostles, we read about the relationship of the Holy Spirit to the infant Church and, in a special way, to Mary and the twelve Apostles. The Acts is often thought of as the Gospel of the Holy Spirit because of the importance it lends to the Spirit's role in the formation and expansion of the early Church.

Mattins

O Lord, † open my lips,

~AND MY MOUTH WILL DECLARE YOUR PRAISE.

Come, Holy Spirit, fill the hearts of your faithful,

~AND KINDLE IN THEM THE FIRE OF YOUR LOVE.

PSALM 95   A CALL TO PRAYER

ANTIPHON Come, LET US WORSHIP THE SPIRIT WHO FILLS THE WHOLE EARTH.

O come, let us sing to the Lord;
let us make a joyful noise to the rock of our
      salvation!
Let us come into God's presence with
      thanksgiving;

let us make a joyful noise with songs of praise!

~COME, LET US WORSHIP THE SPIRIT
WHO FILLS THE WHOLE EARTH.

For the Lord is a great God,
a great Ruler above all gods,
in whose hands are the depths of the earth
and also the heights of the mountains.
The sea belongs to God who made it,
and the dry land, because God formed it.

~COME, LET US WORSHIP THE SPIRIT
WHO FILLS THE WHOLE EARTH.

O come, let us worship and bow down,
let us kneel before the Lord, our Maker!
For the Lord is our God,
we are the people of God's pasture,
the sheep of God's hand.

~COME, LET US WORSHIP THE SPIRIT
WHO FILLS THE WHOLE EARTH.

Glory to the Father, and to the Son,
and to the Holy Spirit:
as it was in the beginning, is now,
and will be for ever. Amen.

~COME, LET US WORSHIP THE SPIRIT
WHO FILLS THE WHOLE EARTH.

HYMN TO THE HOLY SPIRIT

Holy Spirit, font of light,
    focus of God's glory bright,

shed on us a shining ray.
Father of the fatherless,
    giver of gifts limitless,
    come and touch our hearts today.

Source of strength and sure relief,
    comforter in time of grief,
    enter in and be our guest.
On our journey grant us aid,
    freshening breeze and cooling shade,
    in our labor inward rest.

Enter each aspiring heart,
    occupy its inmost part,
    with your dazzling purity.
All that gives to us our worth,
    all that benefits the earth,
    you bring to maturity.

With your soft refreshing rains,
    break our drought, remove our stains;
    bind up all our injuries.
Shake with rushing wind our will;
    melt with fire our icy chill;
    bring to light our perjuries.

As you promise we believe,
    make us ready to receive
    gifts from your unbounded store.
Grant enabling energy,
    courage in adversity,
    joys that last forevermore.
        Amen.[29]

ANTIPHON By the word of the Lord THE HEAVENS
    WERE MADE!

The Lord loves justice and righteousness;
the earth is full of the steadfast love of the Lord.
By the word of the Lord the heavens were made,
and all their host by the breath of God's mouth.
The Lord gathered the waters of the sea as in a
    bottle
and put the deeps in storehouses.

Let the earth fear the Lord,
let all the inhabitants of the world stand in awe.
For the Lord spoke, and it came to be,
the Lord commanded, and it stood forth.

The Lord brings the counsel of the nations to
    nothing
and frustrates the plans of the peoples.
The counsel of the Lord stands forever,
the thoughts of God's heart to all generations.

Blessed is the nation whose God is the Lord,
the people whom the Lord has chosen as his
    heritage!
The Lord looks down from heaven,
and sees all peoples;

the Lord sits enthroned and looks forth
on all the inhabitants of the earth,
fashioning the hearts of them all,
and observing all their deeds.

ANTIPHON BY THE WORD OF THE LORD THE
HEAVENS WERE MADE!

PSALM PRAYER
Let us pray *(pause for quiet prayer)*:
Creator Spirit,
you made the world and all that is in it.
Fashion the hearts of your people
whom you have created to praise you,
and bring them into the courts of our heavenly
    home.
We ask this through Christ our Lord.
~AMEN.

READING   NO ORPHANS   JOHN 14:18–20
Jesus said to his disciples: "I will not leave you
orphaned; I am coming to you. In a little while the
world will no longer see me, but you will see me;
because I live, you also will live. On that day you
will know that I am in my Father, and you in me,
and I in you."

RESPONSE
Peace I leave with you;
~MY PEACE I GIVE TO YOU.

CANTICLE OF THE CHURCH
We praise you, O God,
We acclaim you as Lord;
all creation worships you,
the Father everlasting.

To you all angels, all the powers of heaven,
the cherubim and seraphim, sing in endless praise:
Holy, holy, holy Lord, God of power and might,
heaven and earth are full of your glory.

The glorious company of apostles praise you.
The noble fellowship of prophets praise you.
The white-robed army of martyrs praise you.

Throughout the world the holy church acclaims
you:
Father of majesty unbounded,
your true and only Son, worthy of all praise,
the Holy Spirit, advocate and guide.

You, Christ, are the king of glory,
the eternal Son of the Father.
When you took our flesh to set us free
you humbly chose the Virgin's womb.

You overcame the sting of death,
and opened the kingdom of heaven to all believers.
You are seated at God's right hand in glory.
We believe that you will come to be our judge.

Come then, Lord, and help your people,
bought with the price of your own blood,
and bring us with your saints
to glory everlasting.[30]

CLOSING PRAYER
Heavenly King, Consoler, Spirit of truth,
present in all places, filling all things,
treasury of blessings and giver of life:

Come and dwell in us,
cleanse us from every stain of sin,
and save our souls,
O gracious Lord.
~AMEN.[31]

May the blessing of almighty God,
the Father, † the Son, and the Holy Spirit,
rest upon us and abide with us for ever.
~AMEN.

Morning Prayer

Our help is † in the name of the Lord,
~THE MAKER OF HEAVEN AND EARTH.
Come, Holy Spirit, fill the hearts of your faithful,
~AND KINDLE IN THEM THE FIRE OF YOUR LOVE.

HYMN

Father, Lord of earth and heaven,
King to whom all gifts belong,
Give your gentlest Gift, your Spirit,
God the holy, God the strong.

Son of God, enthroned in glory,
Send your promised Gift of grace,
Make your Church your holy Temple,
God the Spirit's dwelling-place.

Spirit, come, in peace descending,
As at Jordan, heavenly Dove,
Seal your Church as God's anointed,
Set our hearts on fire with love.

Stay among us, God the Father,
Stay among us, God the Son,
Stay among us, Holy Spirit:
Dwell within us, make us one.[32]

PSALM 36:5–11   RIVERS OF LIVING WATER

ANTIPHON O God, HOW PRECIOUS IS YOUR
    STEADFAST LOVE!

Your steadfastness, O Lord, extends to the
    heavens,
your faithfulness to the clouds.
Your righteousness is like the mighty mountains,
your judgments are like the great deep;
O Lord, you save humans and animals!

O God, how precious is your steadfast love!
All people may take refuge in the shadow of your
    wings.
They feast on the abundance of your house,
and you give them drink from the river of your
    delights.
For with you is the fountain of life;
in your light do we see light.

O continue your steadfast love to those who know
    you,
and your salvation to the upright of heart.
Do not let the foot of the arrogant come upon me,
nor the hand of the wicked drive me away.

ANTIPHON O God, HOW PRECIOUS IS YOUR
    STEADFAST LOVE!

Psalm Prayer

Let us pray (pause for quiet prayer):

Lord Jesus,
you promised that "Out of the believer's heart
shall flow rivers of living water."
Now that you are glorified by the Father,
be the fountain of life for us
as we walk in the Spirit.
You live and reign, now and for ever.
~Amen.

Reading   Love One Another   John 15:12–16

Jesus said to his disciples, "This is my
commandment, that you love one another as I
have loved you. No one has greater love than this,
to lay down one's life for one's friends. You are my
friends if you do what I command you. I do not
call you servants any longer, because the servant
does not know what the master is doing; but I have
called you friends, because I have made known to
you everything that I have heard from my Father.
You did not choose me but I chose you."

Response

The Father will give you, alleluia!
~Whatever you ask in my name, alleluia!

The Canticle of Zachary   Luke 1:68–79

Antiphon Love one another as I have loved
   you.

Blessed ✝ are you, Lord, the God of Israel,
you have come to your people and set them free.
You have raised up for us a mighty Savior,
born of the house of your servant David.

Through your holy prophets, you promised of old
     to save us from our enemies,
     from the hands of all who hate us,
     to show mercy to our forebears,
     and to remember your holy covenant.

This was the oath you swore to our father Abraham:
     to set us free from the hands of our enemies,
     free to worship you without fear,
     holy and righteous before you,
     all the days of our life.

And you, child, shall be called the prophet
     of the Most High,
for you will go before the Lord to prepare the way,
to give God's people knowledge of salvation
by the forgiveness of their sins.

In the tender compassion of our God
the dawn from on high shall break upon us,
to shine on those who dwell in darkness
     and the shadow of death,
and to guide our feet into the way of peace.

Glory to the Holy and Undivided Trinity:
now and always, and for ever and ever. Amen.

ANTIPHON LOVE ONE ANOTHER AS I HAVE LOVED
    YOU.

THE LORD'S PRAYER

Lord, have mercy.
~CHRIST, HAVE MERCY. LORD, HAVE MERCY.

Our Father in heaven,
    ~HALLOWED BE YOUR NAME,
    YOUR KINGDOM COME,
    YOUR WILL BE DONE,
       ON EARTH AS IN HEAVEN.
GIVE US TODAY OUR DAILY BREAD.
FORGIVE US OUR SINS
    AS WE FORGIVE THOSE WHO SIN AGAINST US.
SAVE US FROM THE TIME OF TRIAL
    AND DELIVER US FROM EVIL.
FOR THE KINGDOM AND THE POWER AND THE
    GLORY ARE YOURS
    NOW AND FOREVER. AMEN.

CLOSING PRAYER

Almighty God and Father,
on the first Pentecost you formed the hearts
of your Son's chosen disciples
by the indwelling of the Holy Spirit.
Under the inspiration of the same Spirit,
infuse our hearts with love for you
and for our friends and neighbors.
We ask this through Christ our Lord.
    ~AMEN.

May the grace of our Lord Jesus Christ,
and the love of God,
and the communion of the Holy Spirit,
✝ be with us, now and for ever.
~AMEN.

Noonday Hour
O God, ✝ come to my assistance.
~O LORD, MAKE HASTE TO HELP ME.
Come, Holy Spirit, fill the hearts of your faithful,
~AND KINDLE IN THEM THE FIRE OF YOUR LOVE.

HYMN
Spirit of the Lord, come down,
Spreading your protecting wing
Over all that you have made,
Over every living thing.

Come in storm-wind, cleansing fire,
Sweeping through a world unclean;
Come in every gentle breeze:
Breath of God, unheard, unseen.

Father of the poor, come down,
In your sight our sins lie bare;
What is naked, clothe with love,
That your likeness we might wear.

Holy Spirit, blessed light,
Guide and strengthen mind and will.
Comfort every grieving heart,
And our inmost being fill.

Through the Father and the Son,
By whose blood our life is bought,
Fill our empty hands with gifts:
Come with grace unearned, unsought.[33]

PSALM 150   UNIVERSAL PRAISE

ANTIPHON Let everything that breathes PRAISE
    THE LORD!

Praise God in the sanctuary;
praise God in the mighty firmament!
Praise God for mighty deeds;
praise God for exceeding greatness!

Praise God with trumpet sound;
praise God with lute and harp!
Praise God with tambourine and dance;
praise God with strings and pipe!

Praise God with sounding cymbals;
praise God with loud clashing cymbals!
Let everything that breathes praise the Lord!

ANTIPHON LET EVERYTHING THAT BREATHES
    PRAISE THE LORD!

PSALM PRAYER

Let us pray *(pause for quiet prayer)*:

With every living creature
may we sing without ceasing
your praise, O God of mighty deeds,
and chant endless alleluias
with the undying host of angels and saints

who worship without stint or stay.
Blest be our great God and Savior Jesus Christ,
now and for ever.
~Amen.

READING
SAMARIA AND THE SPIRIT
ACTS 8:14–17

When the apostles at Jerusalem heard that
Samaria had accepted the word of God, they sent
Peter and John to them. The two went down and
prayed for them that they might receive the Holy
Spirit (for as yet the Spirit had not come upon any
of them; they had only been baptized in the name
of the Lord Jesus). Then Peter and John laid their
hands on them, and they received the Holy Spirit.

RESPONSE
They were all filled with the Holy Spirit, alleluia!
~AND SPOKE THE WORD OF GOD WITH BOLDNESS,
ALLELUIA!

CLOSING PRAYER
You are the King of glory, O Lord,
put to death in the flesh,
but made alive in the Spirit.
By your victory over death and hell,
help us proclaim the Holy Gospel
at every time and in every place;
for the sake of your holy Name.
~Amen.

Let us bless the Lord, alleluia!
~THANKS BE TO GOD, ALLELUIA!

Evening Prayer
Light and peace ✝ in Jesus Christ our Lord.
~THANKS BE TO GOD.
Come, Holy Spirit, fill the hearts of your faithful,
~AND KINDLE IN THEM THE FIRE OF YOUR LOVE.

HYMN TO THE HOLY SPIRIT
O Holy Spirit, by whose breath
Life rises vibrant out of death:
Come to create, renew, inspire;
Come, kindle in our hearts your fire.

You are the seeker's sure resource,
Of burning love the living source,
Protector in the midst of strife,
The giver and the Lord of life.

In you God's energy is shown,
To us your varied gifts made known.
Teach us to speak, teach us to hear;
Yours is the tongue and yours the ear.

Flood our dull senses with your light;
In mutual love our hearts unite.
Your power the whole creation fills;
Confirm our weak, uncertain wills.

From inner strife grant us release;
Turn nations to the ways of peace,
To fuller life your people bring

That as one body we may sing:

Praise to the Father, Christ his Word,
And to the Spirit, God the Lord;
To them all honor, glory be
Both now and in eternity. Amen.[34]

PSALM 145:1–13   AWESOME DEEDS

ANTIPHON The Spirit of the Lord FILLS THE WHOLE
    WORLD.

I will extol you, my God and Ruler,
and bless your name forever and ever.
Every day I will bless you,
and praise your name forever and ever.
Great is the Lord, and greatly to be praised,
whose greatness is unsearchable.

One generation shall laud your works to another,
and shall declare your mighty acts.
On the glorious splendor of your majesty,
and on your wondrous works, I will meditate.

The might of your awesome deeds shall be
        proclaimed,
and I will declare your greatness.
They shall celebrate the memory
    of your great goodness,
and shall sing aloud of your righteousness.

The Lord is gracious and merciful,
slow to anger and abounding in steadfast love.
The Lord is good to all

and has compassion over all creation.

All your works shall give thanks to you, O Lord,
and the faithful shall bless you!
They shall speak of the glory of your realm,
and tell of your power,
to make known to all people your mighty deeds,
and the glorious splendor of your realm.
Your realm is an everlasting realm,
and your dominion endures throughout all
      generations.

ANTIPHON THE SPIRIT OF THE LORD FILLS THE
      WHOLE WORLD.

PSALM PRAYER

Let us pray *(pause for quiet prayer):*

Gracious and merciful God,
you continually teach your Church
the beautiful truths of the Gospel
by the Spirit who brings us light and life.
Inspire us each day to listen attentively
to the inner movements of the heart
that lead us toward the will of God in all things.
We ask this through Christ our Lord.
~AMEN.

READING   **THE ADVOCATE**   **JOHN 15:26–27**

Jesus said to his disciples: "When the Advocate
comes, whom I will send to you from the Father, the
Spirit of truth who comes from the Father, he will

testify on my behalf. You also are to testify because you have been with me from the beginning."

RESPONSE

If I do not go away, alleluia!
~THE ADVOCATE WILL NOT COME TO YOU,
    ALLELUIA!

THE CANTICLE OF THE VIRGIN MARY   LUKE 1:46–55

ANTIPHON Peace I leave with you;
MY PEACE I GIVE TO YOU, ALLELUIA!

My soul † proclaims the greatness of the Lord,
my spirit rejoices in God my Savior,
for you, Lord, have looked with favor on your
        lowly servant.

From this day all generations will call me blessed:
    you, the Almighty, have done great things for me,
    and holy is your name.
    You have mercy on those who fear you,
    from generation to generation.

You have shown strength with your arm
and scattered the proud in their conceit,
casting down the mighty from their thrones
and lifting up the lowly.
You have filled the hungry with good things
and sent the rich away empty.

You have come to the aid of your servant Israel,
to remember the promise of mercy,
the promise made to our forebears,

to Abraham and his children forever.

Glory to the Holy and Undivided Trinity:
now and always and for ever and ever. Amen.

ANTIPHON PEACE I LEAVE WITH YOU;
MY PEACE I GIVE TO YOU, ALLELUIA!

LITANY OF THE HOLY SPIRIT

Lord and life-giving Spirit, in the beginning
    you swept over the primeval waters.
~COME, FILL OUR HEARTS.

You led the people of Israel out of slavery
    and into the land of milk and honey.
~COME, FILL OUR HEARTS.

You overshadowed Mary of Nazareth
    and made her the Mother of the Messiah.
~COME, FILL OUR HEARTS.

You descended on Jesus like a dove in bodily form
    at his baptism in the Jordan.
~COME, FILL OUR HEARTS.

You raised Jesus out of death and proclaimed him
    Son of God in all his power.
~COME, FILL OUR HEARTS.

You appeared in tongues of flame on Pentecost
    and enriched the church with precious gifts.
~COME, FILL OUR HEARTS.

You sent your apostles out across the world
    to testify to the Good News.
~COME, FILL OUR HEARTS.

(Pause for special intentions.)

THE LORD'S PRAYER
Lord, have mercy.
~CHRIST, HAVE MERCY. LORD, HAVE MERCY.

Our Father in heaven,
  ~HALLOWED BE YOUR NAME,
  YOUR KINGDOM COME,
  YOUR WILL BE DONE,
    ON EARTH AS IN HEAVEN.
GIVE US TODAY OUR DAILY BREAD.
FORGIVE US OUR SINS
  AS WE FORGIVE THOSE WHO SIN AGAINST US.
SAVE US FROM THE TIME OF TRIAL
  AND DELIVER US FROM EVIL.
FOR THE KINGDOM AND THE POWER AND THE
    GLORY ARE YOURS
  NOW AND FOREVER. AMEN.

CLOSING PRAYER
Heavenly Father,
on the fiftieth day after Easter,
you poured out your Holy Spirit
on Mary and the twelve apostles.
By their loving prayers,
strengthen the apostolic faith in us
and grant us the peace
that passes all understanding;
for the sake of Christ our Lord.
~AMEN.

May the divine Trinity, Father, Son, and Holy
    Spirit,
✝ bless and keep us, now and for ever.
~AMEN.

Night Prayer

Our help ✝ is in the name of the Lord,
~THE MAKER OF HEAVEN AND EARTH.
Come, Holy Spirit, fill the hearts of your faithful,
~AND KINDLE IN THEM THE FIRE OF YOUR LOVE.

HYMN

O radiant Light, O Sun divine
Of God the Father's deathless face,
O Image of the Light sublime
That fills the heavenly dwelling place:

O Son of God, the source of life,
Praise is your due by night and day.
Unsullied lips must raise the strain
Of your esteemed and splendid name.

Lord Jesus Christ, as daylight fades,
As shine the lights of eventide,
We praise the Father with the Son,
The Spirit blest and with them one.[35]

PSALM 145:1–2, 13–21   BLESS GOD

ANTIPHON Great is the LORD AND WORTHY OF
      PRAISE!

I will extol you, my God and Ruler,
and bless your name forever and ever.

Every day I will bless you,
and praise your name forever and ever.

The Lord's words are faithful.
The Lord's deeds are gracious.
The Lord holds up all who are falling,
and raises up all who are bowed down.

The eyes of all look to you,
and you give them their food in due season.
You open your hand,
you satisfy the desire of every living thing.

All the Lord's ways are just,
to all who call upon the Lord in truth.
The Lord fulfills the desire of all the faithful,
and hears their cry and saves them.

The Lord preserves all who love the Lord,
the Lord destroys all the wicked.
My mouth will speak the praise of the Lord;
let all flesh bless God's holy name forever and ever.

ANTIPHON GREAT IS THE LORD AND WORTHY OF
 PRAISE!

PSALM PRAYER

Let us pray *(pause for quiet prayer)*:

Risen Lord and Savior,
you are worthy of all praise
in heaven and on earth.
By your glorious resurrection,
lift our hearts on high

and fill us with your empowering Spirit,
now and for ever.

~AMEN.

READING THE SPIRIT OF TRUTH JOHN 16:12–15

Jesus said to his disciples, "I still have many things to
say to you, but you cannot bear them now. When the
Spirit of truth comes, he will guide you into all the
truth; for he will not speak on his own, but will speak
whatever he hears, and he will declare to you the
things that are to come. He will glorify me, because
he will take what is mine and declare it to you. All
that the Father has is mine. For this reason I said that
he will take what is mine and declare it to you."

RESPONSE

If you ask anything of the Father in my name,
~HE WILL GIVE IT TO YOU.

THE CANTICLE OF SIMEON THE PROPHET LUKE 2:29–32

ANTIPHON I will ask the Father,
AND HE WILL GIVE YOU ANOTHER ADVOCATE.

Now, Lord, † let your servant go in peace:
your word has been fulfilled.

My own eyes have seen your salvation
which you have prepared in the sight
   of every people:

a light to reveal you to the nations

and the glory of your people Israel.

Glory to the Father, and to the Son,
and to the Holy Spirit:

as it was in the beginning, is now,
and will be forever. Amen.

ANTIPHON I WILL ASK THE FATHER,
AND HE WILL GIVE YOU ANOTHER ADVOCATE.

CLOSING PRAYER
Send the Holy Spirit, O Lord,
to overshadow us forever.
By his abiding presence,
absolve our hearts of every sin
and defend us from every danger.
We ask this through Christ our Lord.
~AMEN.

May the Father of glory bless us and keep us.
~AMEN.

May the Savior of the world graciously smile upon
       us.
~AMEN.

May the holy and life-giving Spirit † grant us peace.
~AMEN.

Tuesday　　Hours of Our Dear Departed

Every traditional Book of Hours contained the Office of the Dead as its second main component. This fostered the almost universal custom of praying the Office of the Dead once a week to commemorate our departed friends, relatives, and benefactors.

The ancient Apostles' Creed speaks of "the communion of saints, the resurrection of the body, and the life everlasting." Over time the Eucharist and other liturgical prayers of the Church evolved through this belief to include all the faithful, the living, and the more than living.

Especially at the time of death, the church prepared people for their departure from this life by the sacraments of reconciliation, final anointing, and Holy Communion (viaticum). Then came the waking of the dead through the celebration of Vespers, a vigil service, and a Mass of Requiem. These services were also used on the third, seventh, and thirtieth days after a death, for an annual commemoration of the departed soul, and on November 2, the universal memorial for all the faithful departed.

Mattins

O Lord, † open my lips,

~AND MY MOUTH WILL DECLARE YOUR PRAISE.

Eternal rest grant to them, O Lord,

~AND LET PERPETUAL LIGHT SHINE UPON THEM.

PSALM 95　　　　　　　　　　　　A CALL TO PRAYER

ANTIPHON　Come, LET US WORSHIP THE LORD OF
　　　　ALL THE LIVING.

O come, let us sing to the Lord;

let us make a joyful noise to the rock of our
    salvation!
Let us come into God's presence with
    thanksgiving;
let us make a joyful noise with songs of praise!

~COME, LET US WORSHIP THE LORD OF ALL THE
    LIVING.

For the Lord is a great God,
a great Ruler above all gods,
in whose hands are the depths of the earth
and also the heights of the mountains.
The sea belongs to God who made it,
and the dry land, because God formed it.

~COME, LET US WORSHIP THE LORD OF ALL THE
    LIVING.

O come, let us worship and bow down,
let us kneel before the Lord, our Maker!
For the Lord is our God,
we are the people of God's pasture,
the sheep of God's hand.

~COME, LET US WORSHIP THE LORD OF ALL THE
    LIVING.

Glory to the Father, and to the Son,
and to the Holy Spirit:
as it was in the beginning, is now,
and will be forever. Amen.

~COME, LET US WORSHIP THE LORD OF ALL THE
    LIVING.

Hymn

O Lord, you died that all might live
And rise to see the perfect day.
The fullness of your mercy give
To these our friends for whom we pray.

Lord, bless our friends who died in you,
As you have given them release.
Enliven them since they were true,
And give them everlasting peace.

In your green pleasant pastures feed
The sheep that you have summoned hence;
And by the still, cool waters lead
Your flock in loving providence.

Direct us with your arm of might,
that with our friends we may all come
To dwell within your city bright,
Jerusalem, our heavenly home.[36]

Psalm 6   We Trust in God

Antiphon The Lord ACCEPTS MY PRAYER.

O Lord, do not rebuke me in your anger,
nor chasten me in your wrath.
Be gracious to me, O Lord, for I languish;
O Lord, heal me, for my bones are stricken.
My whole being also is stricken with terror.
But you, O Lord—how long?

Turn, O Lord, save my life;
deliver me for the sake of your steadfast love.

For in death there is no remembrance of you;
in Sheol who can give you praise?

I am weary with my moaning;
every night I flood my bed with tears;
I drench my couch with weeping.
My eye wastes away because of grief,
it grows weak because of all my foes.

Depart from me, all you workers of evil,
for the Lord has heard the sound of my weeping.
The Lord has heard my supplication;
the Lord accepts my prayer.

All my enemies shall be ashamed
    and stricken with terror;
they shall turn back, and be put to shame
    in a moment.

ANTIPHON THE LORD ACCEPTS MY PRAYER.

PSALM PRAYER
Let us pray *(pause for quiet prayer)*:

God of mercy and compassion,
your ears are always open to our prayers.
We trust in your care for us
and beg you to multiply your mercies
toward the faithful departed
that they may rest in peace and pray for us.
We ask this through Christ our Lord.
~AMEN.

The LORD of hosts will destroy on this mountain
the shroud that is cast over all peoples, the sheet
that is spread over all nations; he will swallow up
death forever. Then the LORD God will wipe away
the tears from all faces, and the disgrace of his
people he will take away from all the earth, for the
LORD has spoken.

RESPONSE

This is the LORD for whom we have waited;
~LET US BE GLAD AND REJOICE IN HIS SALVATION.

THE CANTICLE OF WISDOM   WISDOM 3:1-7, 9

ANTIPHON God tested them AND FOUND THEM
    WORTHY.

The souls of the righteous are in the hand of God,
and no torment will ever touch them.
In the eyes of the foolish they seemed to have
    died,
and their departure was thought to be a disaster,
and their going from us to be their destruction;
but they are at peace.

For though in the sight of others they were
    punished,
their hope is full of immortality.
Having been disciplined a little, they will receive
    great good,

because God tested them and found them worthy
    of himself;
like gold in the furnace he tried them,
and like a sacrificial burnt offering he accepted
    them.
In the time of their visitation they will shine forth,
and will run like sparks through the stubble.
Grace and mercy are upon his holy ones,
and he watches over his elect.

Eternal rest grant to them, O LORD;
and let perpetual light shine upon them.

ANTIPHON GOD TESTED THEM AND FOUND THEM
    WORTHY.

CLOSING PRAYER
God of mercy and compassion,
your promises endure forever.
For the sake of our risen Savior,
make us worthy of immortality
with all your saints and angels,
through all the ages of ages.
~AMEN.

May the souls of the faithful departed
through the mercy of God † rest in peace.
~AMEN.

Morning Prayer
O God, † come to my assistance.
~O LORD, MAKE HASTE TO HELP ME.

If we live, we live to the Lord;
~IF WE DIE, WE DIE TO THE LORD.

HYMN

Praise the Lord, all you nations,
praise the Lord, all you peoples:
we have witnessed his mercy,
he is faithful forever.

Praise the Father, who made us,
praise his Son, who redeemed us,
praise their life-giving Spirit,
praise one God through all ages.[37]

PSALM 90   A PRAYER OF MOSES

ANTIPHON May we rejoice AND BE GLAD ALL OUR
   DAYS.

Lord, you have been our dwelling place
in all generations.
Before the mountains were brought forth,
or ever you had formed the earth and the world,
from everlasting you are God.

You turn us back to the dust,
and say, "Turn back, you mortals!"
For a thousand years in your sight
are as yesterday when it is past,
or as a watch in the night.

You sweep them away; they are like a dream,
like grass which is renewed in the morning:
in the morning it flourishes and is renewed;

in the evening it fades and withers.

Satisfy us in the morning with your steadfast love,
that we may rejoice and be glad all our days.
Make us glad as many days as you have afflicted
       us,
and as many years as we have seen evil.

Let your work be manifest to your servants,
and your glorious power to their children.
Let the favor of the Lord our God be upon us,
and establish the work of our hands;
yes, establish the work of our hands.

ANTIPHON MAY WE REJOICE AND BE GLAD ALL
       OUR DAYS.

PSALM PRAYER
Let us pray *(pause for quiet prayer)*:
Merciful God,
you are from everlasting to everlasting.
When you turn us back to dust
you promise us life everlasting.
In the morning of your promise
we shall be renewed and refreshed
in our risen Christ,
who lives and reigns with you,
in the unity of the Holy Spirit,
now and for ever.
~AMEN.

READING   CHILDREN OF GOD   1 JOHN 3:1–2

Sisters and brothers, see what love the Father has given us, that we should be called children of God; and that is what we are. The reason the world does not know us is that it did not know him. Beloved, we are God's children now; what we will be has not yet been revealed. What we do know is this: when he is revealed, we will be like him, for we will see him as he is.

RESPONSE

The Son of God was revealed for this purpose,
~TO DESTROY THE WORKS OF THE DEVIL.

THE CANTICLE OF ZACHARY   LUKE 1:68–79

ANTIPHON I am the living bread THAT CAME
DOWN FROM HEAVEN. WHOEVER EATS OF
THIS BREAD WILL LIVE FOREVER.

Blessed † are you, Lord, the God of Israel,
you have come to your people and set them free.
You have raised up for us a mighty Savior,
born of the house of your servant David.

Through your holy prophets, you promised of old
    to save us from our enemies,
      from the hands of all who hate us,
      to show mercy to our forebears,
      and to remember your holy covenant.

This was the oath you swore to our father Abraham:
    to set us free from the hands of our enemies,
    free to worship you without fear,

holy and righteous before you,
all the days of our life.

And you, child, shall be called the prophet
of the Most High,
for you will go before the Lord to prepare the way,
to give God's people knowledge of salvation
by the forgiveness of their sins.

In the tender compassion of our God
the dawn from on high shall break upon us,
to shine on those who dwell in darkness
and the shadow of death,
and to guide our feet into the way of peace.

Eternal rest grant to them, O Lord;
and let perpetual light shine upon them.

ANTIPHON I AM THE LIVING BREAD THAT CAME
DOWN FROM HEAVEN. WHOEVER EATS OF
THIS BREAD WILL LIVE FOREVER.

LITANY FOR THE FAITHFUL DEPARTED

By the holy incarnation of Jesus, your only Son,
~GOOD LORD, DELIVER THEM.
By his blessed cross and bitter suffering,
~GOOD LORD, DELIVER THEM.
By his precious death and burial,
~GOOD LORD, DELIVER THEM.
By his glorious resurrection and wonderful
ascension,
~GOOD LORD, DELIVER THEM.

By the priceless gift of the Holy Spirit in every age,
~GOOD LORD, DELIVER THEM.

(Pause for personal petitions.)

By the prayers of the Blessed Virgin Mary
   and of all the saints in glory,
~GOOD LORD, DELIVER THEM.

THE LORD'S PRAYER
Lord, have mercy.
~CHRIST, HAVE MERCY. LORD, HAVE MERCY.

Our Father in heaven,
   ~HALLOWED BE YOUR NAME,
   YOUR KINGDOM COME,
   YOUR WILL BE DONE,
      ON EARTH AS IN HEAVEN.
GIVE US TODAY OUR DAILY BREAD.
FORGIVE US OUR SINS
      AS WE FORGIVE THOSE WHO SIN AGAINST US.
SAVE US FROM THE TIME OF TRIAL
      AND DELIVER US FROM EVIL.
FOR THE KINGDOM AND THE POWER AND THE
      GLORY ARE YOURS
      NOW AND FOREVER. AMEN.

CLOSING PRAYER
Lord Jesus, Bread of Life,
by the power of the Holy Eucharist
and its promise of everlasting life,

deliver those for whom we pray
from the death that lasts for ever.
May our joy and gladness
be that of the saints in glory
where we shall enjoy eternal bliss,
for ever and ever.
~AMEN.

May the souls of the faithful departed
through the mercy of God † rest in peace.
~AMEN.

Noonday Hour
O God, † come to my assistance.
~O LORD, MAKE HASTE TO HELP ME.
When the Son of Man comes in his glory,
~THEN HE WILL SIT ON THE THRONE OF HIS
   GLORY.

HYMN
God be in my head
and in my understanding;
God be in my eyes
and in my looking;
God be in my mouth
and in my speaking;
God be in my heart,
and in my thinking;
God be at my end,
and my departing.[38]

ANTIPHON With the Lord THERE IS GREAT
REDEMPTION.

Out of the depths I cry to you, O Lord!
Lord, hear my voice!
Let your ears be attentive
to the voice of my supplications!

If you, O Lord, should mark iniquities,
Lord, who could stand?
But there is forgiveness with you,
that you may be worshipped.

I wait for the Lord, my soul waits,
in the Lord's word I hope;
my soul waits for the Lord
more than watchers for the morning,
more than watchers for the morning.

O Israel, hope in the Lord!
For with the Lord there is steadfast love;
with the Lord there is great redemption.
The Lord alone will redeem Israel
from all iniquities.

ANTIPHON WITH THE LORD THERE IS GREAT
REDEMPTION.

PSALM PRAYER

Let us pray *(pause for quiet prayer):*

Lord of the living and the dead,
with you there is great redemption
for all who die in the Christian faith.

May all our friends, relatives, and benefactors
enjoy your divine presence,
O Savior of the world,
now and for ever.
~Amen.

	OUR INNER	2 CORINTHIANS
READING	NATURE	4:16–18

Brothers and sisters, even though our outer nature
is wasting away, our inner nature is being renewed
day by day. For this slight momentary affliction is
preparing us for an eternal weight of glory beyond
all measure, because we look not at what can be
seen but at what cannot be seen; for what can
be seen is temporary, but what cannot be seen is
eternal.

RESPONSE
We walk by faith,
~NOT BY SIGHT.

CLOSING PRAYER
Almighty and everlasting God,
for the sake of Jesus our blessed Redeemer,
you promised us eternal life with you.
By the power of Christ's glorious resurrection,
raise us to new life in him,
uniting us with all the martyrs and saints in glory.
~Amen.

Eternal rest grant unto them, O Lord,
~AND LET PERPETUAL LIGHT SHINE UPON THEM.

Evening Prayer

Light and peace † in Jesus Christ our Lord.
~THANKS BE TO GOD.
Even darkness is not dark to you, O Lord,
~THE NIGHT IS BRIGHT AS DAY.

HYMN

Come, my Way, my Truth, my Life:
Such a way as gives us breath;
Such a truth as ends all strife;
Such a life as killeth death.

Come, my Light, my Feast, my Strength:
Such a light as shows a feast;
Such a feast as mends in length;
Such a strength as makes his guest.

Come, my Joy, my Love, my Heart:
Such a joy as none can move;
Such a love as none can part;
Such a heart as joys in love.[39]

PSALM 139:1–12   DIVINE PRESENCE

ANTIPHON Search me, O God, AND KNOW MY
      HEART!

O Lord, you have searched me and known me!
You know me when I sit down and when I rise up;
you discern my thoughts from afar.

You search out my path and my lying down,
and are acquainted with all my ways.

Even before a word is on my tongue, O Lord,
you know it completely.

You pursue me behind and before,
and lay your hand upon me.
Such knowledge is too wonderful for me;
it is so high, I cannot attain it.

Where shall I go from your Spirit?
Or where shall I flee from your presence?
If I ascend to heaven, you are there!
If I make my bed in Sheol, you are there!

If I take the wings of the morning
and dwell in the deepest parts of the sea,
even there your hand shall lead me,
and your right hand shall hold me.

If I say, "Let only darkness cover me,
and the light about me be night,"
even darkness is not dark to you,
the night is bright as day;
for darkness is as light to you.

Antiphon Search me, O God, and know my
heart!

Psalm Prayer

Let us pray *(pause for quiet prayer)*:

All-knowing God,
we are fearfully and wonderfully made
by your omnipotent majesty.

Rule and guide our hearts
that you know so perfectly,
that we may walk in your way
and be at peace with you
and with our fellow human beings,
now and for ever.
~AMEN.

READING   JUDGMENT DAY   REVELATION 20:11–13

I saw a great white throne and the one who sat
on it; the earth and the heaven fled from his
presence, and no place was found for them. And
I saw the dead, great and small, standing before
the throne, and books were opened. Also another
book was opened, the book of life. And the dead
were judged according to their works, as recorded
in the books. Death and Hades gave up the dead
that were in them, and all were judged according
to what they had done.

RESPONSE

Christ must reign, Christ must rule,
~CHRIST MUST BE THE LORD OF ALL.

THE CANTICLE OF THE VIRGIN MARY   LUKE 1:46–55

ANTIPHON Peace I leave with you;
MY PEACE I GIVE TO YOU, ALLELUIA!

My soul † proclaims the greatness of the Lord,
my spirit rejoices in God my Savior,

for you, Lord, have looked with favor on your
   lowly servant.

From this day all generations will call me blessed:
   you, the Almighty, have done great things for
      me
   and holy is your name.
   You have mercy on those who fear you,
   from generation to generation.

You have shown strength with your arm
and scattered the proud in their conceit,
casting down the mighty from their thrones
and lifting up the lowly.
You have filled the hungry with good things
and sent the rich away empty.

You have come to the aid of your servant Israel,
to remember the promise of mercy,
the promise made to our forebears,
to Abraham and his children forever.

Eternal rest grant to them, O Lord;
and may perpetual light shine upon them.

Antiphon Peace I leave with you;
my peace I give to you, alleluia!

Litany of the Faithful Departed
By the precious blood of your circumcision,
   O Child of Israel,
~Grant them eternal rest.

By the precious blood that oozed from your pores
   in the Garden of Gethsemane,
~Grant them eternal rest.
By the precious blood that spattered Pilate's court
   at your brutal scourging,
~Grant them eternal rest.
By the precious blood that flowed from beneath
   your cruel crown of thorns,
~Grant them eternal rest.
By the precious blood that spilled to the ground
   on your way to Golgotha,
~Grant them eternal rest.
By the precious blood that poured from your
      hands and feet
   when they were nailed to the cross,
~Grant them eternal rest.
By the precious blood that streamed
   from your heart opened by a Roman spear,
~Grant them eternal rest.

(Pause and pray for special friends.)

By the prayers of the Mother of Sorrows
   and of all who mourned for you,
~Grant them eternal rest.

The Lord's Prayer
Lord, have mercy.
~Christ, have mercy. Lord, have mercy.

Our Father in heaven,
~HALLOWED BE YOUR NAME,
YOUR KINGDOM COME,
YOUR WILL BE DONE,
ON EARTH AS IN HEAVEN.
GIVE US TODAY OUR DAILY BREAD.
FORGIVE US OUR SINS
AS WE FORGIVE THOSE WHO SIN AGAINST US.
SAVE US FROM THE TIME OF TRIAL
AND DELIVER US FROM EVIL.
FOR THE KINGDOM AND THE POWER AND THE
GLORY ARE YOURS
NOW AND FOREVER. AMEN.

CLOSING PRAYER

Creator and Redeemer of the world,
have mercy on all our friends, relatives,
and benefactors
who stand in need of our prayers.
You are good and you love the human race
for whom you died and rose again,
O Savior of the world,
living and reigning with the Father,
in the unity of the Holy Spirit,
one God, for ever and ever.
~AMEN.

May the souls of the faithful departed
through the mercy of God † rest in peace.
~AMEN.

Night Prayer

Our help † is in the name of the Lord,

~The Maker of heaven and earth.

Search me, O God, and know my heart!

~Test me and know my thoughts.

Hymn

May God the Father look on you with love,
and call you to himself in bliss above.
May God the Son, good Shepherd of the sheep,
stretch out his hand and waken you from sleep.
May God the Spirit breathe on you his peace,
where joys beyond all knowing never cease.

May flights of angels lead you on your way
to paradise, and heaven's eternal day!
May martyrs greet you after death's dark night,
and bid you enter into Zion's light!
May choirs of angels sing you to your rest
with once poor Lazarus, now for ever blest.[40]

Psalm 13   **Rely on the Lord**

Antiphon My heart shall rejoice in your
        salvation.

How long, O Lord? Will you forget me forever?
How long will you hide your face from me?
How long must I bear pain in my soul,
and have sorrow in my heart all the day?
How long shall my enemy be exalted over me?

Consider and answer me, O Lord my God;
lighten my eyes, lest I sleep the sleep of death;
lest my enemy say, "I have prevailed";
lest my foes rejoice because I am shaken.

But I trusted in your steadfast love;
my heart shall rejoice in your salvation.
I will sing to the Lord,
for the Lord has dealt richly with me.

ANTIPHON MY HEART SHALL REJOICE IN YOUR
SALVATION.

PSALM PRAYER

Let us pray *(pause for quiet prayer):*

All-knowing God,
in Christ we know you as you are,
always seeing, always listening.
Please give us full confidence
lest we sleep the sleep of death
and lose sight of your face
and your loving care for us.
We ask this through the same Christ our Lord.
~AMEN.

READING **DEATH WILL BE NO MORE** **REVELATION 21:3–4**

See, the home of God is among mortals. He will
dwell with them as their God; they will be his
peoples, and God himself will be with them; he
will wipe every tear from their eyes. Death will be

no more; mourning and crying and pain will be
no more, for the first things have passed away.

RESPONSE

I am the Alpha and the Omega,
~THE BEGINNING AND THE END.

THE CANTICLE OF
SIMEON THE PROPHET   LUKE 2:29–32

ANTIPHON See, I AM MAKING ALL THINGS NEW.

Now, Lord, ✝ let your servant go in peace:
your word has been fulfilled.

My own eyes have seen your salvation
which you have prepared in the sight
    of every people:

a light to reveal you to the nations
and the glory of your people Israel.

Eternal rest grant to them, O Lord;
and let perpetual light shine upon them.

ANTIPHON SEE, I AM MAKING ALL THINGS NEW.

CLOSING PRAYER

Lord Jesus Christ,
you are the resurrection and life.
You raised Lazarus from the grave
four days after he died
and promised that everyone
who believes in you will never die.
Be with us at the hour of our death

and bring to fulfillment your divine promises
of the resurrection of the body
and the life everlasting.
You live and reign, now and for ever.
~Amen.

May the souls of the faithful departed
through the mercy of God ✝ rest in peace.
~Amen.

Since by holy baptism we are all united in the one Body of Christ, one of the central teachings of the Church is the communion of saints. Those living in the Church on earth are indivisibly united with those who have gone before us into glory—and with all the holy angels, too!

The proliferation in the Church of martyrs and saints sparked a pious desire to commemorate *all* the saints, known and unknown. When the Roman Pantheon was converted into a Christian church in the sixth century, it was dedicated to St. Mary and all the martyrs, encouraging a further feast of all saints. In the later Middle Ages this feast was observed each year on November 1 and became deeply connected to All Souls' Day on November 2.

Many of the famous Books of Hours contained an Office of All Saints and numerous commemorations of a great variety of popular saints.

Mattins

O Lord, † open my lips,
~AND MY MOUTH WILL DECLARE YOUR PRAISE.
Precious in the sight of the Lord
~IS THE DEATH OF THE FAITHFUL.

PSALM 100   **A CALL TO PRAYER**

ANTIPHON Come, LET US ADORE THE LORD
        CHRIST,

WHO REWARDS ALL THE SAINTS, ALLELUIA!

Make a joyful noise to the Lord, all the lands!
Serve the Lord with gladness!
Come into God's presence with singing!

~Come, let us adore the Lord Christ,
who rewards all the saints, alleluia!

Know that the Lord, who made us, is God.
We are the Lord's;
we are the people of God,
the sheep of God's pasture.

~Come, let us adore the Lord Christ,
who rewards all the saints, alleluia!

Enter God's gates with thanksgiving,
and God's courts with praise!
Give thanks and bless God's name!

~Come, let us adore the Lord Christ,
who rewards all the saints, alleluia!

For the Lord is good;
God's steadfast love endures forever,
God's faithfulness to all generations.

~Come, let us adore the Lord Christ,
who rewards all the saints, alleluia!

Glory to the Father, and to the Son,
and to the Holy Spirit:
as it was in the beginning, is now,
and will be forever. Amen.

~Come, let us adore the Lord Christ,
who rewards all the saints, alleluia!

Hymn

For all the saints who from their labors rest,
All who by faith before the world confessed.

Your name, O Jesus, be for ever blest.
Alleluia! Alleluia!

You were their rock, their fortress, and their
    might;
You, Lord, their Captain in their well-fought fight;
You in the darkness drear, their one true light.
Alleluia! Alleluia!

O may your soldiers, faithful, true, and bold,
Fight as the saints who nobly fought of old,
And win with them, the victor's crown of gold.
Alleluia! Alleluia![41]

PSALM 149:1–6   THE SAINTS IN GLORY

ANTIPHON Praise God IN THE ASSEMBLY OF THE
    SAINTS, ALLELUIA!

Sing to the Lord a new song,
God's praise in the assembly of the faithful!
Let Israel be glad in its Maker,
let the children of Zion rejoice in their Ruler!

Let them praise God's name with dancing,
making melody with tambourine and lyre!
For the Lord takes pleasure in his people;
and adorns the humble with victory.

Let the faithful exult in glory;
let them sing for joy on their couches.
Let the high praise of God be in their throats
and two-edged swords in their hands.

ANTIPHON PRAISE GOD IN THE ASSEMBLY OF THE
SAINTS, ALLELUIA!

PSALM PRAYER

Let us pray *(pause for quiet prayer)*:

God of all holiness,
in baptism we are set apart
for you alone.
May the saints in glory be our intercessors
as we rejoice in their presence
and bless you for their victory over death.
We ask this through Christ our Lord.
~AMEN.

READING   THE SON OF MAN   REVELATION 1:13–16

I saw one like the Son of Man, clothed with a
long robe and with a golden sash across his chest.
His head and his hair were white as white wool,
white as snow; his eyes were like a flame of fire,
his feet were like burnished bronze, refined as in a
furnace, and his voice was like the sound of many
waters. In his right hand he held seven stars, and
from his mouth came a sharp, two-edged sword,
and his face was like the sun shining with full
force.

RESPONSE

See, I am alive forever and ever, alleluia!
~AND I HAVE THE KEYS OF DEATH AND OF
HADES, ALLELUIA!

CANTICLE OF THE CHURCH

We praise you, O God,
We acclaim you as Lord;
all creation worships you,
the Father everlasting.

To you all angels, all the powers of heaven,
the cherubim and seraphim, sing in endless praise:
  Holy, holy, holy Lord, God of power and might,
  heaven and earth are full of your glory.

The glorious company of apostles praise you.
The noble fellowship of prophets praise you.
The white-robed army of martyrs praise you.

Throughout the world the holy Church acclaims
    you:
  Father of majesty unbounded,
  your true and only Son, worthy of all praise,
  the Holy Spirit, advocate and guide.

You, Christ, are the king of glory,
the eternal Son of the Father.
When you took our flesh to set us free
you humbly chose the Virgin's womb.

You overcame the sting of death,
and opened the kingdom of heaven to all believers.
You are seated at God's right hand in glory.
We believe that you will come to be our judge.

Come then, Lord, and help your people,
bought with the price of your own blood,
and bring us with your saints

to glory everlasting.[42]

CLOSING PRAYER
Almighty ever-living God,
by whose gift we venerate in one celebration
the merits of all the Saints,
bestow on us, we pray,
through the prayers of so many intercessors,
an abundance of the reconciliation with you
for which we earnestly long.
Through our Lord Jesus Christ, your Son,
who lives and reigns with you in the unity of the
    Holy Spirit,
one God, for ever and ever.
~AMEN.[43]

May the divine assistance † remain always with
    us.
~AMEN.

Morning Prayer
O God, † come to my assistance.
~O LORD, MAKE HASTE TO HELP ME.
Let us join all the saints and angels
~IN PRAISING THE SON OF GOD.

HYMN
O blest communion, family divine!
We feebly struggle, they in glory shine;
Yet all are one within your great design.
Alleluia! Alleluia!

And when the strife is fierce, the warfare long,
Steals on the ear the distant triumph song,
And hearts are brave again and arms are strong.
Alleluia! Alleluia!

The golden evening brightens in the west;
Soon, soon to faithful warriors comes their rest;
Sweet is the calm of paradise the blest.
Alleluia! Alleluia!

But then there breaks a yet more glorious day;
The saints triumphant rise in bright array;
The King of glory passes on his way.
Alleluia! Alleluia![44]

PSALM 148   OUR GREAT LORD

ANTIPHON You are worthy, our Lord and God,
TO RECEIVE HONOR AND GLORY AND POWER,
    ALLELUIA!

Praise the Lord from the heavens;
praise the Lord, in the heights!
Praise the Lord, all angels;
praise the Lord, all hosts!

Praise the Lord, sun and moon;
praise the Lord, all shining stars!
Praise the Lord, highest heavens,
and all waters above the heavens!

Let them praise the name of the Lord,
who commanded and they were created,
who established them for ever and ever,
and fixed their bounds that cannot be passed.

Praise the Lord from the earth,
sea monsters and all deeps,
fire and hail, snow and smoke,
stormy wind fulfilling God's command.

Mountains and hills,
fruit trees and all cedars!
Wild animals and all cattle,
creeping things and flying birds!

Monarchs of the earth and all peoples,
nobles and all rulers of the earth!
Young men and women together,
old and young alike!

Let them praise the name of the Lord
whose name alone is exalted,
whose glory is above earth and heaven.

God has raised up a horn for the people,
praise for all God's faithful,
for the people of Israel who are near to God.

ANTIPHON YOU ARE WORTHY, OUR LORD AND
GOD,
TO RECEIVE HONOR AND GLORY AND POWER,
ALLELUIA!

PSALM PRAYER
Let us pray *(pause for quiet prayer):*

Praise the Lord of all the saints and angels
who dwell in light inaccessible

but come to us in Christ Jesus,
the one Mediator between heaven and earth.
By the prayers of the Blessed Virgin Mary
and the whole company of heaven,
may we strive for the holiness
that purifies and exalts all God's chosen ones.
We ask this through the same Christ our Lord.
~AMEN.

	THE THRONE	REVELATION
READING	OF GOD	4:2–3, 5–6

There in heaven stood a throne, with one seated
on the throne! And the one seated there looks like
jasper and carnelian, and around the throne is a
rainbow that looks like an emerald. Coming from
the throne are flashes of lightning, and rumblings
and peals of thunder, and in front of the throne
burn seven flaming torches, which are the seven
spirits of God; and in front of the throne there is
something like a sea of glass, like crystal.

RESPONSE

Holy, holy, holy Lord, God of power and might,
~HEAVEN AND EARTH ARE FULL OF YOUR GLORY.

THE CANTICLE OF ZACHARY   LUKE 1:68–79

ANTIPHON The glorious company of the apostles,
THE NOBLE FELLOWSHIP OF PROPHETS,
THE WHITE-ROBED ARMY OF MARTYRS
ALL SING YOUR PRAISE, O HOLY TRINITY, ONE
    ONLY GOD.

Blessed ✝ are you, Lord, the God of Israel,
you have come to your people and set them free.
You have raised up for us a mighty Savior,
born of the house of your servant David.

Through your holy prophets, you promised of old
    to save us from our enemies,
    from the hands of all who hate us,
    to show mercy to our forebears,
    and to remember your holy covenant.

This was the oath you swore to our father
    Abraham:
    to set us free from the hands of our enemies,
    free to worship you without fear,
    holy and righteous before you,
    all the days of our life.

And you, child, shall be called the prophet
    of the Most High,
for you will go before the Lord to prepare the way,
to give God's people knowledge of salvation
by the forgiveness of their sins.

In the tender compassion of our God
the dawn from on high shall break upon us,
to shine on those who dwell in darkness
    and the shadow of death,
and to guide our feet into the way of peace.

Glory to the Holy and Undivided Trinity:
now and always and for ever and ever. Amen.

ANTIPHON THE GLORIOUS COMPANY OF THE
  APOSTLES,
THE NOBLE FELLOWSHIP OF PROPHETS,
THE WHITE-ROBED ARMY OF MARTYRS
ALL SING YOUR PRAISE, O HOLY TRINITY, ONE
  ONLY GOD.

LITANY

Holy is God, holy and strong, holy and living for
  ever!

~LORD, HAVE MERCY.

By the prayers of the great Mother of God,
  Mary most holy, Queen of all saints:

~LORD, HAVE MERCY.

By the prayers of all the holy apostles of Christ
  in every age:

~LORD, HAVE MERCY.

By the prayers of all the heroic martyrs
  who shed their blood for Christ's sake:

~LORD, HAVE MERCY.

By the prayers of all the men and women
  who boldly professed their faith before the
  world:

~LORD, HAVE MERCY.

By the prayers of all the saints, known and
  unknown, in every age:

~LORD, HAVE MERCY.

(Pause for personal petitions.)

Holy is God, holy and strong, holy and living for
ever!
~LORD, HAVE MERCY.

THE LORD'S PRAYER
Lord, have mercy.
~CHRIST, HAVE MERCY. LORD, HAVE MERCY.

Our Father in heaven,
~HALLOWED BE YOUR NAME,
YOUR KINGDOM COME,
YOUR WILL BE DONE,
ON EARTH AS IN HEAVEN.
GIVE US TODAY OUR DAILY BREAD.
FORGIVE US OUR SINS
AS WE FORGIVE THOSE WHO SIN AGAINST US.
SAVE US FROM THE TIME OF TRIAL
AND DELIVER US FROM EVIL.
FOR THE KINGDOM AND THE POWER AND THE
GLORY ARE YOURS
NOW AND FOREVER. AMEN.

CLOSING PRAYER
God our Father,
source of all holiness,
the work of your hands is manifest in your saints,
the beauty of your truth is reflected in their faith.
May we who aspire to have part in their joy
be filled with the Spirit that blessed their lives,
so that having shared their faith on earth
we may also know their peace in your kingdom.

Grant this through Christ our Lord.
~Amen.[45]

May Christ Jesus, Lord of all the saints,
† bless us and keep us.
~Amen.

Noonday Hour
O God, † come to my assistance.
~O Lord, make haste to help me.
Come, Lord, with all your saints
~And bring us into glory everlasting.

Hymn
O white-robed King of glory,
You come to seek your own;
With angel hosts around you,
You claim your altar-throne.
A hundred-thousand welcomes
We give you, God most high;
With loving hearts we greet you,
High King of earth and sky.

You come yourself to bring us
The hope of Paradise;
You come to lead us homeward
To joy beyond the skies.
You come in hidden glory
Who yet will come again
In majesty and splendor
To be our great Amen.

O King of kings, in wonder
We wait for that blest morn,
New springtime of creation,
When all shall be reborn.
Then by your Word almighty
The promised heav'n and earth
In glory and in gladness
At last shall come to birth.[46]

PSALM 124   SAINTS AND MARTYRS

ANTIPHON The righteous shall shine like the sun
IN THE KINGDOM OF THE FATHER, ALLELUIA!

If it had not been the Lord who was on our side—
let Israel now say—
if it had not been the Lord who was on our side,
when foes rose up against us,
then they would have swallowed us up alive,
when their anger was kindled against us;

then the flood would have swept us away,
the torrent would have gone over us;
then the raging waters
would have gone over us.

Blessed be the Lord who has not given us
as prey to their teeth!
We have escaped as a bird
from the snare of the fowlers;

the snare is broken,
and we have escaped!

Our help is in the name of the Lord
who made heaven and earth.

ANTIPHON THE RIGHTEOUS SHALL SHINE LIKE THE
   SUN
IN THE KINGDOM OF THE FATHER, ALLELUIA!

PSALM PRAYER
Let us pray *(pause for quiet prayer)*:

Gracious God,
always on our side,
always kind and loving:
Be our escape from all evil
like birds from their snares,
trusting in your infinite love.
We ask this through Christ our Lord.
~AMEN.

READING   **TESTING**   **SIRACH 2:1–6**
My child, when you come to serve the Lord,
prepare yourself for testing. Set your heart right
and be steadfast, and do not be impetuous in time
of calamity. Cling to him and do not depart, so
that your last days may be prosperous. Accept
whatever befalls you, and in times of humiliation
be patient. For gold is tested in the fire, and those
found acceptable, in the furnace of humiliation.
Trust in him, and he will help you; make your
ways straight, and hope in him.

RESPONSE
You who fear the Lord, hope for good things,
~FOR LASTING JOY AND MERCY.

CLOSING PRAYER
Lord Jesus, King of glory,
by the blood of your holy cross,
come and help your people,
keep us from all sin,
and bring us with your saints
into glory everlasting.
Blest be your holy Name, now and for ever.
~AMEN.

Govern † and uphold us, O Lord,
in the communion of your blessed saints.
~AMEN.

Evening Prayer
Light and peace † in Jesus Christ our Lord.
~THANKS BE TO GOD.
Light dawns for the righteous,
~AND JOY FOR THE UPRIGHT IN HEART.

HYMN
The Father's holy ones, the blest,
Who drank the chalice of the Lord,
Have learned that bitterness is sweet
And courage keener than the sword.

In darkness they were unafraid,
And kept alight their living fire;

They now keep timeless days of joy,
Where God gives all their hearts desire.

May all that splendid company
Whom Christ in glory came to meet,
Help us on our uneven road
Made smoother by their passing feet.

O Father, Son, and Spirit blest,
May we keep faith till time shall cease;
Grant us a place among your saints,
The poor who served the prince of peace.[47]

PSALM 126   REAPING AND REJOICING

ANTIPHON The Lord HAS DONE GREAT THINGS FOR
    THEM, ALLELUIA!

When the Lord restored the fortunes of Zion,
we were like those in a dream.
Then our mouth was filled with laughter,
and our tongue with shouts of joy;
then it was said among the nations,
"The Lord has done great things for them."

The Lord has done great things for us,
and we are glad.
Restore our fortunes, O Lord,
like the watercourses in the Negeb!

May those who sow in tears
reap with shouts of joy!
Those who go out weeping,
bearing the seed for sowing,

shall come home with shouts of joy,
carrying their sheaves.

ANTIPHON THE LORD HAS DONE GREAT THINGS
    FOR THEM, ALLELUIA!

PSALM PRAYER
Let us pray *(pause for quiet prayer)*:

Great and holy God,
you have done great things in all your saints.
May we come to share their glory
and their unceasing praise
of the Father, the Son, and the Holy Spirit,
now and always and for ever and ever.
~AMEN.

READING   **THE BEATITUDES**   **LUKE 6:20–23**
Jesus looked up at his disciples and said:
"Blessed are you who are poor,
    for yours is the kingdom of God.
Blessed are you who are hungry now,
    for you will be filled.
Blessed are you who weep now,
    for you will laugh.
Blessed are you when people hate you, and when
they exclude you, revile you, and defame you on
account of the Son of Man. Rejoice in that day
and leap for joy, for surely your reward is great in
heaven; for that is what their ancestors did to the
prophets.

Holy is God, holy and strong,
~HOLY AND LIVING FOR EVER.

THE CANTICLE OF THE VIRGIN MARY   LUKE 1:46–55

ANTIPHON   How glorious is the kingdom
WHERE ALL THE SAINTS REJOICE WITH CHRIST;
CLOTHED IN WHITE ROBES, THEY FOLLOW THE
    LAMB WHEREVER HE GOES, ALLELUIA!

My soul † proclaims the greatness of the Lord,
my spirit rejoices in God my Savior,
for you, Lord, have looked with favor
   on your lowly servant.

From this day all generations will call me blessed:
   you, the Almighty, have done great things for
     me,
   and holy is your name.
   You have mercy on those who fear you,
   from generation to generation.

You have shown strength with your arm
and scattered the proud in their conceit,
casting down the mighty from their thrones
and lifting up the lowly.
You have filled the hungry with good things
and sent the rich away empty.

You have come to the aid of your servant Israel,
to remember the promise of mercy,

the promise made to our forebears,
to Abraham and his children forever.

Glory to the Father, and to the Son,
and to the Holy Spirit:
as it was in the beginning, is now,
and will be forever. Amen.

ANTIPHON HOW GLORIOUS IS THE KINGDOM
WHERE ALL THE SAINTS REJOICE WITH CHRIST;
CLOTHED IN WHITE ROBES, THEY FOLLOW THE
    LAMB WHEREVER HE GOES, ALLELUIA!

LITANY OF PEACE
Let us conclude our evening prayer to the Lord.
~LORD, HAVE MERCY.
For peace from on high and for our salvation,
    let us pray to the Lord.
~LORD, HAVE MERCY.
For the peace of the world, the welfare
    of the Church of God, and for all its ministers,
    let us pray to the Lord.
~LORD, HAVE MERCY.
For all those who meet together in faith
    and stand in awe of God, let us pray to the
        Lord.
~LORD, HAVE MERCY.
For our nation, its government,
    and for all who serve and protect us,
    let us pray to the Lord.
~LORD, HAVE MERCY.

For the safety of travelers, the recovery of the sick,
   the liberation of the oppressed, and the release
   of prisoners, let us pray to the Lord.
~LORD, HAVE MERCY.
Help, save, pity, and defend us, O God, by your
   grace.
~LORD, HAVE MERCY.

(Pause for personal petitions.)

With the prayers of the great Mother of God,
of St. Joseph, her spouse, and of all the saints in
   glory,
let us commend ourselves, one another,
and our whole life to Christ our Lord.
~TO YOU, O LORD.

THE LORD'S PRAYER
Lord, have mercy.
~CHRIST, HAVE MERCY. LORD, HAVE MERCY.

Our Father in heaven,
   ~HALLOWED BE YOUR NAME,
   YOUR KINGDOM COME,
   YOUR WILL BE DONE,
      ON EARTH AS IN HEAVEN.
GIVE US TODAY OUR DAILY BREAD.
FORGIVE US OUR SINS
   AS WE FORGIVE THOSE WHO SIN AGAINST US.
SAVE US FROM THE TIME OF TRIAL
   AND DELIVER US FROM EVIL.

FOR THE KINGDOM AND THE POWER AND THE
      GLORY ARE YOURS
   NOW AND FOREVER. AMEN.

CLOSING PRAYER

Lord and Savior of the world,
hear the prayers we offer to you
to bring before your God and our God.
May we rejoice in the communion of saints
and share with them the light of glory
in the new and heavenly Jerusalem.
By their prayers rescue us from every evil
and draw us to walk in their footsteps,
now and always and for ever and ever.
~AMEN.

May the divine assistance † remain always with
      us,
and may the souls of the faithful departed,
through the mercy of God, rest in peace.
~AMEN.

Night Prayer

Our help † is in the name of the Lord,
~THE MAKER OF HEAVEN AND EARTH.
In peace I will lie down and sleep,
~FOR YOU ALONE MAKE ME LIE DOWN IN SAFETY.

HYMN

O radiant Light, O Sun divine
Of God the Father's deathless face,

O Image of the Light sublime
That fills the heavenly dwelling place:

O Son of God, the source of life,
Praise is your due by night and day.
Our happy lips must raise the strain
Of your esteemed and splendid name.

Lord Jesus Christ, as daylight fades,
As shine the lights of eventide,
We praise the Father with the Son,
The Spirit blest and with them one.[48]

PSALM 3   **OUR SHIELD**

ANTIPHON You have redeemed us, O Lord,
BY YOUR BLOOD.

How many are my foes!
Many are rising against me;
many are saying of me,
"There is no help from God for that one."

But you, O Lord, are a shield about me,
my glory, and the lifter of my head.
I cry aloud to the Lord
who answers me from God's holy hill.

I lie down and sleep;
I wake again, for the Lord sustains me.
I am not afraid of ten thousand people
who have set themselves against me
    on every side.

Arise, O Lord!
Deliver me, O God!
For you strike all my enemies on the cheek,
you break the teeth of the wicked.
Deliverance belongs to the Lord;
your blessing be upon your people!

ANTIPHON YOU HAVE REDEEMED US, O LORD,
BY YOUR BLOOD.

PSALM PRAYER
Let us pray *(pause for quiet prayer):*

By the power of God, Lord Jesus,
you awoke again from the sleep of death
and delivered the souls of the righteous
from their darkness and ignorance.
Save us now from the second death
and raise us with your saints to glory everlasting.
You live and reign, now and for ever.
~AMEN.

READING   **A CLOUD OF WITNESSES**   **HEBREWS 12:1–2**

Brothers and sisters, since we are surrounded by
so great a cloud of witnesses, let us also lay aside
every weight and the sin that clings so closely,
and let us run with perseverance the race that
is set before us, looking to Jesus the pioneer and
perfecter of our faith, who for the sake of the
joy that was set before him endured the cross,

disregarding its shame, and has taken his seat at
the right hand of the throne of God.

RESPONSE
Pursue peace with everyone and the holiness
~WITHOUT WHICH NO ONE WILL SEE THE LORD.

**THE CANTICLE OF
SIMEON THE PROPHET**   **LUKE 2:29–32**

ANTIPHON The righteous WILL BE REMEMBERED
        FOR EVER.

Now, Lord, ✝ let your servant go in peace:
your word has been fulfilled.

My own eyes have seen your salvation
which you have prepared in the sight
    of every people:

a light to reveal you to the nations
and the glory of your people Israel.

Glory to the Holy and Undivided Trinity:
now and always and for ever and ever. Amen.

ANTIPHON THE RIGHTEOUS WILL BE REMEMBERED
        FOR EVER.

CLOSING PRAYER
God of all holiness,
we glorify you in all your holy ones
and see that in crowning their merits
you are but crowning your own gifts.

Surrounded by such a crowd of witnesses,
help us run our appointed race
and with them receive a never-fading garland of
    glory,
through Jesus Christ our Lord.
~Amen.

May Christ, the King of glory,
✝ grant us life and peace.
~Amen.

The Holy Eucharist is a banquet, a sacrifice, and a living memorial of the passion, death, and resurrection of our Lord. The Lord's Supper on the Lord's Day is the high point of our weekly worship. The body and blood, soul and divinity of Jesus, our complete and living Lord dwelling in our tabernacles, makes every church and chapel a true temple of his abiding presence. Visits to the Blessed Sacrament and other forms of eucharistic devotion center our lives on Jesus who promised to stay with us always, "to the end of the age" (Matthew 28:20).

Jesus instituted the Eucharist on Holy Thursday evening. Traditional piety singles out this day of the week for an Office of the Blessed Sacrament.

Mattins

O Lord, † open my lips,

~AND MY MOUTH WILL DECLARE YOUR PRAISE.

Blessed be Jesus in the most holy Sacrament
of the Altar!

~BLESSED BE HIS HOLY NAME, NOW AND FOR
EVER!

PSALM 100   **A CALL TO PRAYER**

ANTIPHON   Come, let us adore Jesus Christ
our Lord, THE HIGH PRIEST OF THE NEW
COVENANT.

Make a joyful noise to the Lord, all the lands!
Serve the Lord with gladness!
Come into God's presence with singing!

~Cᴄᴀᴇ, ʟᴇᴛ ᴘˢ ᴀᴅᴄʀᴇ Jᴇˢᴘˢ Cʰʀᴀˢᴛ ᴄᴘʀ Lᴄʀᴅ,
ᴛʰᴇ ʰіɠʰ ᴘʀіᴇˢᴛ ᴡʙ ᴛʰᴇ ᴀᴇᴡ ᴄᴡᴠᴇʀᴀᴀᴛ.

Know that the Lord, who made us, is God.
We are the Lord's;
the sheep of God's pasture.

~Cᴄᴀᴇ, ʟᴇᴛ ᴘˢ ᴀᴅᴄʀᴇ Jᴇˢᴘˢ Cʰʀᴀˢᴛ ᴄᴘʀ Lᴄʀᴅ,
ᴛʰᴇ ʰіɠʰ ᴘʀіᴇˢᴛ ᴡʙ ᴛʰᴇ ᴀᴇᴡ ᴄᴡᴠᴇʀᴀᴀᴛ.

Enter God's gates with thanksgiving,
and God's courts with praise!
Give thanks and bless God's name!

~Cᴄᴀᴇ, ʟᴇᴛ ᴘˢ ᴀᴅᴄʀᴇ Jᴇˢᴘˢ Cʰʀᴀˢᴛ ᴄᴘʀ Lᴄʀᴅ,
ᴛʰᴇ ʰіɠʰ ᴘʀіᴇˢᴛ ᴡʙ ᴛʰᴇ ᴀᴇᴡ ᴄᴡᴠᴇʀᴀᴀᴛ.

For the Lord is good;
God's steadfast love endures for ever,
God's faithfulness to all generations.

~Cᴄᴀᴇ, ʟᴇᴛ ᴘˢ ᴀᴅᴄʀᴇ Jᴇˢᴘˢ Cʰʀᴀˢᴛ ᴄᴘʀ Lᴄʀᴅ,
ᴛʰᴇ ʰіɠʰ ᴘʀіᴇˢᴛ ᴡʙ ᴛʰᴇ ᴀᴇᴡ ᴄᴡᴠᴇʀᴀᴀᴛ.

Glory to the Father, and to the Son,
and to the Holy Spirit:
as it was in the beginning, is now,
and will be for ever. Amen.

~Cᴄᴀᴇ, ʟᴇᴛ ᴘˢ ᴀᴅᴄʀᴇ Jᴇˢᴘˢ Cʰʀᴀˢᴛ ᴄᴘʀ Lᴄʀᴅ,
ᴛʰᴇ ʰіɠʰ ᴘʀіᴇˢᴛ ᴡʙ ᴛʰᴇ ᴀᴇᴡ ᴄᴡᴠᴇʀᴀᴀᴛ.

Hymn
O Priest and Victim, Lord of life,
Throw wide the gates of paradise!

We face our foes in mortal strife;
You are our strength: O heed our cries.

To Father, Son, and Spirit blest,
One only God, be ceaseless praise!
May God in goodness grant us rest
In heaven, our home, for endless days![49]

St. Thomas Aquinas, OP (1225–1274)

PSALM 116:12–19 THE HOLY SACRIFICE

ANTIPHON I will offer you THE SACRIFICE
OF THANKSGIVING.

What shall I return to the Lord
for all God's gifts to me?
I will lift up the cup of salvation
and call on the name of the Lord.
I will pay my vows to the Lord
in the presence of all God's people.

Precious in the sight of the Lord
is the death of the faithful.
O Lord, I am your servant;
I am your servant, the child of your handmaid.
You have loosed my bonds.

I will offer you the sacrifice of thanksgiving
and call on the name of the Lord.
I will pay my vows to the Lord,
in the presence of all God's people,
in the courts of the house of the Lord,
in your midst, O Jerusalem.

PSALM PRAYER

Let us pray *(pause for quiet prayer)*:

It is right and fitting, Lord our God,
to thank you unceasingly
for the gifts of your heart.
In the presence of your people,
we promise to honor our baptismal vows
and to embrace the living presence of Jesus
in the holy sacrament of the altar,
now and for ever.
~AMEN.

READING	**THE BODY OF CHRIST**	**1 CORINTHIANS 10:16–17**

Brothers and sisters, the cup of blessing that we
bless, is it not a sharing in the blood of Christ?
The bread that we break, is it not a sharing in the
body of Christ? Because there is one bread, we
who are many are one body, for we all partake of
the one bread.

RESPONSE

You fed your people, O Lord, alleluia!
~WITH THE FOOD OF ANGELS, ALLELUIA!

CANTICLE OF THE CHURCH

We praise you, O God,
we acclaim you as Lord;

all creation worships you,
the Father everlasting.

To you all angels, all the powers of heaven,
the cherubim and seraphim, sing in endless praise:
    Holy, holy, holy Lord, God of power and might,
    heaven and earth are full of your glory.

The glorious company of apostles praise you.
The noble fellowship of prophets praise you.
The white-robed army of martyrs praise you.

Throughout the world the holy Church acclaims
      you:
    Father, of majesty unbounded,
    your true and only Son, worthy of all praise,
    the Holy Spirit, advocate and guide.

You, Christ, are the king of glory,
the eternal Son of the Father.
When you took our flesh to set us free
you humbly chose the Virgin's womb.

You overcame the sting of death
and opened the kingdom of heaven to all believers.
You are seated at God's right hand in glory.
We believe that you will come to be our judge.

Come then, Lord, and help your people,
bought with the price of your own blood,
and bring us with your saints
to glory everlasting.[50]

Closing Prayer

O God, who in this wonderful Sacrament
have left us a memorial of your Passion,
grant us, we pray,
so to revere the sacred mysteries of your Body and
      Blood
that we may always experience in ourselves
the fruits of your redemption.
Who live and reign with God the Father
in the unity of the Holy Spirit,
one God, for ever and ever.
~Amen.[51]

May Christ, the true bread from heaven,
† bless us and keep us.
~Amen.

Morning Prayer

O God, † come to my assistance.
~O Lord, make haste to help me.
Blessed be Jesus in the most holy Sacrament
      of the Altar!
~Blessed be his holy Name, now and for
      ever!

Hymn

Your Body, Jesus, once for us was broken,
Your Blood outpoured to heal a broken world.
You rose from death in glory of the Spirit,
Your royal flag victoriously unfurled.

So now these signs of Bread and Wine, retelling
Your dying gift, your living self proclaim.
Until you come in splendor at earth's ending
Your people, Lord, your hidden presence here
      acclaim.[52]

PSALM 84:1–5, 8–11   GOD'S HOME AMONG US

ANTIPHON O God, LOOK UPON THE FACE OF YOUR
     ANOINTED.

How lovely is your dwelling place,
O Lord of hosts!
My soul longs, indeed it faints
for the courts of the Lord;
my heart and flesh sing for joy
to the living God.

O Lord of hosts, my Ruler and my God,
at your altars even the sparrow finds a home,
and the swallow a nest for herself,
where she may lay her young.

Blessed are those who dwell in your house,
ever singing your praise.
Blessed are those whose strength is in you,
in whose heart are the highways to Zion.

O Lord God of hosts, hear my prayer;
O God of Jacob, hear!
Behold our shield, O God;
look upon the face of your anointed!

For a day in your courts is better
than a thousand elsewhere.
I would rather be a doorkeeper in the house of my
    God
than dwell in the tents of wickedness.

ANTIPHON O GOD, LOOK UPON THE FACE OF YOUR
    ANOINTED.

PSALM PRAYER

Let us pray *(pause for quiet prayer):*

Lord God of hosts,
look on the face of your Christ
who tabernacles among us
in his divine and human presence
and causes our rejoicing hearts
to hallow his name, now and for ever.
~AMEN.

1 CORINTHIANS
READING   **THE LAST SUPPER**   **11:23–25**
Brothers and sisters, I received from the Lord what
I also handed on to you, that the Lord Jesus on the
night when he was betrayed took a loaf of bread,
and when he had given thanks, he broke it and
said, "This is my body that is broken for you. Do
this in remembrance of me. In the same way he
took the cup also, after supper, saying, "This cup
is the new covenant in my blood. Do this, as often
as you drink it, in remembrance of me."

As often as you eat this bread and drink the cup,
~YOU WILL PROCLAIM THE LORD'S DEATH UNTIL
HE COMES.

WISDOM

A CANTICLE OF WISDOM   **16:20–21, 26; 17:1A**

ANTIPHON It is my Father WHO GIVES YOU
THE TRUE BREAD FROM HEAVEN.

You gave your people food of the angels,
and without their toil
you supplied them from heaven
with bread ready to eat,
providing every pleasure
and suited to every taste.

For your sustenance manifested your sweetness
toward your children;
and the bread ministering to the desire
of the one who took it,
was changed to suit everyone's liking.

Glory to the Holy and Undivided Trinity:
now and always and for ever and ever. Amen.

ANTIPHON IT IS MY FATHER WHO GIVES YOU
THE TRUE BREAD FROM HEAVEN.

LITANY OF THE BLESSED SACRAMENT
Word made flesh and living among us,
~HAVE MERCY ON US.

Pure and acceptable sacrifice,
~HAVE MERCY ON US.
Hidden manna from above,
~HAVE MERCY ON US.
Living bread that came down from heaven,
~HAVE MERCY ON US.
Bread of life for a hungry world,
~HAVE MERCY ON US.
Chalice of blessing,
~HAVE MERCY ON US.
Precious blood that washes away our sins,
~HAVE MERCY ON US.
Memorial of God's undying love,
~HAVE MERCY ON US.

(Pause for special intentions.)

THE LORD'S PRAYER
Lord, have mercy.
~CHRIST, HAVE MERCY. LORD, HAVE MERCY.
Our Father in heaven,
~HALLOWED BE YOUR NAME,
YOUR KINGDOM COME,
YOUR WILL BE DONE,
ON EARTH AS IN HEAVEN.
GIVE US TODAY OUR DAILY BREAD.
FORGIVE US OUR SINS
AS WE FORGIVE THOSE WHO SIN AGAINST US.
SAVE US FROM THE TIME OF TRIAL
AND DELIVER US FROM EVIL.

For the kingdom and the power and the
glory are yours
now and forever. Amen.

Closing Prayer
Lord Jesus Christ,
we worship you living among us
in the sacrament of your body and blood.
May we offer to our Father in heaven
a solemn pledge of undivided love.
May we offer to our brothers and sisters
a life poured out in loving service of that kingdom
where you live with the Father and the Holy Spirit,
one God, forever and ever.
~Amen.[53]

May the Word made flesh living in our
tabernacles
✝ bless us and keep us.
~Amen.

Noonday Hour
Blessed ✝ be Jesus in the most holy Sacrament of
the Altar!
~Blessed be his holy Name, now and for
ever!

Hymn
King of angels, you are welcome,
Risen Body that feeds my own,

Take my body, take my spirit,
Make them yours and yours alone.

Body born of Virgin Mother,
Child of promise, yet God the Son,
Welcome, heart's desire, true Wisdom,
Make us holy, make us one.[54]

PSALM 150   UNIVERSAL PRAISE

ANTIPHON Let everything that breathes PRAISE
    THE LORD!
Praise God in the sanctuary;
praise God in the mighty firmament!
Praise God for mighty deeds;
praise God for exceeding greatness!

Praise God with trumpet sound;
praise God with lute and harp!
Praise God with tambourine and dance;
praise God with strings and pipe!

Praise God with sounding cymbals;
praise God with loud clashing cymbals!
Let everything that breathes praise the Lord!

ANTIPHON LET EVERYTHING THAT BREATHES
    PRAISE THE LORD!

PSALM PRAYER

Let us pray *(pause for quiet prayer)*:

With the great Mother of God
and the whole company of heaven,
we men and women praise you unceasingly

with all that lives and breathes.
May the melodious music
of your singing Church
be music to all human ears.
We ask this through Christ our Lord.
~Amen.

THE PASSOVER SUPPER

READING Luke 22:15–18

Jesus said to his apostles: "I have eagerly desired
to eat this Passover with you before I suffer; for I
tell you, I will not eat it until it is fulfilled in the
kingdom of God." Then he took a cup, and after
giving thanks he said, "Take this and divide it
among yourselves; for I tell you that from now on
I will not drink of the fruit of the vine until the
kingdom of God comes."

RESPONSE

This is my body which is given for you.
~Do this in remembrance of me.

LITANY OF THE BLESSED SACRAMENT

Food that lasts for eternal life,
~Have mercy on us.
Mystery of faith,
~Have mercy on us.
Medicine of immortality,
~Have mercy on us.
Food of God's chosen,
~Have mercy on us.

Perpetual presence in our tabernacles,
~Have mercy on us.
Viaticum of those who die in the Lord,
~Have mercy on us.
Pledge of future glory,
~Have mercy on us.

(Pause for special intentions.)

Closing Prayer
O God, who in this wonderful Sacrament
have left us a memorial of your Passion,
grant us, we pray,
so to revere the sacred mysteries of your Body and
    Blood
that we may always experience in ourselves
the fruits of your redemption.
Who live and reign with God the Father
in the unity of the Holy Spirit,
one God, for ever and ever.
~Amen.[55]

May the Word made flesh,
Son of God and Son of Mary,
✝ bless us and keep us.
~Amen.

Evening Prayer
Light and peace ✝ in Jesus Christ our Lord!
~Thanks be to God.

Blessed be Jesus in the most holy Sacrament of the
   Altar!
~Blessed be the name of Jesus, now and for
   ever!

HYMN TO THE BLESSED SACRAMENT

Hail our Savior's glorious Body,
Which his Virgin Mother bore;
Hail the Blood, which shed for sinners,
Did a broken world restore;
Hail the sacrament most holy,
Flesh and Blood of Christ adore!

To the Virgin, for our healing,
His own Son the Father sends;
From the Father's love proceeding
Sower, seed, and Word descends;
Wondrous life of Word incarnate
With his greatest wonder ends!

On that paschal evening see him
With the chosen twelve recline,
To the old law still obedient
In its feast of love divine;
Love divine the new law giving,
Gives himself as Bread and Wine!

By his word the Word almighty
Makes of bread his flesh indeed;
Wine becomes his very life-blood:
Faith God's living Word must heed!

Faith alone may safely guide us
Where the senses cannot lead!⁵⁶

St. Thomas Aquinas, OP (1225–1274)

PSALM 42:1–4; 43:3–4   **TO GOD'S ALTAR**

ANTIPHON I will go to the altar of God,
TO GOD MY EXCEEDING JOY!

As the deer longs for flowing streams,
so I long for you, O God.
My whole being thirsts for God,
for the living God.
When shall I come and behold
the face of God?

My tears have been my food
day and night,
while people say to me continually,
"Where is your God?"

These things I remember
as I pour out my life:
how I went with the throng
and led them in procession to the house of God,
with glad shouts and songs of thanksgiving,
a multitude celebrating festival.

O send out your light and your truth;
let them lead me,
let them bring me to your holy hill
and to your dwelling!

Then I will go to the altar of God,
to God my exceeding joy;
and I will praise you with the lyre,
O God, my God.

ANTIPHON I WILL GO TO THE ALTAR OF GOD,
TO GOD MY EXCEEDING JOY!

PSALM PRAYER
Let us pray *(pause for quiet prayer)*:

Lord Jesus, present on our altars,
lift our hearts above the sorrows of this life,
send out your light and your truth,
and be our God of exceeding joy,
now and for ever.
~AMEN.

READING   LIVING BREAD   JOHN 6:47–51
Jesus said to his friends, "Very truly, I tell you,
whoever believes has eternal life. I am the bread
of life. Your ancestors ate the manna in the
wilderness, and they died. This is the bread that
comes down from heaven, so that one may eat of it
and not die. I am the living bread that came down
from heaven. Whoever eats of this bread will live
forever; and the bread that I will give for the life of
the world is my flesh."

RESPONSE
You gave them bread from heaven to be their food.
~BREAD CONTAINING ALL GOODNESS.

The Canticle of the Virgin Mary Luke 1:46–55

ANTIPHON How sacred is the banquet
IN WHICH CHRIST IS OUR FOOD,
THE MEMORIAL OF HIS PASSION IS CELEBRATED
    AGAIN,
OUR HEARTS ARE FILLED WITH GRACE,
AND WE ARE GIVEN A PLEDGE OF FUTURE GLORY,
    ALLELUIA!

My soul † proclaims the greatness of the Lord,
my spirit rejoices in God my Savior,
for you, Lord, have looked with favor on your
    lowly servant.

From this day all generations will call me blessed:
    you, the Almighty, have done great things for
      me
    and holy is your name.
    You have mercy on those who fear you,
    from generation to generation.

You have shown strength with your arm
and scattered the proud in their conceit,
casting down the mighty from their thrones
and lifting up the lowly.
You have filled the hungry with good things
and sent the rich away empty.

You have come to the aid of your servant Israel,
to remember the promise of mercy,
the promise made to our forebears,
to Abraham and his children forever.

Glory to the Holy and Undivided Trinity:
now and always and for ever and ever. Amen.

ANTIPHON HOW SACRED IS THE BANQUET
IN WHICH CHRIST IS OUR FOOD,
THE MEMORIAL OF HIS PASSION IS CELEBRATED
    AGAIN,
OUR HEARTS ARE FILLED WITH GRACE,
AND WE ARE GIVEN A PLEDGE OF FUTURE GLORY,
    ALLELUIA!

LITANY OF THE BLESSED SACRAMENT

By the eager desire you had to eat the Passover
    with your disciples,
~HAVE MERCY ON US.
By your utter humility in washing their feet,
~HAVE MERCY ON US.
By your loving gift of this divine sacrament,
~HAVE MERCY ON US.
By the five wounds of your pierced body,
~HAVE MERCY ON US.
By your sacrificial death on the cross,
~HAVE MERCY ON US.
By the lancing of your sacred heart,
~HAVE MERCY ON US.
By your holy resurrection and ascension into
        heaven,
~HAVE MERCY ON US.
By the gift of the Spirit of truth and consolation,
~HAVE MERCY ON US.

By your return in glory to judge the living and the
     dead,
~HAVE MERCY ON US.

(Pause for special intentions.)

Lamb of God, you take away the sins of the world,
     ~HAVE MERCY ON US.
Lamb of God, you take away the sins of the world,
     ~HAVE MERCY ON US.
Lamb of God, you take away the sins of the world,
     ~GRANT US YOUR PEACE.

CLOSING PRAYER
O God, who in this wonderful Sacrament
have left us a memorial of your Passion,
grant us, we pray,
so to revere the sacred mysteries of your Body and
     Blood
that we may always experience in ourselves
the fruits of your redemption.
Who live and reign with God the Father
in the unity of the Holy Spirit,
one God, for ever and ever.
~AMEN.[57]

May Christ, the bread of life,
✝ be our strength and our stay.
~AMEN.

Night Prayer

Blessed † be Jesus reigning in our tabernacles!
~He is a priest for ever, according to
    Melchizedek.

Hymn

Come, adore this wondrous presence,
Bow to Christ, the source of grace.
Here is kept the ancient promise
Of God's earthly dwelling-place.
Sight is blind before God's glory,
Faith alone may see his face.

Glory be to God the Father,
Praise to his co-equal Son,
Adoration to the Spirit,
Bond of love, in Godhead one.
Blest be God by all creation
joyously while endless ages run. Amen.[58]

St. Thomas Aquinas, OP (1225–1274)

Psalm 23   Shepherd and Host

Antiphon I am the good shepherd; I know mine
and mine know me.

The Lord is my shepherd, I shall not want;
the Lord makes me lie down in green pastures,
leads me beside the still waters;
restores my life, leads me in right paths
for the sake of the Lord's name.

Even though I walk through the darkest valley,
I fear no evil; for you are with me;
your rod and your staff they comfort me.

You prepare a table before me
in the presence of my enemies;
you anoint my head with oil,
my cup overflows.

Only goodness and mercy shall follow me
all the days of my life;
and I shall dwell in the house of the Lord
as long as I live.

ANTIPHON I AM THE GOOD SHEPHERD; I KNOW
MINE AND MINE KNOW ME.

PSALM PRAYER

Let us pray *(pause for quiet prayer):*

Lord Jesus,
good shepherd of your flock of rational sheep,
you are with us even in the darkest valley.
Anoint us with your strength and courage
and make us live for you and with you,
now and for ever.
~AMEN.

READING

TRUE FOOD AND DRINK   **JOHN 6:53–55**

Jesus said to them, "Very truly, I tell you, unless
you eat the flesh of the Son of Man and drink his
blood, you have no life in you. Those who eat my
flesh and drink my blood have eternal life, and I

will raise them up on the last day; for my flesh is true food and my blood is true drink."

RESPONSE

No one can come to me
~UNLESS IT IS GRANTED BY THE FATHER.

THE CANTICLE OF
SIMEON THE PROPHET

LUKE 2:29–32

ANTIPHON Remember, I AM WITH YOU ALWAYS, TO THE END OF THE AGE.

Now, Lord, † let your servant go in peace:
your word has been fulfilled.

My own eyes have seen your salvation
which you have prepared in the sight
   of every people:

a light to reveal you to the nations
and the glory of your people Israel.

Glory to the Father, and to the Son,
and to the Holy Spirit:

as it was in the beginning, is now,
and will be forever. Amen.

ANTIPHON REMEMBER, I AM WITH YOU ALWAYS, TO THE END OF THE AGE.

CLOSING PRAYER

Lord Jesus Christ,
in the blessed Sacrament of the Altar
you have left us a living memorial

of your passion, death, and resurrection.
We worship you in these holy mysteries
and ask you in all humility
to reveal to us all they contain.
Blessed be the name of Jesus, now and for ever!
~AMEN.

May the heart of Jesus in the most Blessed
      Sacrament
be praised, adored, and loved
with grateful affection, at every moment,
in all the tabernacles of the world,
even to the end of time.
~AMEN.

Friday   Hours of the Holy Cross

As early as the second century, the passion and death of our Savior were commemorated every week on Friday with special prayer and fasting. As pieces of the true cross circulated throughout the Catholic world, devotion to this supreme relic of Jesus' passion and death increased, and the Office of the Cross became an important part of the Books of Hours.

"See the glory of the Cross: the world was not subdued by iron weapons but by the wood of the Cross."

St. Augustine of Hippo Regius, *On Psalm 55, verse 1*

"Fasting is not only good for us personally but our fasting supplies the needs of the poor, for by abstaining from food we feed the poor."

St. Leo the Great, *Sermon 2 on the December Fast*

Mattins   Grief in the Garden

O Lord, † open my lips,
~AND MY MOUTH WILL DECLARE YOUR PRAISE.
We adore you, O Christ, and we bless you,
~FOR BY YOUR HOLY CROSS YOU HAVE REDEEMED
  THE WORLD.

PSALM 95   A CALL TO PRAYER

ANTIPHON Come, LET US WORSHIP CHRIST
WHO DIED ON THE CROSS FOR OUR SALVATION.

O come, let us sing to the Lord;
let us make a joyful noise to the rock of our
      salvation!

Let us come into God's presence with
        thanksgiving;
let us make a joyful noise with songs of praise!

~Come, let us worship Christ who died
on the cross for our salvation.

For the Lord is a great God,
a great Ruler above all gods,
in whose hands are the depths of the earth
and also the heights of the mountains.
The sea belongs to God who made it,
and the dry land, because God formed it.

~Come, let us worship Christ who died
on the cross for our salvation.

O come, let us worship and bow down,
let us kneel before the Lord, our Maker!
For the Lord is our God,
we are the people of God's pasture,
the sheep of God's hand.

~Come, let us worship Christ
who died on the cross for our salvation.

Glory to the Father, and to the Son,
and to the Holy Spirit:
as it was in the beginning, is now,
and will be forever. Amen.

~Come, let us worship Christ
who died on the cross for our salvation.

Hymn to the Cross

O Cross of Christ, immortal tree
On which our Savior died,
The world is sheltered by your arms
That bore the Crucified.

From bitter death and barren wood
The tree of life is made;
Its branches bear unfailing fruit
And leaves that never fade.

O faithful Cross, you stand unmoved
While ages run their course:
Foundation of the universe,
Creation's binding force.

Give glory to the risen Christ
And to his Cross give praise,
The sign of God's unfathomed love,
The hope of all our days.
    Amen.[59]

Psalm 13   Gethsemane

ANTIPHON Jesus prayed IN GREAT AGONY AND
      DISTRESS TO HIS FATHER.

How long, O Lord? Will you forget me forever?
How long will you hide your face from me?
How long must I bear pain in my soul,
and have sorrow in my heart all the day?
How long shall my enemy be exalted over me?

Consider and answer me, O Lord my God;
lighten my eyes, lest I sleep the sleep of death;

lest my enemy say, "I have prevailed";
lest my foes rejoice because I am shaken.

But I trusted in your steadfast love;
my heart shall rejoice in your salvation.
I will sing to the Lord,
for the Lord has dealt richly with me.

ANTIPHON JESUS PRAYED IN GREAT AGONY AND
DISTRESS TO HIS FATHER.

PSALM PRAYER

Let us pray *(pause for quiet prayer):*

Lord Jesus, man of sorrows,
you were deeply grieved in the Garden,
betrayed by Judas with a kiss,
and deserted by your friends:
Help us to meditate on your sufferings,
embrace the cross daily with you,
and die to ourselves.
Your reign is a reign for all ages.
~AMEN.

THE AGONY IN

READING **THE GARDEN** **MARK 14:32–36**

Jesus and his disciples went to a place called
Gethsemane; and he said to his disciples, "Sit here
while I pray." He took with him Peter and James
and John, and began to be distressed and agitated.
And he said to them, "I am deeply grieved, even to
death; remain here, and keep awake." And going
a little farther, he threw himself on the ground

and prayed that, if it were possible, the hour might pass from him. He said, "Abba, Father, for you all things are possible; remove this cup from me; yet, not what I want, but what you want."

RESPONSE

Judas went up to Jesus and said,
~"RABBI!" AND KISSED HIM.

A CANTICLE OF
PAUL THE APOSTLE   PHILIPPIANS 2:6–11

ANTIPHON Jesus said to Simon Peter,
"BEFORE THE COCK CROWS YOU WILL DENY ME
        THREE TIMES."

Though he was in the form of God,
Christ Jesus did not regard equality with God
as something to be exploited,
but emptied himself, taking the form of a slave,
being born in human likeness.

And being found in human form,
he humbled himself
and became obedient to the point of death—
even death on a cross.

Therefore God also highly exalted him
and gave him the name
that is above every name,
so that at the name of Jesus
every knee should bend
in heaven and on earth and under the earth,
and every tongue should confess

that Jesus Christ is Lord,
to the glory of God the Father.

ANTIPHON JESUS SAID TO SIMON PETER,
"BEFORE THE COCK CROWS YOU WILL DENY ME
THREE TIMES."

CLOSING PRAYER
Heavenly Father,
in the Garden of Gethsemane
your Son was deeply grieved even to death
and asked you to spare him the cross
while still accepting your holy will.
Permit us to share his agony with him
and promise to be more faithful
than Judas who betrayed him
or the disciples who abandoned him.
Blest be Jesus, true God and true Man!
~AMEN.

May the glorious passion of our Lord Jesus Christ
† bring us to the joys of paradise.
~AMEN.

Morning Prayer   **Jesus Is Tried and Condemned**

O God, † come to my assistance.
~O LORD, MAKE HASTE TO HELP ME.
We adore you, O Christ, and we bless you,
~FOR BY THE HOLY CROSS YOU HAVE REDEEMED
THE WORLD.

Hymn

O love, how deep, how broad, how high,
How passing thought and fantasy,
That God, the Son of God should take
Our mortal form for mortals' sake.

For us to evil power betrayed,
Scourged, mocked, in purple robe arrayed,
He bore the shameful cross and death,
For us gave up his dying breath.

For us he rose from death again;
For us he went on high to reign;
For us he sent the Spirit here
To guide, to strengthen, and to cheer.

All glory to our Lord and God
For love so deep, so high, so broad:
The Trinity whom we adore
For ever and for evermore.[60]

Psalm 51   A Broken, Contrite Heart

ANTIPHON Jesus was arrested, BOUND,
AND TAKEN TO CAIAPHAS, THE HIGH PRIEST.

Have mercy on me, O God,
according to your steadfast love;
according to your abundant mercy
blot out my transgressions.

Wash me thoroughly of my iniquity,
and cleanse me from my sin!
For I know my transgressions,
and my sin is ever before me.

Against you, you only, I have sinned,
and done that which is evil in your sight,
so that you are justified in your sentence
and blameless in your judgment.

Surely, you desire truth in the inward being;
therefore teach me wisdom in my secret heart.
Purge me with hyssop, and I shall be clean;
wash me, and I shall be whiter than snow.

Let me hear with joy and gladness;
let the bones which you have broken rejoice.
Hide your face from my sins,
and blot out all my iniquities.

Create in me a clean heart, O God,
and put a new and right spirit within me.
Cast me not away from your presence,
and take not your holy spirit from me.

Restore to me the joy of your salvation,
and sustain in me a willing spirit.
Then I will teach transgressors your ways,
and sinners will return to you.

Deliver me from bloodshed, O God,
    God of my salvation,
and my tongue will sing aloud of your deliverance.
O Lord, open my lips,
and my mouth shall show forth your praise.

For you have no delight in sacrifice;
were I to give you a burnt offering,
    you would not be pleased.

The sacrifice acceptable to God is a broken spirit;
a broken and contrite heart, O God,
  you will not despise.

ANTIPHON JESUS WAS ARRESTED, BOUND,
AND TAKEN TO CAIAPHAS, THE HIGH PRIEST.

PSALM PRAYER

Let us pray *(pause for quiet prayer):*

Lord Jesus Christ,
during the night Caiaphas, the high priest,
and the whole council conspired against you,
urging your death for blasphemy.
By your silence before your lying accusers,
give us the grace to speak the truth
and stand up for your Gospel
in all circumstances.
You live and reign, now and for ever.
~AMEN.

MATTHEW
READING   **FALSE WITNESSES**   **26:57–68**

Those who had arrested Jesus took him to
Caiaphas the high priest, in whose house the
scribes and the elders had gathered. Now the chief
priests and the whole council were looking for
false testimony against Jesus so that they might
put him to death, but they found none, though
many false witnesses came forward. Then the high
priest said to him, "I put you under oath before
the living God, tell us if you are the Messiah, the

Son of God." Jesus said to him, "You have said so. But I tell you, from now on you will see the Son of Man seated at the right hand of Power and coming on the clouds of heaven." Then the high priest tore his clothes and said, "He has blasphemed! Why do we still need witnesses? You have now heard his blasphemy. What is your verdict?" They answered, "He deserves death." Then they spat in his face and struck him; and some slapped him, saying, "Prophesy to us, you Messiah! Who is it that struck you?"

RESPONSE

Even though I must die with you,
~I WILL NOT DENY YOU, SAID SIMON PETER.

THE CANTICLE OF ZACHARY   LUKE 1:68–79

ANTIPHON You will see THE SON OF MAN SEATED
        AT THE RIGHT HAND OF POWER AND
        COMING ON THE CLOUDS OF HEAVEN.

Blessed are you, † Lord, the God of Israel,
you have come to your people and set them free.
You have raised up for us a mighty Savior,
born of the house of your servant David.

Through your holy prophets, you promised of old
    to save us from our enemies,
    from the hands of all who hate us,
    to show mercy to our forebears,
    and to remember your holy covenant.

This was the oath you swore to our father
     Abraham:
   to set us free from the hands of our enemies,
   free to worship you without fear,
   holy and righteous before you,
   all the days of our life.

And you, child, shall be called the prophet
     of the Most High,
for you will go before the Lord to prepare the way,
to give God's people knowledge of salvation
by the forgiveness of their sins.

In the tender compassion of our God
the dawn from on high shall break upon us,
to shine on those who dwell in darkness
     and the shadow of death,
and to guide our feet into the way of peace.

Glory to the Holy and Undivided Trinity:
now and always and forever and ever. Amen.

ANTIPHON YOU WILL SEE THE SON OF MAN
     SEATED AT THE RIGHT HAND OF POWER AND
     COMING ON THE CLOUDS OF HEAVEN.

LITANY OF THE PASSION
Jesus, man of sorrows, you were betrayed by Judas
     with a kiss.
~LORD, HAVE MERCY ON US.
Jesus, man of sorrows, you were led before
     Annas and Caiaphas, the high priests.
~LORD, HAVE MERCY ON US.

170 A Book of Hours

Jesus, man of sorrows, you were accused
   by many false witnesses.
~LORD, HAVE MERCY ON US.
Jesus, man of sorrows, you were condemned
   for blasphemy.
~LORD, HAVE MERCY ON US.
Jesus, man of sorrows, you were spit upon,
      slapped, mocked, and beaten in the house of
      the high priest.
~LORD, HAVE MERCY ON US.
Jesus, man of sorrows, you were bound, led away,
   and handed over to Pilate the governor.
~LORD, HAVE MERCY ON US.

(Pause for special intentions.)

THE LORD'S PRAYER
Lord, have mercy.
~CHRIST, HAVE MERCY. LORD, HAVE MERCY.
Our Father in heaven,
   ~HALLOWED BE YOUR NAME,
   YOUR KINGDOM COME,
   YOUR WILL BE DONE,
      ON EARTH AS IN HEAVEN.
GIVE US TODAY OUR DAILY BREAD.
FORGIVE US OUR SINS
   AS WE FORGIVE THOSE WHO SIN AGAINST US.
SAVE US FROM THE TIME OF TRIAL
   AND DELIVER US FROM EVIL.

FOR THE KINGDOM AND THE POWER AND THE
  GLORY ARE YOURS
    NOW AND FOREVER. AMEN.

CLOSING PRAYER

Lord Jesus, man of sorrows
and acquainted with grief,
lodge in our hearts the image of your betrayal,
your arrest and trial before the high priests,
and your mockery and mistreatment.
By the first miseries of your passion,
grant us contrition for all our sins,
and heartfelt compassion for your sufferings
at the hand of wicked men.
Your reign is a reign for all ages.
~AMEN.

May the glorious passion of our Lord Jesus Christ
✝ bring us to the joys of paradise.
~AMEN.

Noonday   The Trial before Pilate

O God, ✝ come to my assistance.
~O LORD, MAKE HASTE TO HELP ME.
We adore you, O Christ, and we bless you,
~FOR BY YOUR HOLY CROSS YOU HAVE REDEEMED
    THE WORLD.

HYMN

Alone, in depths of woe,
Upon that scornful tree

Hangs Christ, redeemer of the world,
In shame and agony.

His feet and hands outstretched
By hammered nails are torn;
In mocking, on his head is thrust
A crown of bitter thorn.

Come, kneel before the Lord:
He shed for us his blood;
He died the victim of pure love
To make us one with God.[61]

PSALM 54   INNOCENCE IN CHAINS

ANTIPHON They bound him, LED HIM AWAY,
AND HANDED HIM OVER TO PILATE THE
GOVERNOR.

Save me, O God, by your name,
and vindicate me by your might.
Hear my prayer, O God;
listen to the words of my mouth.

For the insolent have risen against me,
the ruthless seek my life;
they do not set God before them.

But surely, God is my helper;
the Lord is the upholder of my life.
God will repay my enemies for their evil.
In your faithfulness, put an end to them.

With a freewill offering I will sacrifice to you;
I will give thanks to your name, O Lord, for it
is good.

For God has delivered me from every trouble,
and my eye has looked in triumph on my enemies.

ANTIPHON THEY BOUND HIM, LED HIM AWAY,
AND HANDED HIM OVER TO PILATE THE
GOVERNOR.

PSALM PRAYER
Let us pray *(pause for quiet prayer)*:

Innocent Jesus,
faithless priests betrayed you,
lying witnesses accused you falsely,
and craven Pilate sent you to your death.
By your holy and silent witness,
give us the courage to meditate
on all the scenes of your bitter passion
and to place our faith and trust in you,
now and for ever.
~AMEN.

READING   **JESUS BEFORE PILATE**   **MATTHEW 27:11–14**

Now Jesus stood before the governor; and the
governor asked him, "Are you the King of the
Jews?" Jesus said, "You say so." But when he was
accused by the chief priests and elders, he did not
answer. Then Pilate said to him, "Do you not hear
how many accusations they make against you?"
But he gave him no answer, not even to a single
charge, so that the governor was greatly amazed.

RESPONSE

After flogging Jesus,

~PILATE HANDED HIM OVER TO BE CRUCIFIED.

THE CANTICLE OF   **REVELATION**
THE LAMB OF GOD   **4:11; 5:9–10, 12**

ANTIPHON Help your people, Lord,

BOUGHT WITH THE PRICE OF YOUR OWN BLOOD.

You are worthy, our Lord and God,
to receive glory and honor and power,
for you created all things,
and by your will they existed and were created.

You are worthy, O Christ,
to take the scroll and to open its seals,
for you were slaughtered,
and by your blood you ransomed for God
saints from every tribe and language
    and people and nation;
you have made them to be a kingdom and priests
serving our God, and they will reign on earth.

Worthy is the Lamb that was slaughtered
to receive power and wealth and wisdom and
     might
and honor and glory and blessing!

ANTIPHON HELP YOUR PEOPLE, LORD,

BOUGHT WITH THE PRICE OF YOUR OWN BLOOD.

CLOSING PRAYER

Lord Jesus Christ, man of sorrows,
condemned to death by Pontius Pilate,
mocked, flogged, crowned with thorns,
pierced with nails, and scorned by unbelievers:
By your holy and glorious wounds,
soften our hard hearts,
teach us true repentance for our sins,
and bring us to the victory you have won for us,
O Savior of the world,
living and reigning, now and for ever.
~AMEN.

By the prayers of Mary, the mother of sorrows,
✝ bring us, O Lord, to the joys that never end.
~AMEN.

Evening Prayer   The Crucifixion

Light and peace ✝ in Jesus Christ our Lord.
~AMEN.
We adore you, O Christ, and we bless you,
~FOR BY YOUR HOLY CROSS YOU HAVE REDEEMED
THE WORLD.

HYMN

Jesus, when faith with constant eyes
Regards your wondrous sacrifice,
Love rises to an ardent flame,
And we all other hope disclaim.

With cold affections who can see
The lash, the thorns, the nails, the tree,
The flowing tears and purple sweat,
The bleeding hands, and head, and feet.

Look, saints, into his gaping side,
The cleft how large, how deep, how wide?
There issues forth a double flood
Of cleansing water, pard'ning blood.

From there, O soul, a balsam flows
To heal your wounds, and cure your woes;
Immortal joys come streaming down,
Joys, like his griefs, immense, unknown.

Thus I could ever, ever sing
The sufferings of my heavenly King:
With growing pleasure spread abroad
The mysteries of a dying God.[62]

PSALM 70   JESUS CRIES OUT ON THE CROSS

ANTIPHON They pierced my hands and my feet
AND LAID MY SOUL IN THE DUST OF DEATH.

Be pleased, O God, to deliver me!
O Lord, make haste to help me!
Let them be put to shame and confusion
who seek my life!

Let them be turned back and dishonored
who desire my pain!
Let them turn back because of their shame
who say, "Aha, Aha!"

May all who seek you
rejoice and be glad in you!
May those who love your salvation
say evermore, "God is great!"

But I am poor and needy;
hasten to help me, O God!
You are my help and my deliverer;
O Lord, do not tarry!

ANTIPHON THEY PIERCED MY HANDS AND MY FEET
AND LAID MY SOUL IN THE DUST OF DEATH.

PSALM PRAYER
Let us pray *(pause for quiet prayer)*:

Lord Jesus Christ, suffering servant of God,
as you hung on the cross, daylight failed,
and the whole land was plunged into darkness.
In the gloom you cried out in desolation
and handed over your spirit to your Father.
By your suffering on the cross,
grant us lasting light for our souls and bodies
and bring us in safety to the unfading glories
of our heavenly home,
where you live and reign, for ever and ever.
~AMEN.

JOHN 19:17–19,
READING   **JESUS CRUCIFIED**   28–30

Carrying the cross by himself, Jesus went out to
what is called The Place of the Skull, which in
Hebrew is called Golgotha. There they crucified

him, and with him two others, one on either side, with Jesus between them. Pilate also had an inscription written and put on the cross. It read, "Jesus of Nazareth, the King of the Jews."

When Jesus knew that all was now finished, he said (in order to fulfill the scripture), "I am thirsty." A jar full of sour wine was standing there. So they put a sponge full of the wine on a branch of hyssop and held it to his mouth. When Jesus had received the wine, he said, "It is finished." Then he bowed his head and gave up his spirit.

RESPONSE

They will look on the one
~WHOM THEY HAVE PIERCED.

THE CANTICLE OF THE VIRGIN MARY   LUKE 1:46–55

ANTIPHON Standing near the cross of Jesus were
    his mother,
AND HIS MOTHER'S SISTER, MARY THE WIFE OF
    CLOPAS, MARY MAGDALENE,
AND THE BELOVED DISCIPLE.

My soul † proclaims the greatness of the Lord,
my spirit rejoices in God my Savior,
for you, Lord, have looked with favor on your
    lowly servant.

From this day all generations will call me blessed:
    you, the Almighty, have done great things for me
    and holy is your name.

You have mercy on those who fear you,
from generation to generation.

You have shown strength with your arm
and scattered the proud in their conceit,
casting down the mighty from their thrones
and lifting up the lowly.
You have filled the hungry with good things
and sent the rich away empty.

You have come to the aid of your servant Israel,
to remember the promise of mercy,
the promise made to our forebears,
to Abraham and his children forever.

Glory to the Holy and Undivided Trinity:
now and always and for ever and ever. Amen.

ANTIPHON STANDING NEAR THE CROSS OF JESUS
WERE HIS MOTHER,
AND HIS MOTHER'S SISTER, MARY THE WIFE OF
CLOPAS, MARY MAGDALENE,
AND THE BELOVED DISCIPLE.

LITANY OF THE PASSION
Lord Jesus, of your own free will you accepted the
cross for our salvation:
~THANK YOU, JESUS.
Friend of humankind, you embraced the tragic
agony of the cross for our sake:
~THANK YOU, JESUS.

You were seen without beauty to restore us
  to the splendor of God:
~THANK YOU, JESUS.
Like a seed you were buried in the ground
  to spring up a hundredfold:
~THANK YOU, JESUS.
Through your divine death we are delivered
  from death and decay:
~THANK YOU, JESUS.
Your holy cross vanquished hell and put dark death
  to flight:
~THANK YOU, JESUS.
By your love and compassion you are the Savior
  of the world:
~THANK YOU, JESUS.

(Pause for special intentions.)

For the prayers of the Mother of Sorrows
  and of all the saints watching near the cross:
~THANK YOU, JESUS.

THE LORD'S PRAYER
Lord, have mercy.
~CHRIST, HAVE MERCY. LORD, HAVE MERCY.

Our Father in heaven,
  ~HALLOWED BE YOUR NAME,
  YOUR KINGDOM COME,
  YOUR WILL BE DONE,
    ON EARTH AS IN HEAVEN.

Give us today our daily bread.
Forgive us our sins
   as we forgive those who sin against us.
Save us from the time of trial
   and deliver us from evil.
For the kingdom and the power and the
      glory are yours
   now and forever. Amen.

Closing Prayer
Lord Jesus Christ,
as you were dying at mid-afternoon,
you promised paradise to a dying criminal,
handed over your spirit to your Father,
and descended among the imprisoned spirits
to enlighten and release them.
By the blood and water that poured
from your broken heart,
wash away all our sins,
renew in us a true and life-giving Spirit,
and bring us at last to the resurrection of the body
and life everlasting in the world to come,
where you live and reign with the Father,
in the unity of the Holy Spirit,
one God, for ever and ever.
~Amen.

By his holy and glorious wounds
may Christ Jesus † protect us and keep us.
~Amen.

Night Prayer　　　　　**Death and Burial**

Our help † is in the name of the Lord,

~The Maker of heaven and earth.

We adore your cross, O Lord,

~And we praise and glorify your holy
　　　resurrection,

For by the wood of the cross,

~Joy came into the whole world!

Hymn

You make your way alone: a victim, Lord,
whose sacrifice will see death overthrown.
What can we say, so wretched, overawed,
when all the pain we bear should be our own?

The sins are ours, and ours should be the blame;
why should you suffer in the sinner's place?
Lord, break our hearts, and make us feel your
　　　shame,
for only such compassion shares your grace.

We see the anguish of the grievous night:
the evening came with weeping, which will last
until the third day breaks, and new delight
comes surging with you, Lord, where grief has
　　　passed.[63]

Psalm 31:1–7　　　Last Words from the Cross

Antiphon　Into your hands, O Lord, I commend
　　　my spirit.

In you, O Lord, I seek refuge;
let me never be put to shame;
in your righteousness, deliver me!
Listen to me,
rescue me speedily!

Be a rock of refuge for me,
a strong fortress to save me!
You are indeed my rock and my fortress;
for your name's sake lead me and guide me,
for you are my refuge.

Into your hands I commend my spirit;
you have redeemed me, O Lord, faithful God.
I will rejoice and be glad in your steadfast love,
because you have seen my affliction,
and have taken heed of my adversities.

ANTIPHON INTO YOUR HANDS, O LORD, I
    COMMEND MY SPIRIT.

PSALM PRAYER

Let us pray *(pause for quiet prayer)*:
Merciful Father,
look on this family of yours
for which our Lord Jesus Christ
did not hesitate to hand himself over
    to the wicked
and to undergo the torment of the cross;
his reign is a reign for all ages.
~AMEN.

THE BURIAL OF JESUS

When it was evening, there came a rich man from Arimathea, named Joseph, who was also a disciple of Jesus. He went to Pilate and asked for the body of Jesus; then Pilate ordered it to be given to him. So Joseph took the body and wrapped it in a clean linen cloth and laid it in his own new tomb, which he had hewn in the rock. He then rolled a great stone to the door of the tomb and went away. Mary Magdalene and the other Mary were there, sitting opposite the tomb.

RESPONSE

Jesus cried out with a loud voice
~AND BREATHED HIS LAST.

A CANTICLE OF PETER THE APOSTLE

1 PETER 2:21–24

ANTIPHON The centurion who stood facing him said, "TRULY THIS MAN WAS GOD'S SON!"

Christ suffered for you, leaving you an example,
so that you should follow in his steps.
"He committed no sin,
and no deceit was found in his mouth."

When he was abused,
he did not return abuse;
when he suffered,
he did not threaten;

but he entrusted himself
to the one who judges justly.

He himself bore our sins
in his body on the cross,
so that, free from sins,
we might live for righteousness;
by his wounds we have been healed.

ANTIPHON THE CENTURION WHO STOOD FACING
    HIM SAID, "TRULY THIS MAN WAS GOD'S
    SON!"

CLOSING PRAYER
Lord Jesus Christ, Son of the living God,
at the end of the day you rested in the tomb
and made the grave a bed of hope
for those who believe in you.
Life of the world,
when our bodies lie in the dust of death,
may our souls live with you,
for ever and ever.
~AMEN.

May the glorious passion of our Lord Jesus Christ,
✝ bring us to the joys of paradise.
~AMEN.

Saturday   Hours of the Virgin Mary

One of the most central and long-lasting of Marian devotions has been the Little Office of the Blessed Virgin Mary and the Saturday Office of Mary. These forms of devotion concentrate on Mary's central role as *Theotokos*, Mother of God, in the incarnation of Christ and help us to understand and appreciate her divine and virginal motherhood.

"Yes, she remained a virgin during it all. A virgin conceiving. A virgin birthing! A virgin while heavy with child. A virgin after she delivered the child. A virgin forever!"

St. Augustine of Hippo Regius (354–430),
Sermons to the People[64]

Mattins   The Annunciation

O Lord, † open my lips.
~AND MY MOUTH WILL DECLARE YOUR PRAISE.
Blest be the great Mother of God, Mary most holy,
~AND BLEST BE HER HOLY AND DIVINE CHILD.

PSALM 95   A CALL TO PRAYER

ANTIPHON Hail, Mary, FULL OF GRACE, THE LORD
    IS WITH YOU.

O come, let us sing to the Lord;
let us make a joyful noise to the rock of our
    salvation!
Let us come into God's presence with
    thanksgiving;
let us make a joyful noise with songs of praise.

~HAIL, MARY, FULL OF GRACE, THE LORD IS WITH
   YOU.

For the Lord is a great God,
and a great Ruler above all gods,
in whose hands are the depths of the earth
and also the heights of the mountains.
The sea belongs to God who made it,
and the dry land, because God formed it.

~HAIL, MARY, FULL OF GRACE, THE LORD IS WITH
   YOU.

O come, let us worship and bow down,
let us kneel before the Lord, our Maker!
For the Lord is our God,
we are the people of God's pasture,
the sheep of God's hand.

~HAIL, MARY, FULL OF GRACE, THE LORD IS WITH
   YOU.

Glory to the Father, and to the Son,
and to the Holy Spirit:
as it was in the beginning, is now,
and will be for ever. Amen.

~HAIL, MARY, FULL OF GRACE, THE LORD IS WITH
   YOU.

HYMN
The God whom earth and sea and sky
Adore and praise and magnify,

Whose might they claim, whose love they tell,
In Mary's body came to dwell.

O Mother blest! the chosen shrine
Wherein the Architect divine,
Whose hand contains the earth and sky,
Has come in human form to lie.

Blest in the message Gabriel brought;
Blest in the work the Spirit wrought;
Most blest, to bring to human birth
The long desired of all the earth.

O Lord, the Virgin-born, to you
Eternal praise and laud are due,
Whom with the Father we adore
And Spirit blest for evermore. Amen.[65]

PSALM 45   **KING JESUS AND QUEEN MARY**

ANTIPHON Christ our Lord, LEAVING HIS ROYAL
        THRONE,
CAME DOWN FROM HEAVEN INTO THE WOMB OF
        HIS VIRGIN MOTHER, ALLELUIA!

You are the most handsome of men;
grace is poured upon your lips;
therefore God has blessed you forever.

Gird your sword upon your thigh, O mighty one,
in your glory and majesty!
In your majesty ride forth victoriously
for the cause of truth and to defend the right;
let your right hand teach you right deeds!

Your arrows are sharp
in the hearts of the king's enemies;
the peoples fall under you.
Your throne, O God, endures forever and ever.
Your royal scepter is a scepter of equity;
you love righteousness and hate wickedness.

Therefore God, your God, has anointed you
with the oil of gladness above your peers;
your robes are all fragrant with myrrh and aloes
    and cassia.

From ivory palaces stringed instruments make
        you glad;
daughters of kings are among your ladies of honor;
at your right hand stands the queen in gold of
        Ophir.

Hear, O daughter, consider and listen;
forget your people and your father's house;
and the king will desire your beauty.

Since he is your lord, bow to him;
the people of Tyre will seek your favor with gifts,
the richest of the people with all kinds of gifts.

The princess in her chamber is decked
    with gold-woven robes;
in many-colored robes she is led to the king;
behind her the virgins, her companions, follow.
With joy and gladness they are led along
as they enter the palace of the king.

In the place of ancestors you shall have sons;
you will make them princes in all the earth.
I will cause your name to be celebrated in all
    generations;
therefore the people will praise you forever and
    ever.

ANTIPHON CHRIST OUR LORD, LEAVING HIS ROYAL
    THRONE,
CAME DOWN FROM HEAVEN INTO THE WOMB OF
    HIS VIRGIN MOTHER, ALLELUIA!

PSALM PRAYER

Let us pray *(pause for quiet prayer):*

Great God and Savior, Jesus Christ,
you made your mother a model of faith,
an obedient servant of your holy will.
By her perpetual prayer on our behalf,
make us true sons and daughters
of the communion of saints.
Your reign is a reign for all ages.
~AMEN.

READING   **GABRIEL'S MESSAGE**   **LUKE 1:35, 38**
The angel said to Mary, "The Holy Spirit will
come upon you, and the power of the Most High
will overshadow you; therefore the child to be
born of you will be holy; he will be called Son of
God." Then Mary said, "Here am I, the servant
of the Lord; let it be with me according to your
word." Then the angel departed from her.

RESPONSE

Blessed are you among women, O Mary,

~AND BLESSED IS THE FRUIT OF YOUR WOMB,
    JESUS.

A CANTICLE TO THE BLESSED VIRGIN MARY

We praise you as our Mother,
we acclaim you as our blessed Lady.
All the earth reveres you,
the eternal Father's daughter.

All the angelic powers sing your praise:
the angels dance for joy, the archangels clap their
    hands,
the virtues sing and shout, the principalities are
    glad,
the powers are joyful, the dominations are delighted,
the thrones make festival, the cherubim and
    seraphim
  cry out without ceasing:

  Holy, holy, holy is the great Mother of God,
    Mary most holy;
  Jesus, the blessed fruit of your womb, is the
    glory of heaven and earth.

The glorious choir of apostles,
the noble company of prophets,
the white-robed army of martyrs,
  all sing your praise.

The holy Church throughout the world celebrates
    you:
the daughter of infinite Majesty,
the mother of God's true and only Son,
the bride of the Spirit of truth and consolation.

You bore Christ, the King of glory,
the eternal Son of the Father.
When he took our flesh to set us free,
he humbly chose your virgin womb.

When he overcame death's sting,
he assumed you into heaven.
You now sit with your Son
at God's right hand in glory.

Intercede for us, O Virgin Mary,
when he comes to be our judge.
Help your chosen people
bought with his precious blood.
And bring us with all the saints
into glory everlasting.

Save your people, O holy Virgin,
and bless your inheritance.
Rule them and uphold them,
now and for ever.

Day by day we salute you;
we acclaim you unceasingly.
In your goodness pray for us sinners;
have mercy on us poor sinners.

May your mercy sustain us always,
for we put our trust in you.
In you, dear Mother, do we trust;
defend us now and for ever.[66]

Pour forth, O Lord, your grace into our hearts,
that we to whom the incarnation of Christ your
      Son
was made known by the message of an angel,
may by his passion and cross
be brought to the glory of his resurrection;
through the same Christ our Lord.
~AMEN.

May the Virgin Mary mild
✝ bless us with her holy Child.
~AMEN.

The Birth and Epiphany of Jesus

Morning Prayer

"On that day we call His birthday, a flock of
shepherds from the Jews saw Him. But this
very day, which has been tagged *Epiphany* or
Manifestation, an embassy of Magi from the
Gentiles paid their respects to Him. Angels
did the announcing in the first instance; in
the second, a star did the honors. Angels hung
around the Heavens, as it were, with the stars as
their pendants. But with both voices over, as the

Psalmist might say, the heavens just couldn't keep
the glory of God to themselves."

St. Augustine of Hippo Regius (354–430),
Sermons to the People[67]

Blessed ✝ is the womb that bore you, O Christ,
~AND THE BREASTS THAT NURSED YOU!
In the womb of the Mother
~RESIDES THE WISDOM OF THE FATHER.

HYMN

Mother of Christ, our hope, our patroness,
Star of the sea, our beacon in distress,
Guide to the shores of everlasting day
God's holy people on their pilgrim way.

Virgin, in you God made his dwelling-place;
Mother of all the living, full of grace,
Blessed are you: God's word you did believe;
"Yes" on your lips undid the "No" of Eve.

Daughter of God, who bore his holy One,
Dearest of all to Christ, your loving Son,
Show us his face, O Mother, as on earth,
Loving us all, you gave our Savior birth.[68]

A MARIAN
ANTHEM
THE SONG OF SOLOMON 6:10,
3:6; PSALMS 24:3–4, 26:6

ANTIPHON A great sign appeared in the sky,
A WOMAN CLOTHED WITH THE SUN,
WITH THE MOON UNDER HER FEET,
AND ON HER HEAD A CROWN OF TWELVE STARS,
   ALLELUIA!

Who is this coming forth like the rising dawn,
fair as the moon, bright as the sun,
as beautiful as all the hosts of heaven?

~THIS IS THE GREAT MOTHER OF GOD, MARY
        MOST HOLY,
    WHO WAS CONCEIVED IN GRACE.

Who is this coming up from the desert
like a column of incense smoke,
breathing of myrrh and frankincense,
and of every fine perfume?

~THIS IS THE GREAT MOTHER OF GOD, MARY
        MOST HOLY,
WHO BORE CHRIST WHOM THE WHOLE WORLD
        CANNOT CONTAIN.

Who is this who ascends God's holy mountain
and stands in his sanctuary
with clean hands and a pure heart?

~THIS IS THE GREAT MOTHER OF GOD, MARY
        MOST HOLY,
    WHO SITS WITH CHRIST ON HIS STARRY
        THRONE.

Who is this who washes her hands in innocence,
joins the procession about the altar,
and proclaims all God's wonders?

~THIS IS THE GREAT MOTHER OF GOD, MARY
        MOST HOLY,
    WHO ALONE, WITHOUT PEER,
    PLEASED OUR LORD JESUS CHRIST.

Who is this exalted above the choirs of angels,
   raised to the heavenly throne,
   and seated beside her divine Son in glory?

~THIS IS THE GREAT MOTHER OF GOD, MARY
      MOST HOLY,
   WHO INTERCEDES FOR US WITH OUR LORD
   JESUS CHRIST.

ANTIPHON A GREAT SIGN APPEARED IN THE SKY,
A WOMAN CLOTHED WITH THE SUN,
WITH THE MOON UNDER HER FEET,
AND ON HER HEAD A CROWN OF TWELVE STARS,
      ALLELUIA!

PRAYER
Let us pray *(pause for quiet prayer):*
O God, who through the fruitful virginity of
      Blessed Mary
bestowed on the human race
the grace of eternal salvation,
grant, we pray,
that we may experience the intercession of her,
through whom we were found worthy
to receive the author of life,
our Lord Jesus Christ, your Son.
Who lives and reigns with you in the unity of the
      Holy Spirit,
one God, for ever and ever.
~AMEN.[69]

READING THE PRINCE OF PEACE ISAIAH 9:6–7

A child has been born for us, a son given to us;
authority rests upon his shoulders; and he is named
Wonderful Counselor, Mighty God, Everlasting
Father, Prince of Peace. His authority shall grow
continually, and there shall be endless peace. . . .
The zeal of the LORD of hosts will do this.

RESPONSE

Blest is the womb that bore you, O Christ,
~AND THE BREASTS THAT NURSED YOU!

A CANTICLE OF MICAH THE PROPHET MICAH 5:2–5

ANTIPHON He shall be called Emmanuel:
"GOD-IS-WITH-US."

You, O Bethlehem of Ephrathah,
who are one of the little clans of Judah,
from you shall come forth for me
one who is to rule in Israel,
whose origin is from of old,
from ancient days.

Therefore he shall give them up until the time
when she who is in labor has brought forth;
then the rest of his kindred shall return
to the people of Israel.

And he shall stand and feed his flock
in the strength of the LORD,
in the majesty of the name
of the LORD his God.

And they shall live secure,
for now he shall be great
to the ends of the earth;
and he shall be the one of peace.

ANTIPHON HE SHALL BE CALLED EMMANUEL:
"GOD-IS-WITH-US."

LITANY

Lord Jesus, Son of the living God and Child of
　　Mary:
~MAY WE LOVE AND SERVE YOU.

Lord Jesus, hymned by angels and adored by
　　shepherds:
~MAY WE LOVE AND SERVE YOU.

Lord Jesus, worshipped by the wise men from the
　　East:
~MAY WE LOVE AND SERVE YOU.

Lord Jesus, revealed to old Simeon and Anna
　　in the temple:
~MAY WE LOVE AND SERVE YOU.

Lord Jesus, baptized by John in the Jordan:
~MAY WE LOVE AND SERVE YOU.

(Pause for special intentions.)

By the prayers of the great Mother of God, Mary
　　most holy,
　　St. Joseph, her spouse, St. John the Baptist,
　　and of all the saints in glory:
~MAY WE LOVE AND SERVE YOU.

THE LORD'S PRAYER

Lord, have mercy.

~CHRIST, HAVE MERCY. LORD, HAVE MERCY.

Our Father in heaven,

~HALLOWED BE YOUR NAME,

YOUR KINGDOM COME,

YOUR WILL BE DONE,

ON EARTH AS IN HEAVEN.

GIVE US TODAY OUR DAILY BREAD.

FORGIVE US OUR SINS

AS WE FORGIVE THOSE WHO SIN AGAINST US.

SAVE US FROM THE TIME OF TRIAL

AND DELIVER US FROM EVIL.

FOR THE KINGDOM AND THE POWER AND THE

GLORY ARE YOURS

NOW AND FOREVER. AMEN.

CLOSING PRAYER

Grant, we pray, almighty God,

that, as we are bathed in the new radiance of your
incarnate Word,

the light of faith, which illumines our minds,

may also shine through in our deeds.

Through our Lord Jesus Christ, your Son,

who lives and reigns with you in the unity of the
Holy Spirit,

one God, for ever and ever.

~AMEN.[70]

May the Virgin Mary mild
† bless us with her holy Child.
~AMEN.

Noonday   **Mary at the Cross**
"I saw part of the compassion of our Lady,
St. Mary, for Christ and she were so united in love
that the greatness of her love was the cause of the
greatness of her pain. For her pain surpassed that
of all others, as much as she loved him more than
all others."

Julian of Norwich (1343–ca. 1423), *Showings*[71]

Blessed † be the great Mother of God, Mary most
    holy,
~WHOSE HEART SUFFERED THE SWORD OF
    SORROW.
Come and see, all you who pass by,
~SEE IF THERE IS ANY SORROW LIKE MINE.

HYMN
The new Eve stands before the Tree;
Her dying Son speaks words of love:
He gives his Mother as our Queen
On earth below, in heaven above.

The second Adam sleeps in death,
His side is pierced, his heart unsealed;
The grace-filled Church, his sinless Bride,
In blood and water is revealed.

We thank you, Father, for the Church,
Where Christ is King and Mary Queen,
Where through your Spirit you unfold
A world of glory yet unseen. Amen.[72]

PSALM 121   MARY LIFTS HER EYES TO GOD

ANTIPHON God so loved the world
THAT HE SENT HIS SON TO SAVE US.

I lift my eyes to the hills—
from where does my help come?
My help comes from the Lord,
who made heaven and earth.

The Lord will not let your foot be moved,
the Lord who keeps you will not slumber.
The One who keeps Israel
will neither slumber nor sleep.

The Lord is your keeper;
the Lord is your shade
on your right hand.
The sun shall not strike you by day,
nor the moon by night.

The Lord will keep you going out
   and coming in
from this time forth and for evermore.

ANTIPHON GOD SO LOVED THE WORLD
THAT HE SENT HIS SON TO SAVE US.

PSALM PRAYER

Let us pray *(pause for quiet prayer):*

Heavenly Father,
you permitted the sword of sorrow
to penetrate Mary's heart and soul,
but as a woman of faith
she looked to you for help,
and you secured her life for your Son's sake.
By her prayers shield us too
that we may serve him with all our hearts,
now and for ever.
~AMEN.

MARY AT THE
READING   **FOOT OF THE CROSS**   **JOHN 19:25–27**

Standing near the cross of Jesus were his mother,
and his mother's sister, Mary the wife of Clopas,
and Mary Magdalene. When Jesus saw his mother
and the disciple whom he loved standing beside
her, he said to his mother, "Woman, here is your
son." Then he said to the disciple, "Here is your
mother." And from that hour the disciple took her
into his own home.

RESPONSE

The Roman spear pierced the heart of Jesus
~AND THE SOUL OF HIS SORROWFUL MOTHER.

CLOSING PRAYER

Lord Jesus Christ,
as old Simeon had predicted,
a sword of sorrow cut her to the heart
as Mary watched you dying on the cross.

By your blood and her tears,
may we share your pains,
repent of all our sins,
and come to the home-haven of heaven
through your saving power.
Your reign is a reign for all ages.
~AMEN.

May the glorious passion of our Lord Jesus Christ
and the prayers of Our Lady of Compassion
† bring us to the joys of paradise.
~AMEN.

Evening Prayer   Easter and Pentecost

"And Jesus, saying this, showed me a spiritual vision
of her [Mary]. Just as before I had seen her small
and simple, now he showed her high and noble and
glorious and more pleasing to him than all creatures.
And so he wishes it to be known that all who take
delight in him should take delight in her, and in the
delight that he has in her and she in him."

Julian of Norwich (1343–ca. 1423), *Showings*[73]

Light and peace † in Jesus Christ our Lord.
~THANKS BE TO GOD.
Blessed † be the great Mother of God, Mary most
holy!
~WHO REJOICED IN THE RESURRECTION OF HER
DIVINE SON.

HYMN

Easter glory fills the sky!
Christ now lives, no more to die!
Darkness has been put to flight
By the living Lord of might.

See the stone is rolled away
From the tomb where once he lay!
He has risen as he said,
Glorious Firstborn from the dead!

Mary, Mother, greet your Son,
Radiant from his triumph won!
By his cross you shared his pain,
So for ever share his reign!

Christ, the Victor over death,
Breathes on us the Spirit's breath!
Paradise is our reward,
Endless Easter with our Lord![74]

PSALM 113   THE HUMBLE VIRGIN AND MOTHER

ANTIPHON   God raises the poor FROM THE DUST,
     ALLELUIA!

Praise, O servants of the Lord,
praise the name of the Lord!
Blessed be the name of the Lord
from this time forth and for evermore!

From the rising of the sun to its setting
the name of the Lord is to be praised!
The Lord is high above all nations,
God's glory above the heavens!

Who is like the Lord our God,
who is seated on high,
who looks far down
upon the heavens and the earth?

God raises the poor from the dust,
and lifts the needy from the ash heap,
to make them sit with nobles,
with the nobles of God's people.

God gives the barren woman a home,
making her the joyous mother of children.

ANTIPHON GOD RAISES THE POOR FROM THE DUST,
   ALLELUIA!

PSALM PRAYER
Let us pray *(pause for quiet prayer):*

Great and gracious Savior,
as we remember your holy Mother
and her steadfast faith in your mission,
may we stand fast in the Gospel of peace
and become the Christians we long to be
by the help of her prayers.
Your reign is a reign for all ages.
~AMEN.

	VICTORY	**1 CORINTHIANS**
READING	**OVER DEATH**	**15:51–53 NAB**

Behold, I tell you a mystery. We shall not all fall
asleep, but we will all be changed, in an instant,
in the blink of an eye, at the last trumpet. For
the trumpet will sound, the dead will be raised

incorruptible, and we shall be changed. For
that which is corruptible must clothe itself with
incorruptibility, and that which is mortal must
clothe itself with immortality.

RESPONSE
This is the day the Lord has made, alleluia!
~LET US REJOICE AND BE GLAD, ALLELUIA!

THE CANTICLE OF THE VIRGIN MARY   LUKE 1:46–55

ANTIPHON
Rejoice, O Queen of heaven, alleluia!
FOR THE SON YOU BORE, ALLELUIA!
HAS ARISEN AS HE PROMISED, ALLELUIA!
PRAY FOR US TO GOD THE FATHER, ALLELUIA!

My soul † proclaims the greatness of the Lord,
my spirit rejoices in God my Savior,
for you, Lord, have looked with favor on your
    lowly servant.

From this day all generations will call me blessed:
    you, the Almighty, have done great things for me
    and holy is your name.
    You have mercy on those who fear you,
    from generation to generation.

You have shown strength with your arm
and scattered the proud in their conceit,
casting down the mighty from their thrones
and lifting up the lowly.
You have filled the hungry with good things
and sent the rich away empty.

You have come to the aid of your servant Israel,
to remember the promise of mercy,
the promise made to our forebears,
to Abraham and his children forever.

Glory to the Holy and Undivided Trinity:
now and always and for ever and ever. Amen.

ANTIPHON
REJOICE, O QUEEN OF HEAVEN, ALLELUIA!
FOR THE SON YOU BORE, ALLELUIA!
HAS ARISEN AS HE PROMISED, ALLELUIA!
PRAY FOR US TO GOD THE FATHER, ALLELUIA!

MARIAN LITANY
Lord Jesus, born of Mary in Bethlehem of Judea:
~HEAR OUR PRAYER.
Lord Jesus, whom Mary presented in the temple:
~HEAR OUR PRAYER.
Lord Jesus, whom Mary lost and found in the
    temple:
~HEAR OUR PRAYER.
Lord Jesus, who did the first of his signs at Cana
    of Galilee:
~HEAR OUR PRAYER.
Lord Jesus, whose blessed mother stood by the
    cross:
~HEAR OUR PRAYER.
Lord Jesus, whose mother rejoiced in his glorious
    resurrection:
~HEAR OUR PRAYER.

Lord Jesus, whose holy mother devoted herself to
    prayer
  with the apostles in the upper room:
~HEAR OUR PRAYER.
Lord Jesus, whose mother stood with your friends
    on the day of Pentecost:
~HEAR OUR PRAYER.

(Pause for personal petitions.)

Lord Jesus, who willed that his mother be praised
    in every generation:
~HEAR OUR PRAYER.

THE LORD'S PRAYER

Lord, have mercy.
~CHRIST, HAVE MERCY. LORD, HAVE MERCY.

Our Father in heaven,
    ~HALLOWED BE YOUR NAME,
    YOUR KINGDOM COME,
    YOUR WILL BE DONE,
        ON EARTH AS IN HEAVEN.
GIVE US TODAY OUR DAILY BREAD.
FORGIVE US OUR SINS
    AS WE FORGIVE THOSE WHO SIN AGAINST US.
SAVE US FROM THE TIME OF TRIAL
    AND DELIVER US FROM EVIL.
FOR THE KINGDOM AND THE POWER AND THE
    GLORY ARE YOURS
    NOW AND FOREVER. AMEN.

CLOSING PRAYER

O God, who have been pleased to gladden the
    world
by the Resurrection of your Son our Lord Jesus
    Christ,
grant, we pray,
that through his Mother, the Virgin Mary,
we may receive the joys of everlasting life.
Through our Lord Jesus Christ, your Son,
who lives and reigns with you in the unity of the
    Holy Spirit,
one God, for ever and ever.
~AMEN.[75]

Christ has risen, alleluia!
~HE HAS RISEN INDEED, ALLELUIA!

May Christ, the King of glory, the Son of Mary,
✝ bless us and keep us.
~AMEN.

Night Prayer   The Assumption of Mary

"In the Ascension, Christ was raised in glory
to the right hand of the Father, while Mary
herself would be raised to that same glory in the
Assumption, enjoying beforehand, by a unique
privilege, the destiny reserved for all the just at
the resurrection of the dead. Crowned in glory,
Mary shines forth as the Queen of the Angels
and Saints, the anticipation and the supreme

realization of the eschatological state of the Church."

Pope John Paul II, *Rosarium Virginis Mariae*[76]

Blessed ✝ be the great Mother of God, Mary most
   holy!
~BLESSED BE HER GLORIOUS ASSUMPTION INTO
   HEAVEN!
O death, where is your victory?
~O DEATH, WHERE IS YOUR STING?

HYMN

Hail, our Queen and Mother blest!
Joy when all was sadness,
Life and hope you brought to earth,
Mother of our gladness.

Children of the sinful Eve,
Sinless Eve, befriend us,
Exiled in this vale of tears:
Strength and comfort send us!

Pray for us, O Patroness,
Be our consolation!
Lead us home to see your Son,
Jesus, our salvation!

Gracious are you, full of grace,
Loving as none other,
Joy of heaven and joy of earth,
Mary, God's own Mother![77]

Psalm 126 A Dream Come True

Antiphon Christ our Lord assumed his Blessed Mother
body and soul into heaven, alleluia!

When the Lord restored the fortunes of Zion,
we were like those who dream.
Then our mouth was filled with laughter,
and our tongue with shouts of joy;

then it was said among the nations,
"the Lord has done great things for them."
The Lord has done great things for us,
and we are glad.

Restore our fortunes, O Lord,
like the watercourses in the Negeb!
May those who sow in tears
reap with shouts of joy!

Those who go out weeping,
bearing the seed for sowing,
shall come home with shouts of joy,
carrying their sheaves.

Antiphon Christ our Lord assumed his
Blessed Mother
body and soul into heaven, alleluia!

Psalm Prayer

Let us pray *(pause for quiet prayer):*

Glorious and ever-Virgin Mary,
celebrated in all generations,

be our loving intercessor before God,
save us from every danger,
and show us the fruit of your womb, Jesus,
by whose merits we find salvation.
Blest be the holy name of Jesus!
~AMEN.

READING   THE BRIDE   SONG OF SOLOMON 2:10–13

My beloved speaks and says to me: "Arise, my
love, my fair one, and come away; for now the
winter is past, the rain is over and gone. The
flowers appear on the earth; the time of singing
has come, and the voice of the turtledove is heard
in our land. The fig tree puts forth its figs, and the
vines are in blossom; they give forth fragrance.
Arise, my love, my fair one, and come away."

RESPONSE

You are more worthy of honor than the cherubim,
     alleluia!

~AND FAR MORE GLORIOUS THAN THE SERAPHIM,
     ALLELUIA!

THE CANTICLE OF SIMEON THE PROPHET   LUKE 2:29–32

ANTIPHON   The holy Mother of God is exalted,
     alleluia!

ABOVE THE CHOIRS OF ANGELS, ALLELUIA!

Now, Lord, † let your servant go in peace:
your word has been fulfilled.

My own eyes have seen your salvation
which you have prepared in the sight
   of every people:

a light to reveal you to the nations
and the glory of your people Israel.

Glory to the Father, and to the Son,
and to the Holy Spirit:

as it was in the beginning, is now,
and will be forever. Amen.

ANTIPHON THE HOLY MOTHER OF GOD IS
       EXALTED, ALLELUIA!
ABOVE THE CHOIRS OF ANGELS, ALLELUIA!

CLOSING PRAYER
Father in heaven,
all creation rightly gives you praise,
for all life and holiness come from you.
In the plan of your wisdom
she who bore Christ in her womb
was raised body and soul to glory
to be with you in heaven.
May we follow her example
in reflecting her holiness
and join with her hymn of endless praise.
We ask this through Christ our Lord.
~AMEN.[78]

May the Queen of heaven
✝ intercede for us with the Lord our God.
~AMEN.

II
Devotions

Eucharistic Devotions

At the final Passover seder that he shared with his disciples on the night he was betrayed, the Lord Jesus inaugurated the Passover meal of the New and Eternal Covenant. By his command, it became the Lord's Supper on the Lord's Day, the weekly celebration of Word and Sacrament that marks all Catholic, Orthodox, and many other Churches.

The following prayers represent seven "days" of eucharistic devotions. They include hymns, psalms, prayers, readings from the Bible and the Holy Fathers, and intercessions. They are designed to help us pause in prayer and contemplation before the Blessed Sacrament whenever we can. They may be prayed by individuals or groups who would like to spend time before the tabernacle. This combination of Word and Sacrament is a devout way of assimilating the Holy Gospel by listening to our Lord's actual words recorded in the Holy Gospels in the very presence of his divine Person in the Blessed Sacrament.

The Holy Eucharist is not only a sacrificial meal but an abiding presence in our tabernacles. The body and the blood of Jesus are reserved primarily for the sick and dying, but the Holy Reserve is also kept in a prominent place in our churches, veiled and attended by a sacrament light, as the focal point of private and public recognition and devotion.

For the last four centuries especially, our churches have been considered more and more as temples of the eucharistic Lord and Savior. Jesus in the Blessed Sacrament is regarded with great awe and reverence because of his full and real presence: body and blood, soul and divinity. The more we meditate on Jesus' supreme gift of himself as the right and fitting extension of the Word made flesh, the more we are drawn to spend time in prayer before the Sacrament. He is *here* in our tabernacles in a unique way that demands our attention and loving devotion.

Visits to the Blessed Sacrament

Day One

LEADER: Blessed † be Jesus in the most holy
   Sacrament of the Altar!

ALL: ~AMEN. ALLELUIA!

HYMN

Hail our Savior's glorious Body,
Which his Virgin Mother bore;
Hail the Blood, which shed for sinners,
Did a broken world restore;
Hail the sacrament most holy,
Flesh and Blood of Christ adore.

To the Virgin for our healing,
His own Son the Father sends;
From the Father's love proceeding
Sower, seed, and Word descends;
Wondrous life of Word incarnate
With his greatest wonder ends!

On that paschal evening see him
With the chosen twelve recline,
To the old law still obedient
In its feast of love divine;
Love divine, the new law giving,
Gives himself as Bread and Wine![79]

St. Thomas Aquinas, OP (1225–1274)

PSALM 42:2–6 NAB LONGING FOR GOD'S PRESENCE

ANTIPHON I will come to the altar of God,
TO GOD, MY JOY, MY DELIGHT.

As the deer longs for streams of water,
   so my soul longs for you, O God.
My being thirsts for God, the living God.
   When can I go and see the face of God?
My tears have been my food day and night,
   as they ask daily, "Where is your God?"

Those times I recall
   as I pour out my soul,
When I went in procession with the crowd,
   I went with them to the house of God,
Amid loud cries of thanksgiving,
   with the multitude keeping festival.

Why are you cast down, my soul;
   why do you groan within me?
Wait for God, whom I shall praise again,
   my savior and my God.

ANTIPHON I WILL COME TO THE ALTAR OF GOD,
TO GOD, MY JOY, MY DELIGHT.

PSALM PRAYER

LEADER: Let us pray *(pause for quiet prayer):*

Our Father, our God,
we remember all you have done for us
because of the great memorial
created by your dear Son, our Savior,

on the night before he died for us.
Give us the grace to praise and adore
   his holy presence
in the blessed Sacrament of the Altar,
now and forever.
ALL: ~AMEN.

FIRST		I CORINTHIANS
READING	THE LAST SUPPER	11:23–26

Brothers and sisters, I received from the Lord what
I also handed on to you, that the Lord Jesus on the
night when he was betrayed took a loaf of bread,
and when he had given thanks, he broke it and
said, "This is my body that is broken for you. Do
this in remembrance of me." In the same way he
took the cup also, after supper, saying, "This cup
is the new covenant in my blood. Do this, as often
as you drink it, in remembrance of me."

SILENT PRAYER

RESPONSE

LEADER: As often as you eat this bread and drink
   this cup,
ALL: ~YOU PROCLAIM THE LORD'S DEATH UNTIL
   HE COMES.

SECOND READING   JUDGE BY FAITH

This teaching of blessed Paul is in itself sufficient
to assure you fully on the divine mysteries. . . .
Since then Christ himself clearly described the
bread to us in the words, "This is my body," who

will dare dispute it? And since he has emphatically said, "This is my blood," who will waver in the slightest and say it is not his blood?

By his own power on a previous occasion he turned water into wine at Cana of Galilee; so it is surely credible that he has changed wine into his blood. If he performed that wonderful miracle just because he had been invited to a human marriage, we shall certainly be much more willing to admit that he has conferred on the wedding guests the savoring of his body and blood. . . .

Do not, then, regard the bread and wine as nothing but bread and wine, for they are the body and blood of Christ, as the Master himself has proclaimed. Though your senses suggest this to you, let faith reassure you. Do not judge the matter by taste but by faith, which brings you certainty without doubting, since you have been found worthy of Christ's body and blood.

St Cyril of Jerusalem (ca. 315–386),
Mystagogical Catecheses[80]

RESPONSE

LEADER: Examine yourself, and only then
ALL: ~EAT OF THE BREAD AND DRINK OF THE CUP.

LITANY OF THE BLESSED SACRAMENT

Lord, have mercy.	~LORD, HAVE MERCY.
Christ, have mercy.	~CHRIST, HAVE MERCY.
Lord, have mercy.	~LORD, HAVE MERCY.

God our Father in heaven,	~HAVE MERCY ON US.
God the Son, Redeemer of the world,	~HAVE MERCY ON US.
God the Holy Spirit,	~HAVE MERCY ON US.
Holy Trinity, one God,	~HAVE MERCY ON US.
Word made flesh and living among us,	~CHRIST, HAVE MERCY ON US.
Pure and acceptable sacrifice,	~CHRIST, HAVE MERCY ON US.
Hidden manna from above,	~CHRIST, HAVE MERCY ON US.
Living bread that came down from heaven,	~CHRIST, HAVE MERCY ON US.
Bread of life for a hungry world,	~CHRIST, HAVE MERCY ON US.
Chalice of blessing,	~CHRIST, HAVE MERCY ON US.
Precious blood that washes away our sins,	~CHRIST, HAVE MERCY ON US.
Memorial of God's undying love,	~CHRIST, HAVE MERCY ON US.
Food that lasts for eternal life,	~CHRIST, HAVE MERCY ON US.
Mystery of faith,	~CHRIST, HAVE MERCY ON US.
Medicine of immortality,	~CHRIST, HAVE MERCY ON US.
Food of God's chosen,	~CHRIST, HAVE MERCY ON US.
Perpetual presence in our tabernacles,	~CHRIST, HAVE MERCY ON US.
Viaticum of those who die in the Lord,	~CHRIST, HAVE MERCY ON US.
Pledge of future glory,	~CHRIST, HAVE MERCY ON US.
By the great longing you had to eat the Passover with your disciples,	~GOOD LORD, DELIVER US.

By your great humility in washing their feet,	~Good Lord, deliver us.
By your loving gift of this divine sacrament,	~Good Lord, deliver us.
By your sacrificial death on the cross,	~Good Lord, deliver us.
By the piercing of your sacred heart,	~Good Lord, deliver us.
By your rising to new life,	~Good Lord, deliver us.
By your gift of the Paraclete Spirit,	~Good Lord, deliver us.
By your return in glory to judge the living and the dead,	~Good Lord, deliver us.
Lamb of God, you take away the sins of the world,	~Have mercy on us.
Lamb of God, you take away the sins of the world,	~Have mercy on us.
Lamb of God, you take away the sins of the world,	~Grant us your peace.

Leader: You gave them bread from heaven to be their food,

All: ~And this bread contained all goodness.

Prayer

O God, who in this wonderful Sacrament
have left us a memorial of your Passion,
grant us, we pray,
so to revere the sacred mysteries of your Body and
Blood
that we may always experience in ourselves

the fruits of your redemption.
Who live and reign with God the Father
in the unity of the Holy Spirit,
one God, for ever and ever.
ALL: ~AMEN.[81]

DOXOLOGY

May the heart of Jesus in the most Blessed
        Sacrament
be praised, adored, and loved,
with grateful affection, at every moment,
in all the tabernacles of the world,
even to the end of time.
ALL: ~AMEN.

Day Two

Blessed † be Jesus in the most holy Sacrament
    of the Altar!

~AMEN. ALLELUIA!

HYMN

By his word the Word almighty
Makes of bread his flesh indeed;
Wine becomes his very life-blood;
Faith God's living Word must heed!
Faith alone may safely guide us
Where the senses cannot lead.

Come, adore his wondrous presence;
Bow to Christ, the source of grace!
Here is kept the sacred promise

Of God's earthly dwelling-place!
Sight is blind before God's glory,
Faith alone may see his face!

Glory be to God the Father,
Praise to his coequal Son,
Adoration to the Spirit,
Bond of love, in Godhead one!
Blest be God by all creation
Joyously while ages run![82]

St. Thomas Aquinas, OP (1225–1274)

PSALM 78:1–4, 23–28 BREAD FROM HEAVEN

ANTIPHON My flesh is true food AND MY BLOOD
IS TRUE DRINK.

Give ear, O my people, to my teaching;
incline your ears to the words of my mouth.
I will open my mouth in a parable;
I will utter dark sayings from of old,
things that we have heard and known,
that our ancestors have told us.

We will not hide them from their children,
but tell to the coming generation
the glorious deeds of the Lord, the might
and wonders God has wrought.

The Lord commanded the skies above,
opened the doors of heaven,
rained down on them manna to eat,
and gave them the grain of heaven.

Mortals ate the bread of angels;
God sent them food in abundance,
caused the east wind to blow in the heavens,
and led out the south wind in power.

God rained flesh down upon them like dust,
winged birds like the sand of the seas;
God let them fall within their camp,
all around their dwellings.

ANTIPHON MY FLESH IS TRUE FOOD AND MY
BLOOD IS TRUE DRINK.

PSALM PRAYER

Let us pray *(pause for quiet prayer)*:

God of our ancestors in the faith,
you provide for us in all our needs.
Remember the deeds you did of old
for the people who put their trust in you
and give the people of the new covenant
the precious body and blood of your dear Son
as food for our journey toward paradise.
Blest be the holy name of Jesus!
~AMEN.

FIRST READING	**MANNA FROM HEAVEN**	**DEUTERONOMY 8:2–3**

Remember the long way that the LORD your God
has led you these forty years in the wilderness, in
order to humble you, testing you to know what
was in your heart, whether or not you would keep
his commandments. He humbled you by letting

you hunger, then by feeding you with manna, with which neither you nor your ancestors were acquainted, in order to make you understand that one does not live by bread alone, but by every word that comes from the mouth of the LORD.

RESPONSE

God rained down manna for their food,
~AND GAVE THEM BREAD FROM HEAVEN.

SECOND READING   CHRIST'S WORDS

Who is the author of the sacraments except the Lord Jesus? These sacraments came from heaven, for all God's purpose is from heaven. Still, it remains true that when God rained down manna for the people from heaven, and the people ate without working for their food, this was a great and divine sign.

Perhaps you say, "The bread I have here is ordinary bread." Yes, before the sacramental words are uttered this bread is nothing but bread. But at the consecration the bread becomes the body of Christ. Let us reason this out. How can something that is bread be the body of Christ? Well, by what words is the consecration effected, and whose words are they? The words of the Lord Jesus. All that is said before are the words of the priest: praise is offered to God, the prayer is offered up, petitions are made for the people, for kings, for all others. But when the moment comes for bringing

the most holy sacrament into being, the priest
does not use his own words any longer: he uses the
words of Christ. Therefore, it is Christ's word that
brings the sacrament into being.

St. Ambrose of Milan (ca. 339–397),
Sermons on the Sacraments[83]

RESPONSE
Jesus said to them, "I am the living bread
~THAT CAME DOWN FROM HEAVEN."

LITANY OF THE BLESSED SACRAMENT (SEE PAGES 220–222)

PRAYER
Gracious Father,
your loving providence
is our strength and our delight.
We thank you from the bottom of our heart
for your great and precious gift of Christ's
abiding presence on our altars.
We believe that Jesus is here for us,
body and blood, soul and divinity,
in the fullness of his divine personhood.
As you fed your ancient people of Israel,
feed us now with the true bread
that comes down from heaven
and gives life to the world.
Your kingdom come!
~AMEN.

DOXOLOGY

May the heart of Jesus in the most Blessed
     Sacrament
be praised, adored, and loved,
with grateful affection, at every moment,
in all the tabernacles of the world,
even to the end of time.
~AMEN.

Day Three

Blessed † be Jesus in the most holy sacrament
  of the altar!
~AMEN. ALLELUIA!

HYMN

Forth from on high the Father sends
His Son, who yet stays by his side.
The Word made us for us then spends
His life till life's last eventide.

While Judas plans the traitor's sign,
The mocking kiss that Love betrays,
Jesus in form of bread and wine
His loving sacrifice displays.

He gives himself that faith may see
The heavenly food on which we feed,
That flesh and blood in us may be
Fed by his Flesh and Blood in deed.

O Priest and Victim, Lord of Life,
Throw wide the gates of Paradise!

We face our foes in mortal strife;
You are our strength! O heed our cries![84]

St Thomas Aquinas, OP (1225–1274)

PSALM 23 TEV   SHEPHERD AND HOST

ANTIPHON You prepare a table before me,
MY CUP OVERFLOWS.

The LORD is my shepherd, I shall not want;
the LORD makes me lie down in green pastures,
leads me beside still waters;
restores my life,
leads me in right paths
for the sake of the LORD's name.

Even though I walk through the darkest valley,
I fear no evil;
for you are with me;
your rod and your staff,
they comfort me.

You prepare a table before me
in the presence of my enemies;
you anoint my head with oil,
my cup overflows.

Only goodness and mercy shall follow me
all the days of my life;
and I shall dwell in the house of the LORD
as long as I live.

ANTIPHON YOU PREPARE A TABLE BEFORE ME,
MY CUP OVERFLOWS.

Psalm Prayer

Let us pray *(pause for quiet prayer):*

Good Shepherd of the flock,
guide us along the right path
and deliver us from all our fears.
Your sacramental presence among us
assures us you are always with us.
You anoint us with the oil of salvation,
feed us with the finest wheat,
and make us sit at your welcome table,
now and forever.
~Amen.

Reading   The Pure Offering   Malachi 1:11

From the rising of the sun till its setting my
name is great among the nations, and in every
place incense is offered to my name, and a pure
offering; for my name is great among the nations,
says the Lord of hosts.

Response

The Lord is my light and my salvation.
~Whom shall I fear?

Second Reading   The Sacrament of the Altar

No other sacrament can be more wholesome. By
it sins are purged away; virtues are increased; and
the soul is enriched with an abundance of every
spiritual gift. The Church offers it for both the
living and the dead so that what was instituted for
all might be to the advantage of all. We cannot

fully express the attractiveness of this sacrament
in which we taste spiritual delight at its source
and in which we renew the surpassing love which
Christ revealed to us in his passion. In order to
impress the immensity of his love for us, at the
last supper, while celebrating the Passover Meal
with his disciples, he instituted this sacrament
as a perpetual memorial of his passion, as the
fulfillment of all the Old Testament types, as
the greatest of his miracles, and as a unique
consolation for his physical absence.

St. Thomas Aquinas, OP (1225–1274),
Immensa divinae largitatis[85]

RESPONSE

As often as you eat this bread and drink this cup,
~YOU SHOW FORTH THE DEATH OF THE LORD
UNTIL HE COME.

LITANY OF THE BLESSED SACRAMENT (SEE PAGES 220–222)

PRAYER

Lord and Savior of the world,
by the reception of Holy Communion,
you nourish us with your life-giving body and
blood
that unites your holy Church in heaven and on
earth.
Make us ever faithful to the vows of our Baptism

and inspire us to celebrate the Holy Eucharist
with increasing faith and fervor
as we pray for the needs of the whole world.
May the tabernacle of your presence
be the ark of the covenant for us
as we adore you unceasingly,
in union with all the saints
who long for the coming of your kingdom.
You live and reign, now and for ever.
~Amen.

Doxology
May the heart of Jesus in the most Blessed
    Sacrament
be praised, adored, and loved,
with grateful affection, at every moment,
in all the tabernacles of the world,
even to the end of time.
~Amen.

Day Four
Blessed ✝ be Jesus in the most holy Sacrament
  of the Altar!
~Amen. Alleluia!

Hymn
At this great feast of love
Let joyful praise resound,
Let heartfelt knowledge now ascend
To heaven's height:
Ring out the reign of sin;

Ring in the reign of grace;
A world renewed acclaims its King,
Though veiled from sight.

Recall the night when Christ
Proclaims his law of love,
And shows himself as Lamb of God
And great high priest:
The sinless One, made sin,
For sinners gives his all,
And shares with us his very self
As Paschal feast.

The bread that angels eat
Becomes our food on earth,
God sends his manna, living Bread,
From heaven above;
What wonders now we see:
Those who are last and least
Receive their Lord as food and drink,
His pledge of love.

Three persons, yet one God,
Be pleased to hear our prayer:
Come down in power to seek your own,
dispel our night;
Teach us your word of truth;
Guide us along your way;
Bring us at last to dwell with you
In endless light.[86]

St. Thomas Aquinas, OP (1225–1274)

ANTIPHON I will come to your altar, O God,
TO GOD, MY JOY, MY DELIGHT.

Grant me justice, God;
    defend me from a faithless people;
    from the deceitful and unjust rescue me.

You, God, are my strength.
    Why then do you spurn me?
Why must I go about mourning,
    with the enemy oppressing me?

Send your light and fidelity,
    that they may be my guide
And bring me to your holy mountain,
    to the place of your dwelling,

That I may come to the altar of God,
    to God, my joy, my delight.
Then I will praise you with the harp,
    O God, my God.

ANTIPHON I WILL COME TO YOUR ALTAR, O GOD,
TO GOD, MY JOY, MY DELIGHT.

PSALM PRAYER

Let us pray *(pause for quiet prayer)*:

God of our joy,
make us rest in the tabernacle
of your loving presence among us.
Give us the spirit of adoration,
defend us from all error,

and be our protector for ever.
We ask this through Christ our Lord.
~Amen.

First Reading   The Last Supper   Mark 14:22–25

While they were eating, Jesus took a loaf of bread, and after blessing it he broke it, gave it to his disciples, and said, "Take; this is my body." Then he took a cup, and after giving thanks he gave it to them, and all of them drank from it. He said to them, "This is my blood of the new covenant, which is poured out for many. Truly I tell you, I will never again drink of the fruit of the vine until that day when I drink it new in the kingdom of God."

Response

Jesus said to his disciples,
~"Do this in remembrance of me."

Second Reading   The Real Presence

You have now been taught and fully instructed that what seems to be bread is not bread, though it appears to be such to the sense of taste, but the body of Christ; that what seems to be wine is not wine, though the taste would have it so, but the blood of Christ; that David was speaking of this long ago when he sang, *Bread strengthens the heart of man, that he may make his face glad with oil* (Psalm 104:15). May you *unveil it with conscience undefiled* and *reflect the glory of the Lord*, and pass *from glory to glory* in Christ Jesus

our Lord. To him be honor, power and glory for
ever and ever. Amen.

St. Cyril of Jerusalem, *Mystagogical Catecheses*[87]

RESPONSE

God opened the gates of heaven;
~MERE MORTALS ATE THE BREAD OF ANGELS.

LITANY OF THE BLESSED SACRAMENT (SEE PAGES 220–222)

PRAYER

Lord Jesus, Redeemer of the world,
you were eager to eat the Passover
with your friends on the night before you died.
Send forth your light and your truth
and lead us to the place where you dwell
in the blessed Sacrament of the Altar.
By the power of your abiding presence,
make us love you with our whole heart
and love and serve our neighbor as ourselves.
You live and reign with the Father,
in the unity of the Holy Spirit,
one God, for ever and ever.
~AMEN.

DOXOLOGY

May the heart of Jesus in the most Blessed
     Sacrament
be praised, adored, and loved,
with grateful affection, at every moment,

in all the tabernacles of the world,
even to the end of time.
~Amen.

Day Five

Blessed † be Jesus in the most holy Sacrament
   of the Altar!
~Amen. Alleluia!

Hymn

Bread of the world in mercy broken,
Wine of the soul, in mercy shed,
By whom the words of life were spoken,
And in whose death our sins are dead:

Look on the heart by sorrow broken,
Look on the tears by sinners shed;
And be your feast to us your token
That by your grace our souls are fed.[88]

Psalm 63:2–9 NAB   Longing for God

Antiphon The words that I have spoken to you
are spirit and life.

O God, you are my God—
   for you I long!
For you my body yearns;
   for you my soul thirsts,
Like a land parched, lifeless,
   and without water.

So I look to you in the sanctuary
   to see your power and glory.

For your love is better than life;
my lips offer you worship.

I will bless you as long as I live;
I will lift up my hands, calling on your name.
My soul shall savor the rich banquet of praise,
with joyous lips my mouth shall honor you!
When I think of you upon my bed,
through the night watches I will recall
That you indeed are my help,
and in the shadow of your wings I shout for joy.
My soul clings fast to you;
your right hand upholds me.

ANTIPHON THE WORDS THAT I HAVE SPOKEN TO
YOU ARE SPIRIT AND LIFE.

PSALM PRAYER

Let us pray *(pause for quiet prayer)*:

Lord God, giver of peace and rest,
you reward those who thirst for you
and look to you in your tabernacle,
where mercy and faithfulness meet,
and justice and peace embrace.
Blest be Christ Jesus our Lord!
~AMEN.

BREAD
FIRST READING **FROM HEAVEN** JOHN 6:27–34

The Lord Jesus said to his disciples, "Do not work
for the food that perishes, but for the food that
endures for eternal life, which the Son of Man will

give you. For it is on him that God the Father has set his seal." So they said to him, "What sign are you going to give us then, so that we may see it and believe you? What work are you performing? Our ancestors ate the manna in the wilderness; as it is written, 'He gave them bread from heaven to eat.'" Then Jesus said to them, "Very truly, I tell you, it was not Moses who gave you the bread from heaven, but it is my Father who gives you the true bread from heaven. For the bread of God is that which comes down from heaven and gives life to the world." They said to him, "Sir, give us this bread always."

RESPONSE
The Lord gave them bread from heaven,
~SENDING DOWN MANNA FOR THEM TO EAT.

SECOND READING   HOLY COMMUNION
When you come forward to receive Holy Communion, do not come with arm extended or fingers parted. Make your left hand a throne for your right, since your right hand is to welcome a King. Cup your palm and receive in it Christ's Body, saying in response, *Amen*. Then carefully bless your eyes with a touch of the holy Body, and consume it, being careful not to drop a particle of it, for to lose any of it is clearly like losing a part of your own body. Tell me, if any one gave you some gold dust, would you not keep it with the greatest

care, ensuring that you did not lose by dropping
any of it? So you should take still greater care not
to drop a fragment of what is more valuable than
gold and precious stones.

St. Cyril of Jerusalem, *Mystagogical Treatise*[89]

RESPONSE
We have come to believe and know
~THAT YOU ARE THE HOLY ONE OF GOD.

LITANY OF THE BLESSED SACRAMENT (SEE PAGES 220–222)

PRAYER
Lord Jesus Christ,
we long and pine for your divine presence
because you have made us for your self
and we are restless until we rest in you.
May your gracious presence on our altars
feed and calm our restless hearts
and unite us with all our fellow believers
in heaven and on earth.
Be praised and thanked,
O Savior of the world,
living and reigning with the Father,
in the unity of the Holy Spirit,
now and for ever.
~AMEN.

May the heart of Jesus in the most Blessed
     Sacrament
be praised, adored, and loved,
with grateful affection, at every moment,
in all the tabernacles of the world,
even to the end of time.
~Amen.

Day Six

Blessed † Jesus in the most holy Sacrament
   of the Altar!
~Amen. Alleluia!

Hymn

Zion sing in exultation,
Sing your song of jubilation,
Sing in praise of Christ your King.
Sing to Christ in adoration,
Sing the new song of salvation,
Homage to our Savior bring.

See the King his table spreading;
See the Lamb his lifeblood shedding;
See in blood the New Law sealed.
All is new, the old has vanished;
All is real, with shadows banished,
What was hidden stands revealed.

Christians, let your faith grow stronger;
What is bread is bread no longer;
Blood is here where once was wine.

Touch and sight are here deceivers,
Mind and heart, be true believers;
Truth is here beneath the sign.

Bread and wine are here concealing
What to faith God is revealing;
Outward signs his glory hide.
Bread becomes its very Giver,
Wine redemption's mighty river,
Flowing from the Savior's side.[90]

PSALM 84:2–5, 11–12 NAB   THE HOUSE OF GOD

ANTIPHON Better one day in your courts
THAN A THOUSAND ELSEWHERE!

How lovely your dwelling,
   O LORD of hosts!
My soul yearns and pines
   for the courts of the LORD.
My heart and flesh cry out
   for the living God.
As the sparrow finds a home
   and the swallow a nest to settle her young,
My home is by your altars,
   LORD of hosts, my king and my God!
Happy are those who dwell in your house!
   They never cease to praise you.

Better one day in your courts
   than a thousand elsewhere.
Better the threshold of the house of my God
   than a home in the tents of the wicked.

For a sun and shield is the LORD God,
    bestowing all grace and glory.

ANTIPHON BETTER ONE DAY IN YOUR COURTS
THAN A THOUSAND ELSEWHERE!

PSALM PRAYER
Let us pray *(pause for quiet prayer):*

Lord God of all the hosts of heaven,
we long for your divine presence
in the temple of your glory.
Look on the face of your Christ
in the blessed Sacrament of the Altar
as we bow before him in adoration.
Blest be Jesus, the King of glory!
~AMEN.

FIRST READING THE BREAD OF LIFE   JOHN 6:45–51
Jesus said to his disciples, "Everyone who has
heard and learned from the Father comes to me.
Not that anyone has seen the Father except the
one who is from God; he has seen the Father. Very
truly, I tell you, whoever believes has eternal life. I
am the bread of life. Your ancestors ate the manna
in the wilderness, and they died. This is the bread
that comes down from heaven, so that one may eat
of it and not die. I am the living bread that came
down from heaven. Whoever eats of this bread
will live forever; and the bread that I will give for
the life of the world is my flesh."

RESPONSE
The bread that we break
~Is a sharing in the body of Christ.

SECOND READING THE AWESOME TABLE OF THE LORD
As soon as they come up from those sacred waters
[of Baptism] all present embrace them, greet
them, kiss them, congratulate and rejoice with
them, because those who were before slaves and
prisoners have all at once become free men and
sons who have been invited to the royal table. For
as soon as they come up from the font, they are
led to the awesome table which is laden with good
things. They taste the body and blood of the Lord
and become the dwelling-place of the Spirit; since
they have put on Christ, they go about appearing
everywhere like angels on earth and shining as
brightly as the rays of the sun.

St. John Chrysostom (ca. 347–407),
Baptismal Homily[91]

RESPONSE
I am with you always, alleluia!
~To the end of the age, alleluia!

LITANY OF THE BLESSED SACRAMENT (SEE PAGES 220–222)

PRAYER
Lord Jesus Christ,
as we stand before your awesome table,

laden with the precious gifts of your body and
    blood,
may we be filled with sentiments
of praise and thanksgiving
for the endless benefits you confer on us.
Fill our hearts to overflowing with the Holy Spirit
who teaches us to pray in spirit and in truth
and to cherish our brothers and sisters
in the mystery of faith.
You live and reign with the Father,
in the unity of the Holy Spirit,
one God, for ever and ever.
~Amen.

Doxology

May the heart of Jesus in the most Blessed
    Sacrament
be praised, adored, and loved,
with grateful affection, at every moment,
in all the tabernacles of the world,
even to the end of time.
~Amen.

Day Seven

Blessed ✝ be Jesus in the most holy Sacrament
    of the Altar!
~Amen. Alleluia!

Hymn

Christ the King, enthroned in splendor,
Comes from heaven to be our priest!

One with him as priest and victim,
One in love, we share his feast!
Praise him in high heaven above!
Praise him in this feast of love!

Light here scatters all our darkness!
Life here triumphs over death!
Come, receive from Christ in glory
God the Spirit's living breath!
Praise Christ for his victory won!
Praise the Father's firstborn Son!

Heaven is here! The gracious Father
Gives to us his only Son!
Here is sent the loving Spirit,
Making all in Christ but one!
Praise the Father, praise the Son,
Praise the Spirit, Godhead one![92]

A CANTICLE OF
ST. PETER THE APOSTLE   1 PETER 2:21–24

ANTIPHON   We adore you, O Christ, and we bless
you, FOR BY YOUR HOLY CROSS YOU HAVE
REDEEMED THE WORLD.

Christ suffered for us,
leaving us an example,
so that we might follow
in his steps.

"He committed no sin,
and no deceit
was found in his mouth."

When he was abused,
he did not return abuse;
when he suffered,
he did not threaten;
but entrusted himself
to the one who judges justly.

He himself bore our sins
in his body on the cross,
so that, freed from our sins,
we might live for righteousness;
by his wounds we have been healed.

ANTIPHON WE ADORE YOU, O CHRIST, AND WE
BLESS YOU, FOR BY YOUR HOLY CROSS YOU
HAVE REDEEMED THE WORLD.

PRAYER

Let us pray *(pause for quiet prayer):*

Lord Christ,
you laid down your life for us
and committed your living presence
in the blessed Sacrament of the Altar
to your holy Catholic Church.
By your five precious wounds
in hands, feet, and side,
free us from our sins
and make us follow in your steps,
now and for ever.
~AMEN.

FIRST READING   TRUE FOOD AND DRINK   JOHN 6:53–58

Jesus said to them, "Very truly, I tell you, unless you eat the flesh of the Son of Man and drink his blood, you have no life in you. Those who eat my flesh and drink my blood have eternal life, and I will raise them up on the last day; for my flesh is true food and my blood is true drink. Those who eat my flesh and drink my blood abide in me, and I in them. Just as the living Father sent me, and I live because of the Father, so whoever eats me will live because of me. This is the bread that came down from heaven, not like that which your ancestors ate, and they died. But the one who eats this bread will live forever."

RESPONSE

By Christ's wounds
~WE HAVE BEEN HEALED.

SECOND READING   CHRIST THE GREAT HIGH PRIEST

The most important thing to grasp is that the food we take is a kind of sacrifice we perform. It is true that we commemorate our Lord's death in food and drink, believing that these are the memorial of his passion, since he says himself: "This is my body which is broken for you." But it is evident also that what we perform in the liturgy is a form of sacrifice. The duty of the High Priest of the New Covenant is to offer this sacrifice which revealed the nature of the New Covenant. It is

248 Devotions

clearly a sacrifice, although it is not something
that is new or accomplished by the efforts of
the bishop; it is a recalling of the true offering
of Christ. Since the bishop performs in symbol
signs of the heavenly realities, the sacrifice must
manifest them, so that he presents, as it were, an
image of the heavenly liturgy.

Theodore of Mopsuestia (ca. 350–428),
Baptismal Homilies[93]

RESPONSE

The cup of blessing that we bless
~IS A SHARING IN THE BLOOD OF CHRIST.

LITANY OF THE BLESSED SACRAMENT (SEE PAGES 220–222)

PRAYER

Power, splendor, greatness, glory,
    and honor are yours,
Lord of the sacred mysteries.
By sharing in the sacrifice of Golgotha
that we commemorate and celebrate
on our altars unceasingly,
may we arrive at the full expression
of our divine resemblance to you
in all the beauty of holiness.
We ask this through Christ Jesus,
our great High Priest,
who lives and reigns with you,

in the unity of the Holy Spirit,
one God, for ever and ever.
~AMEN.

DOXOLOGY

May the heart of Jesus in the most Blessed
    Sacrament
be praised, adored, and loved,
with grateful affection, at every moment,
in all the tabernacles of the world,
even to the end of time.
~AMEN.

A Devotion to the
Holy Name of Jesus

In Hebrew and in many languages, the *name* stands for and expresses the person. In the case of Jesus, his name indicates his mission in life, to be the Savior of the human race. Out of loving devotion to our blessed Savior, let us bend the knee to Jesus whose name is above every other and is the only name by which we must be saved. The steady repetition of the holy Name is recommended before beginning any other form of prayer, by way of conclusion to formal prayers, as an immediate preparation for the reception of Holy Communion, and especially during the precious moments just after receiving the Eucharist.

In the fifteenth century, St. Bernardino of Siena (1380–1444), the most famous preacher of his day, promoted a warm devotion to the holy Name as he addressed the crowds who came to hear him throughout Italy. During his sermons he held a plaque with the monogram of Jesus—I.H.S.—which he also reproduced on tablets and cards to distribute among his listeners in order to rekindle fervent devotion to Jesus. Such devotion spread rapidly throughout Europe and became especially popular in the British Isles in the form of the Jesus Psalter in the Books of Hours.

The Orthodox churches of the East have a special formula that they recommend for frequent use: "Lord Jesus Christ, Son of the living God, have mercy on me, a sinner." For its use and benefits, see the great spiritual classic, *The Way of a Pilgrim*, translated from the Russian by R. M. French (New York: Seabury Press, 1965).

This devotion is influenced by the English Psalter of Jesus and by Orthodox principles and practice of the Jesus Prayer.

The Latin hymn used in this devotion was composed in the twelfth century and exists in several translations.

> *God highly exalted Christ Jesus*
> *and gave him the name*
> *that is above every name,*
> *so that at the name of Jesus*
> *every knee should bend,*
> *in heaven and on earth and under the earth,*
> *and every tongue should confess*
> *that Jesus Christ is Lord,*
> *to the glory of God the Father.*[94]

I. Gabriel Announces the Holy Name

Our help † is in the name of the Lord,
~The Savior of heaven and earth.
There is no other name under heaven
~By which we must be saved.

Hymn

Jesus, the very thought of you
With sweetness fills my breast,
But sweeter far your face to see
And in your presence rest.

No voice can sing, no heart can frame,
Nor can the memory find
A sweeter sound than your blest name,
O help of humankind!

The angel said to her, "Do not be afraid, Mary, for you have found favor with God. And now, you will conceive in your womb and bear a son, and you will name him Jesus. He will be great, and will be called the Son of the Most High, and the Lord God will give to him the throne of his ancestor David."

OR THIS **MATTHEW**
READING **NAME HIM JESUS** **1:20–21**

An angel of the Lord appeared to him in a dream and said, "Joseph, son of David, do not be afraid to take Mary as your wife, for the child conceived in her is from the Holy Spirit. She will bear a son, and you are to name him Jesus, for he will save his people from their sins."

RESPONSE
The Mighty One has done great things for me
~AND HOLY IS HIS NAME.

PRAYER
Merciful God,
you appointed your only-begotten Son
to be the Savior of the human race
and asked Mary and Joseph to name him Jesus.
By this holy and awesome Name,
may we honor and praise him in this mortal life

and enjoy the vision of him in heaven
through all eternity.
~AMEN.

As I live every knee shall bow to me,
~AND EVERY TONGUE SHALL GIVE PRAISE.

II. Jesus Is Assigned His Holy Name
Our help † is in the name of the Lord,
~THE SAVIOR OF HEAVEN AND EARTH.
There is no other name under heaven
~BY WHICH WE MUST BE SAVED.

HYMN
Jesus, our only joy be now
As you our prize will be;
Jesus, be our glory now
And through eternity.

O Jesus, King most wonderful,
A Conqueror renowned,
A sweetness most ineffable
In whom all joys are found!

READING   THE HOLY NAME   LUKE 2:21
After eight days had passed since his birth, it was
time to circumcise the child; and he was called
Jesus, the name given by the angel before he was
conceived in the womb.

RESPONSE
Come, let us adore the holy name of Jesus
~WHICH IS ABOVE EVERY OTHER NAME.

PRAYER

God of the new and everlasting covenant,
your dear Son was dedicated to you
and took the name of Jesus
to express his unique role
in our salvation.
By this holy and awesome Name,
may we embrace the covenant established in his
      blood
and be faithful members of his mystical body,
now and throughout eternity.
~AMEN.

As I live every knee shall bow to me,
~AND EVERY TONGUE SHALL GIVE PRAISE.

III. The Unclean Spirit Recognizes the Holy Name

Our help † is in the name of the Lord,
~THE SAVIOR OF HEAVEN AND EARTH.
There is no other name under heaven
~BY WHICH WE MUST BE SAVED.

HYMN

May every heart confess your Name
And ever you adore;
And seeking you, itself excite
To seek you more and more.

May our tongues forever bless you,
May we love you all alone,

And ever in our lives express
The image of your own.

READING   JESUS OF NAZARETH   MARK 1:23–27

There was in their synagogue a man with an
unclean spirit, and he cried out, "What have you
to do with us, Jesus of Nazareth? Have you come
to destroy us? I know who you are, the Holy One
of God." But Jesus rebuked him, saying, "Be silent,
and come out of him!" And the unclean spirit,
convulsing him and crying with a loud voice,
came out of him. They were all amazed, and they
kept on asking one another, "What is this? A new
teaching—with authority! He commands even the
unclean spirits, and they obey him."

RESPONSE

If it is by the Spirit of God that I cast out demons,
~THEN THE KINGDOM OF GOD HAS COME TO YOU.

PRAYER

Lord of all the spirits,
at the name of Jesus
unclean spirits recognized him
as the Holy One of God
and fled before his face.
By this holy and awesome Name,
bid the unholy spirits to leave our souls and
      bodies
and give way to the holy and life-giving Spirit

who inhabits all the children of God,
both now and for ever.
~Amen.

As I live every knee shall bow to me,
~And every tongue shall give praise.

IV. Deeds of Power in the Holy Name
Our help † is in the name of the Lord,
~The Savior of heaven and earth.
There is no other name under heaven
~By which we must be saved.

Hymn
When once you visited the heart,
Then truth begins to shine,
Then earthly vanities depart,
And kindles love divine.

O Jesus, light of all below,
A fount of light and fire,
Surpassing all the joys we know,
And all we can desire!

Reading
Casting Out Demons
Mark 9:38–40

"Teacher, we saw someone casting out demons in
your name, and we tried to stop him, because he
was not following us." But Jesus said, "Do not stop
him; for no one who does a deed of power in my
name will be able soon afterward to speak evil of
me. Whoever is not against us is for us."

Response

Signs and wonders are performed
~Through the holy Name of your servant
 Jesus.

Prayer

Gracious Father,
through the mediation of your divine Son
you intervene in the world
to deliver us from evil.
By his holy and awesome Name,
come to our rescue
when we feel overwhelmed by physical or moral
 evil
and deliver us from grief, gloom, and despair,
through the invincible name of Jesus.
~Amen.

As I live every knee shall bow to me,
~And every tongue shall give praise.

V. The Continuing Power of the Holy Name

Our help ✝ is in the name of the Lord,
~The Savior of heaven and earth.
There is no other name under heaven
~By which we must be saved.

Hymn

Your wondrous mercies are untold,
Through each returning day;

Your love exceeds a thousandfold,
Whatever we can say.

May every heart confess your Name;
And ever you adore;
And seeking you, itself inflame,
To seek you more and more.

| | **HEALING IN THE** | |
| **READING** | **NAME OF JESUS** | **ACTS 3:3–8** |

When he [the man lame from birth] saw Peter and
John about to go into the temple, he asked them
for alms. Peter looked intently at him, as did John,
and said, "Look at us." And he fixed his attention
on them, expecting to receive something from
them. But Peter said, "I have no silver or gold,
but what I have I give you; in the name of Jesus
Christ of Nazareth, stand up and walk." And he
took him by the right hand and raised him up;
and immediately his feet and ankles were made
strong. Jumping up, he stood and began to walk,
and he entered the temple with them, walking and
leaping and praising God.

RESPONSE

The God of our ancestors has glorified his servant
    Jesus,
~THE AUTHOR OF LIFE WHOM GOD RAISED FROM
    THE DEAD.

God of our ancestors in the faith,
by the power of Jesus' Name
you did signs and wonders
through the hands of the holy apostles.
By this holy and awesome Name,
raise up the lame who cannot walk firmly
in the path of your holy Gospel
and make them walk and leap and praise God
for the gift of spiritual healing
that leads them toward eternal life.
~Amen.

As I live every knee shall bow to me,
~And every tongue shall give praise.

VI. Living Out the Holy Name

Our help † is in the name of the Lord,
~The Savior of heaven and earth.
There is no other name under heaven
~By which we must be saved.

Hymn

O Jesus, you the beauty are
Of angel worlds above!
Your Name is music to the heart,
Enchanting it with love!

Celestial sweetness unalloyed!
Who eat you hunger still,

Who drink of you still feel a void
Which naught but you can fill!

Let the word of Christ dwell in you richly; teach
and admonish one another in all wisdom; and
with gratitude in your hearts sing psalms, hymns,
and spiritual songs to God. And whatever you do,
in word or deed, do everything in the name of
the Lord Jesus, giving thanks to God the Father
through him.

RESPONSE
O Lord, our Sovereign,
~HOW MAJESTIC IS YOUR NAME IN ALL THE
     EARTH!

PRAYER
Gracious God and Father,
by the power of Jesus' name
you empower us to live in and by him
to the glory of your majestic presence.
By this holy and awesome Name,
save and deliver us from sin
and have us walk the straight and narrow path
that leads to everlasting life.
~AMEN.

As I live every knee shall bow to me,
~AND EVERY TONGUE SHALL GIVE PRAISE.

VII. The Glory of the Holy Name

Our help † is in the name of the Lord,

~THE SAVIOR OF HEAVEN AND EARTH.

There is no other name under heaven

~BY WHICH WE MUST BE SAVED.

HYMN

O my sweet Jesus! hear the sighs
Which unto you I send!
To you my inmost spirit cries,
My being's hope and end!

Stay with us, Lord, and with your light
Illume the soul's abyss;
Scatter the darkness of our night
And fill the world with bliss.[95]

READING

THE SEAL ON THE FOREHEAD

REVELATION 22:1–4

The angel showed me the river of the water of life, bright as crystal, flowing from the throne of God and of the Lamb through the middle of the street of the city. Nothing accursed will be found there any more. But the throne of God and of the Lamb will be in it, and his servants will worship him; they will see his face, and his name will be on their foreheads.

RESPONSE

The seal of the living God

~IS ON THEIR FOREHEADS.

PRAYER

Holy, immortal, and living God,
to glorify your only Son
and seal your chosen people,
you graced their foreheads
with the radiant Name of Jesus.
By this holy and awesome Name,
claim us as your sacred possession
and brand us as sheep of your flock,
now and forever.
~Amen.

As I live every knee shall bow to me,
~And every tongue shall give praise.

Blest be the holy name of Jesus, now and for ever!
~Amen.

Litany of the Holy Name of Jesus

This litany may be attached to the "Devotion to the Holy Name of Jesus" or used as a separate devotion.

Lord, have mercy	~LORD, HAVE MERCY
Christ, have mercy	~CHRIST, HAVE MERCY
Lord, have mercy	~LORD, HAVE MERCY
God our Father in heaven	~HAVE MERCY ON US
God the Son, Redeemer of the world	~HAVE MERCY ON US
God the Holy Spirit	~HAVE MERCY ON US
Holy Trinity, one God	~HAVE MERCY ON US
Jesus, Son of the living God	~HAVE MERCY ON US
Jesus, splendor of the Father	~HAVE MERCY ON US
Jesus, brightness of everlasting light	~HAVE MERCY ON US
Jesus, king of glory	~HAVE MERCY ON US
Jesus, dawn of justice	~HAVE MERCY ON US
Jesus, Son of the Virgin Mary	~HAVE MERCY ON US
Jesus, worthy of our love	~HAVE MERCY ON US
Jesus, worthy of our wonder	~HAVE MERCY ON US
Jesus, mighty God	~HAVE MERCY ON US
Jesus, father of the world to come	~HAVE MERCY ON US
Jesus, prince of peace	~HAVE MERCY ON US
Jesus, all-powerful	~HAVE MERCY ON US
Jesus, pattern of patience	~HAVE MERCY ON US
Jesus, model of obedience	~HAVE MERCY ON US
Jesus, gentle and humble of heart	~HAVE MERCY ON US
Jesus, lover of chastity	~HAVE MERCY ON US
Jesus, lover of us all	~HAVE MERCY ON US
Jesus, God of peace	~HAVE MERCY ON US
Jesus, author of life	~HAVE MERCY ON US
Jesus, model of goodness	~HAVE MERCY ON US
Jesus, seeker of souls	~HAVE MERCY ON US
Jesus, our God	~HAVE MERCY ON US
Jesus, our Refuge	~HAVE MERCY ON US

Jesus, father of the poor	~HAVE MERCY ON US
Jesus, treasure of the faithful	~HAVE MERCY ON US
Jesus, Good Shepherd	~HAVE MERCY ON US
Jesus, the true light	~HAVE MERCY ON US
Jesus, eternal wisdom	~HAVE MERCY ON US
Jesus, infinite goodness	~HAVE MERCY ON US
Jesus, our way and our life	~HAVE MERCY ON US
Jesus, joy of angels	~HAVE MERCY ON US
Jesus, king of patriarchs	~HAVE MERCY ON US
Jesus, teacher of apostles	~HAVE MERCY ON US
Jesus, master of evangelists	~HAVE MERCY ON US
Jesus, courage of martyrs	~HAVE MERCY ON US
Jesus, light of confessors	~HAVE MERCY ON US
Jesus, purity of virgins	~HAVE MERCY ON US
Jesus, crown of all saints	~HAVE MERCY ON US
Lord, be merciful	~JESUS, SAVE YOUR PEOPLE
From all evil	~JESUS, SAVE YOUR PEOPLE
From every sin	~JESUS, SAVE YOUR PEOPLE
From the snares of the devil	~JESUS, SAVE YOUR PEOPLE
From your anger	~JESUS, SAVE YOUR PEOPLE
From the spirit of infidelity	~JESUS, SAVE YOUR PEOPLE
From everlasting death	~JESUS, SAVE YOUR PEOPLE
From neglect of your Holy Spirit	~JESUS, SAVE YOUR PEOPLE
By the mystery of your incarnation	~JESUS, SAVE YOUR PEOPLE
By your birth	~JESUS, SAVE YOUR PEOPLE
By your childhood	~JESUS, SAVE YOUR PEOPLE
By your hidden life	~JESUS, SAVE YOUR PEOPLE
By your public ministry	~JESUS, SAVE YOUR PEOPLE
By your agony and crucifixion	~JESUS, SAVE YOUR PEOPLE
By your abandonment	~JESUS, SAVE YOUR PEOPLE
By your grief and sorrow	~JESUS, SAVE YOUR PEOPLE
By your death and burial	~JESUS, SAVE YOUR PEOPLE

By your rising to new life	~JESUS, SAVE YOUR PEOPLE
By your return in glory to the Father	~JESUS, SAVE YOUR PEOPLE
By your gift of the holy eucharist	~JESUS, SAVE YOUR PEOPLE
By your joy and glory	~JESUS, SAVE YOUR PEOPLE
Christ, hear us	~CHRIST, HEAR US
Lord Jesus, hear our prayer	~LORD JESUS, HEAR OUR PRAYER
Lamb of God, you take away the sins of the world	~HAVE MERCY ON US
Lamb of God, you take away the sins of the world	~HAVE MERCY ON US
Lamb of God, you take away the sins of the world	~HAVE MERCY ON US

Let us pray:

Lord,
may we who honor the holy name of Jesus
enjoy his friendship in this life
and be filled with eternal joy in the kingdom
where he lives and reigns forever and ever.
~AMEN.[96]

A Devotion to the
Five Wounds of Jesus

Stretched between heaven and earth, the Lord Jesus displayed his five precious wounds to believers and unbelievers alike. Though priests, soldiers, criminals, and passersby scoffed at him and scorned him, the faithful few stood by him as he died in agony and dereliction. By faith we know that his death is our life and that his wounds are the profound signs of complete compassion for our sins and offenses.

Devotion to the wounds of Jesus is an ancient and honored practice. As he was dying, St. Richard de Wyche (1197–1253) asked for a crucifix and, kissing the Five Wounds, said, "Thanks be to thee, my Lord Jesus Christ, for all the benefits which thou hast given me, for the pains and insults which thou hast suffered for me; so great were they, that that mournful cry suited thee right well, 'There is no grief like my grief.'"[97]

In the same thirteenth century St. Francis of Assisi (1181–1226) crowned his life of voluntary poverty and devotion to Jesus crucified by receiving in his own body the five wounds of Jesus. He became the exemplary Christian of the Middle Ages and heavily influenced the style of crucifixes forever. A later disciple of Francis, St. Leonard Casnova (1676–1751) became the founder and preacher of the stations of the cross, the most popular devotion to the sufferings of Jesus from the court of Pilate to the rock-hewn tomb. Another disciple of Francis, Padre Pio of Pietrelcina (1887–1968) became another living crucifix in our own time. He stirred up fresh devotion to the Five Wounds and urged people to call upon God in virtue of these wounds for all their spiritual and temporal needs.

THE MOTHER OF SORROWS

O, teach those wounds to bleed
In me; me, so to read
This book of loves, thus writ
In lines of death, my life may copy it
    with loyal cares.
O, let me here, here, claim shares!
Yield something in thy sad prerogative,
    Great Queen of griefs, and give
    Me to my tears; who, though all stone,
Think much that Thou should'st mourn alone.

Richard Crashaw (1613–1649)

I. To the Wound in the Right Hand

Blest be † the holy wound in the right hand
    of Jesus, our wounded Savior!

~AMEN.

	WHITE	ISAIAH
READING	AS WOOL	1:18–20

Come now, let us argue it out, says the LORD:
though your sins are like scarlet, they shall be like
snow; though they are red like crimson, they shall
become like wool. If you are willing and obedient,
you shall eat the good of the land; but if you refuse
and rebel, you shall be devoured by the sword; for
the mouth of the LORD has spoken.

RESPONSORY   PSALM 51:1–3, 7, 9–11, 15, 16

LEADER: Create in me a clean heart, O God,

ALL: AND PUT A NEW AND RIGHT SPIRIT WITHIN
    ME.

Have mercy on me, O God,
according to your steadfast love;
according to your abundant mercy
blot out my transgressions.
~CREATE IN ME A CLEAN HEART, O GOD,
AND PUT A NEW AND RIGHT SPIRIT WITHIN ME.

Wash me thoroughly from my iniquity,
and cleanse me from my sin!
For I know my transgressions,
and my sin is ever before me.
~CREATE IN ME A CLEAN HEART, O GOD,
AND PUT A NEW AND RIGHT SPIRIT WITHIN ME.

Purge me with hyssop, and I shall be clean;
wash me, and I shall be whiter than snow.
Hide your face from my sins,
and blot out all my iniquities.
~CREATE IN ME A CLEAN HEART, O GOD,
AND PUT A NEW AND RIGHT SPIRIT WITHIN ME.

Create in me a clean heart, O God,
and put a new and right spirit within me.
Cast me not away from your presence,
and take not your Holy Spirit from me.
~CREATE IN ME A CLEAN HEART, O GOD,
AND PUT A NEW AND RIGHT SPIRIT WITHIN ME.

O Lord, open my lips,
and my mouth shall show forth your praise.

The sacrifice acceptable to God is a broken spirit;
a broken and contrite heart, O God, you will not
despise.
~Create in me a clean heart, O God,
and put a new and right spirit within me.

To the One seated on the throne and to the Lamb
be blessing and honor and glory and might
forever and ever!
~Create in me a clean heart, O God,
and put a new and right spirit within me.

Psalm Prayer
God of love and compassion,
by the wound of love in the right hand
of your dear Son, our Savior,
you show us how merciful you are
in forgiving and forgetting our sins.
Though our sins are like scarlet,
make them whiter than snow;
though they are as red as crimson,
make them as clean as wool,
for you wash us in the blood of Jesus
and make us acceptable in your sight.
Blest be Jesus, true God and true Man.
~Amen.

II. To the Wound in the Left Hand
Blest be ✝ the holy wound in the left hand
of Jesus, our wounded Savior!
~Amen.

To him who loves us and freed us from our sins by
his blood, and made us to be a kingdom, priests
serving his God and Father, to him be glory and
dominion forever and ever. Amen. Look! He is
coming with the clouds; every eye will see him,
even those who pierced him; and on his account
all the tribes of the earth will wail. So it is to be.
Amen.

RESPONSORY   **PSALM 130**

LEADER: With the Lord ~THERE IS GREAT
    REDEMPTION!

Out of the depths I cry to you, O Lord!
Lord, hear my voice!
Let your ears be attentive
to the voice of my supplications!
~WITH THE LORD THERE IS GREAT REDEMPTION!

If you, O Lord, should mark iniquities,
Lord, who could stand?
But there is forgiveness with you,
that you may be worshipped.
~WITH THE LORD THERE IS GREAT REDEMPTION!

I wait for the Lord, my soul waits,
in the Lord's word I hope;
my soul waits for the Lord
more than watchers for the morning.
~WITH THE LORD THERE IS GREAT REDEMPTION!

O Israel, hope in the Lord!
For with the Lord there is steadfast love.
The Lord alone will redeem Israel
from all iniquities.
~WITH THE LORD THERE IS GREAT REDEMPTION!

To the One seated on the throne and to the Lamb
be blessing and honor and glory and might
forever and ever!
~WITH THE LORD THERE IS GREAT REDEMPTION!

PSALM PRAYER
Great and gracious God,
by the wound of love in the left hand
of your dear Son, our Savior,
have mercy on us all
and take away every sin from our hearts.
Save us from the time of trial
and deliver us from the evil one
who roams around like a roaring lion
seeking to devour us.
By the power of his five precious wounds,
save us from all that may threaten
our commitment to Jesus the Messiah
and bring us under the shadow of his cross.
Blest be Jesus, true God and true Man!
~AMEN.

III. To the Wound in the Right Foot

Blest be † the holy wound in the right foot
of Jesus, our wounded Savior!

~AMEN.

	THE PRECIOUS BLOOD	1 PETER
READING	OF CHRIST	1:18–20

Brothers and sisters, you know that you were
ransomed from the futile ways inherited from
your ancestors, not with perishable things like
silver or gold, but with the precious blood of
Christ, like that of a lamb without defect or
blemish. He was destined before the foundation of
the world, but was revealed at the end of the ages
for your sake.

RESPONSORY   **PSALM 36:5–12**

LEADER: With you ~IS THE FOUNTAIN OF LIFE,
O LORD; IN YOUR LIGHT WE SEE LIGHT.

Your steadfast love, O Lord, extends to the
heavens,
your faithfulness to the clouds.
Your righteousness is like the mighty mountains,
your judgments are like the great deep;
O Lord, you save humans and animals!
~WITH YOU IS THE FOUNTAIN OF LIFE, O LORD;
IN YOUR LIGHT WE SEE LIGHT.

O God, how precious is your steadfast love!
All people take refuge in the shadow of your
wings.

They feast on the abundance of your house,
and you give them to drink from the river of your
    delights.
~With you is the fountain of life, O Lord;
in your light we see light.

Do not let the foot of the arrogant come upon me,
nor the hand of the wicked drive me away.
There the evildoers lie prostrate,
they are thrust down unable to rise.
~With you is the fountain of life, O Lord;
in your light we see light.

To the One seated on the throne and to the Lamb
be blessing and honor and glory and might
forever and ever!
~With you is the fountain of life, O Lord;
in your light we see light.

Psalm Prayer
Great and gracious God,
by the wound of love in the right foot
of your dear Son, our Savior,
have mercy on us and absolve all our sins.
Through this wound of love,
grant us the gift of true repentance
with profound sorrow for all our sins.
You are the fountain of life, O Lord,
and in your light we see light
to walk in Christ's footsteps
that lead by the straight and narrow path

to the heavenly home prepared for us.
Blest be Jesus, true God and true Man!
~Amen.

IV. To the Wound in the Left Foot
Blest be † the holy wound in the left foot
    of Jesus, our wounded Savior!
~Amen.

READING   **BLOOD AND WATER**   **HEBREWS 10:19–22**
My friends, since we have confidence to enter
the sanctuary by the blood of Jesus, by the new
and living way that he opened for us through the
curtain (that is, through his flesh), and since we
have a great priest over the house of God, let us
approach with a true heart in full assurance of
faith, with our hearts sprinkled clean from an
evil conscience and our bodies washed with
pure water.

RESPONSORY   **PSALM 142**
LEADER: Let my prayer arise before you like
    incense,
~THE LIFTING UP OF MY HANDS LIKE AN EVENING
    OBLATION.

With my voice I cry to the Lord,
I make supplication;
Before the Lord I tell my trouble,
I pour out my complaint.

When my spirit is faint,
you know my way.
~Let my prayer arise before you like
   incense, the lifting up of my hands like
   an evening oblation.

In the path where I walk
they have hidden a trap for me.
Look on my right hand and see;
there is no one who takes notice of me;
no refuge remains for me,
no one takes care of me.
~Let my prayer arise before you like
   incense, the lifting up of my hands like
   an evening oblation.

I cry to you, O Lord;
I say, "You are my refuge,
my portion in the land of the living.
Give heed to my cry;
for they are too strong for me."
~Let my prayer arise before you like
   incense, the lifting up of my hands like
   an evening oblation.

Bring me out of prison,
so that I may give thanks to your name!
The righteous will surround me,
for you will deal richly with me.
~Let my prayer arise before you like
   incense, the lifting up of my hands like
   an evening oblation.

276 Devotions

To the One seated on the throne and to the Lamb
be blessing and honor and glory and might
forever and ever!

~LET MY PRAYER ARISE BEFORE YOU LIKE
INCENSE, THE LIFTING UP OF MY HANDS LIKE
AN EVENING OBLATION.

PSALM PRAYER
Good and gracious God,
by the wound of love in the left foot
of your dear Son, our Savior,
have mercy on us and absolve all our sins.
Through this wound of love,
deliver us from every trial and tribulation,
from every fear and temptation,
so that we may serve you wholeheartedly
and hold fast to you in our dying hour
by the intercession of your sorrowful Mother
and of all the saints in glory.
Blest be Jesus, true God and true Man!
~AMEN.

V. To the Wound in the Side
Blest be ✝ the holy wound in the side
of Jesus, our wounded Savior!
~AMEN.

READING   **THE BROKEN HEART**   **JOHN 19:31–35**
So they asked Pilate to have the legs of the
crucified men broken and the bodies removed.
Then the soldiers came and broke the legs of the

first and of the other who had been crucified with him. But when they came to Jesus and saw that he was already dead, they did not break his legs. Instead, one of the soldiers pierced his side with a spear, and at once blood and water came out. (He who saw this has testified so that you also may believe. His testimony is true, and he knows that he tells the truth.)

RESPONSORY **PSALM 22:1–2, 6–8, 14–15**
LEADER: They have pierced my hands and my feet;
~I CAN COUNT ALL MY BONES.

My God, my God, why have you forsaken me?
Why are you so far from helping me,
from the words of my groaning?
O my God, I cry by day, but you do not answer;
and by night, but find no rest.
~THEY HAVE PIERCED MY HANDS AND MY FEET; I
CAN COUNT ALL MY BONES.

But I am a worm, not human;
scorned by others, and despised by the people.
All who see me mock at me,
they make mouths at me,
they wags their heads and say:
~THEY HAVE PIERCED MY HANDS AND MY FEET; I
CAN COUNT ALL MY BONES.

"You committed your cause to the Lord;
let the Lord deliver you.

Let the Lord rescue you,
for the Lord delights in you!"
~THEY HAVE PIERCED MY HANDS AND MY FEET; I
    CAN COUNT ALL MY BONES.

I am poured out like water,
and all my bones are out of joint;
my heart is like wax
within my breast;
my tongue sticks to my jaws;
you lay me in the dust of death.
~THEY HAVE PIERCED MY HANDS AND MY FEET; I
    CAN COUNT ALL MY BONES.

To the One seated on the throne and to the Lamb
be blessing and honor and glory and might
forever and ever!
~THEY HAVE PIERCED MY HANDS AND MY FEET;
I CAN COUNT ALL MY BONES.

PSALM PRAYER
Good and gracious God,
by the wound of love in the side
of your dear Son, our Savior,
have mercy on us and absolve all our sins.
Through this wound of love,
you showed your great kindness
both to the Roman centurion
and to all sinful souls.
By the precious blood and water
that poured from your pierced heart,

deliver us from every evil,
past, present, and still to come,
and conduct us in safety
to our heavenly home.
Blest be Jesus, true God and true Man!
~AMEN.

By his holy and glorious wounds,
may Jesus-Messiah † protect us and keep us.
~AMEN.

The Seven Last Words

As Jesus hung on the cross, he uttered seven last words of great meaning to those who contemplate his passion and death. For centuries these words have been built into various forms of devotion for the consideration and consolation of the Christian people. English Catholics of the late Middle Ages were especially devoted to this pious exercise and passed it on in latter-day prayer books.

Hear the famous English mystic, Julian of Norwich:

Suddenly it came into my mind that I ought to wish for the second wound, that our Lord, of his gift and of his grace, would fill my body full with recollection and feeling of his blessed Passion, as I had prayed before, for I wished that his pains might be my pains, with compassion which would lead to longing for God. . . . And at this suddenly I saw the red blood trickling down from under the crown, all hot, flowing freely and copiously, a living stream, just as it seemed to me that it was at the time when the crown of thorns was thrust down upon his blessed head. . . . With this sight of his blessed Passion and with his divinity, I saw that this was strength enough for me, yes, and for all living creatures who will be protected from all the devils from hell and from all spiritual enemies. [98]

This devotion may be spread over a week, commemorating one of the seven last words each day, or it may be prayed as a whole devotion in a single day.

The First Word

LEADER: We adore you, O Christ, and we bless you,

ALL: FOR BY YOUR HOLY CROSS YOU HAVE
    REDEEMED THE WORLD.

LEADER: Your word is a lamp to our feet

ALL: AND A LIGHT TO OUR PATH.

HYMN

Glory be to Jesus,
who in bitter pains
poured for me the lifeblood
from his sacred veins!

Grace and life eternal
in that blood I find,
blest be his compassion
infinitely kind!

Blest through endless ages
be the precious stream
which for sin and sorrow
does the world redeem.

Lift now then your voices;
swell the mighty flood;
louder still and louder
praise the precious blood.[99]

READING   LUKE 23:33–34

When the soldiers came to the place that is called
The Skull, they crucified Jesus there with the
criminals, one on his right and one on his left.

Then Jesus said, "Father, forgive them; for they do not know what they are doing."

Response
Leader: I held out my hands all day long
All: ~To a disobedient and contrary people.

Prayer
Merciful Savior,
and friend of the human race,
in your compassion
you forgave your mortal enemies
who sentenced you and nailed you to the cross.
By your gracious example,
help us to forgive our enemies from the heart
and make friends even with the sinful.
Blest be your forgiving heart, now and for ever.
All: ~Amen.

May the bitter passion of our Lord Jesus Christ
† bring us to the joys of paradise.
All: ~Amen.

The Second Word
The noble tree of the cross
~Stands in the midst of paradise.
Your word is a lamp to our feet
~And a light to our path.

Hymn (SEE PAGE 282)

Reading   Luke 23:39–43

One of the criminals who were hanged there
kept deriding him and saying, "Are you not
the Messiah? Save yourself and us!" But the
other rebuked him, saying, "Do you not fear
God, since you are under the same sentence
of condemnation? And we indeed have been
condemned justly, for we are getting what we
deserve for our deeds, but this man has done
nothing wrong." Then he said, "Jesus, remember
me when you come into your kingdom." He
replied, "TRULY I TELL YOU, TODAY YOU WILL BE
WITH ME IN PARADISE."

Response

By a tree we were enslaved;
~BY A TREE WE ARE SET FREE.

Prayer

Merciful Savior,
and friend of the human race,
you heard the repentant plea
of the criminal on your right hand
and promised him paradise for his faith.
As we are dying in the midst of our sins,
let us hear this same word from your lips
in response to our prayer of faith
and the life-giving power of your holy sacraments.

Blest be your undying mercy,
now and for ever.
~Amen.

May the bitter passion of our Lord Jesus Christ
† bring us to the joys of paradise.
~Amen.

The Third Word

Sweet wood, sweet nails, bearing so sweet a load;
~Save us who sing your praises.
Your word is a lamp to our feet
~And a light to our path.

Hymn (see page 282)

Reading   John 19:25–27

Standing near the cross of Jesus were his mother,
and his mother's sister, Mary the wife of Clopas,
and Mary Magdalene. When Jesus saw his mother
and the disciple whom he loved standing beside
her, he said to his mother, "Woman, here is your
son." Then he said to the disciple, "Here is your
mother." And from that hour the disciple took
her into his own home.

Response

Mary's canticle puts an end
~To the lamentations of Eve.

PRAYER

Merciful Savior,
and friend of the human race,
on Golgotha you pitied your martyred mother
and bequeathed her to your beloved disciple.
By her tears and prayers,
break our proud hearts
as we worship your cross and passion
and let us take her into our hearts and homes,
now and forever.
~AMEN.

May the bitter passion of our Lord Jesus Christ
† bring us to the joys of paradise.
~AMEN.

The Fourth Word

We adore you, O Christ, and we bless you,
~FOR BY YOUR HOLY CROSS YOU HAVE REDEEMED
    THE WORLD.
Your word is a lamp to our feet
~AND A LIGHT TO OUR PATH.

HYMN (SEE PAGE 282)

READING   MARK 15:33–34

When it was noon, darkness came over the whole
land until three in the afternoon. At three o'clock
Jesus cried out with a loud voice, "Eloi, Eloi, lema
sabachthani?" which means, "MY GOD, MY GOD,
WHY HAVE YOU FORSAKEN ME?"

RESPONSE
Holy cross, you alone were counted worthy
~To bear the ransom of the world.

PRAYER
Merciful Savior,
and friend of the human race,
as darkness came over the whole land
you cried out in agony to your Father.
By this cry of dereliction,
rescue us from the torments of despair,
and entrust us to your sacrificial death.
You live and reign with the Father,
in the unity of the Holy Spirit,
one God, for ever and ever.
~Amen.

May the bitter passion of our Lord Jesus Christ
† bring us to the joys of paradise.
~Amen.

The Fifth Word
The sign of the cross will appear in the heavens
~When the Lord Jesus returns in glory.
Your word is a lamp to our feet
~And a light to our path.

HYMN (SEE PAGE 282)

READING   JOHN 19:28–29
When Jesus knew that all was now finished,
he said (in order to fulfill the scripture), "I am

THIRSTY." A jar full of sour wine was standing there. So they put a sponge full of the wine on a branch of hyssop and held it to his mouth.

RESPONSE
My mouth is dried up like a potsherd;
~AND MY TONGUE STICKS TO MY JAWS.

PRAYER
Merciful Savior,
and friend of the human race,
as your life drew near its end,
you cried out in thirst,
a thirst for souls.
By this dreadful and abiding thirst,
draw our hearts and minds
to your great love for us,
and especially at the hour of our death.
Blest be your merciful love,
now and for ever.
~AMEN.

May the bitter passion of our Lord Jesus Christ
✝ bring us to the joys of paradise.
~AMEN.

The Sixth Word
Reign from the noble tree of the cross,
~AND ESTABLISH THE REIGN OF GOD IN OUR
	HEARTS.

Your word is a lamp to our feet
~And a light to our path.

Hymn (see page 282)

Reading   John 19:30
When Jesus had received the wine, he said, "It is
finished." Then he bowed his head and gave up
his spirit.

Response
They have pierced my hands and my feet
~And lay me in the dust of death.

Prayer
Merciful Savior,
and friend of the human race,
as darkness closed in on you,
you gave a loud cry,
bowed your head, and died.
By your perfect surrender to the Father,
make us worthy disciples of the cross
and defend us from our spiritual enemies,
now and for ever.
~Amen.

May the bitter passion of our Lord Jesus Christ
† bring us to the joys of paradise.
~Amen.

The Seventh Word

Come, let us adore Christ crucified;
~Come, let us adore him.
Your word is a lamp to our feet
~And a light to our path.

Hymn (see page 282)

Reading   Luke 23:44–46

Darkness came over the whole land until three in the afternoon, while the sun's light failed; and the curtain of the temple was torn in two. Then Jesus, crying with a loud voice, said, "Father, into your hands I commend my spirit." Having said this, he breathed his last.

Response

The Roman centurion, who stood facing him,
       said,
~"Truly this man was God's Son!"

Prayer

Merciful Savior,
and friend of the human race,
in a final act of surrender
you breathed forth your spirit
into your Father's hands.
By this ultimate commitment
to the Father's loving care,
deliver us from despair in our dying hour
and help us die in hope and full confidence

in your precious blood poured out for us.
Blest be your gracious caring,
now and for ever.
~AMEN.

May the bitter passion of our Lord Jesus Christ
† bring us to the joys of paradise.
~AMEN.

Litany of the Sacred Passion

This litany may be used in conjunction with the "Seven Last Words" or as a separate devotion. It draws together all the events of Jesus' dying day.

Lord Jesus, at the Last Supper you knew
   that Judas, one of the Twelve, would betray you.
~GOOD LORD, DELIVER US FROM FALSE FRIENDS
   AND TREACHERY.

Lord Jesus, during the supper, you humbly
   washed the feet of your disciples.
~GOOD LORD, MAKE US MEEK AND HUMBLE OF
   HEART.

Lord Jesus, at the Last Supper, you gave us
   the sacrament of your broken body
   and outpoured blood.
~GOOD LORD, WE WORSHIP THE SEAL
   OF THE NEW AND ETERNAL COVENANT.

Lord Jesus, you asked your disciples to watch
   and pray with you in the Garden of
      Gethsemane.
~GOOD LORD, KEEP US AWAKE AND WATCHFUL
   WITH YOU.

Lord Jesus, at your betrayal and arrest all your
   friends fled in fear and deserted you.
~GOOD LORD, GIVE US COURAGE IN TIME OF
   TRIAL.

Lord Jesus, you were falsely accused
and condemned for speaking the truth
before Caiaphas, the high priest.
~GOOD LORD, MAY WE SPEAK TRUTH
IN THE FACE OF INJUSTICE.

Lord Jesus, in the courtyard of the high priest,
Simon Peter swore three times
that he did not know you.
~GOOD LORD, MAKE US FAITHFUL IN TIME
OF TEMPTATION.

Lord Jesus, Pilate traded you for a murderer
and handed you over to crucifixion.
~GOOD LORD, HAVE MERCY ON US SINNERS.

Lord Jesus, you were beaten, mocked,
and humiliated by Pilate's soldiers.
~GOOD LORD, MAY WE SUFFER GLADLY FOR YOUR
SAKE.

Lord Jesus, on the cross you were taunted
and derided as King of the Jews.
~GOOD LORD, MAY WE ALWAYS LIVE IN
OBEDIENCE TO YOU.

Lord Jesus, on the cross you forgave your
enemies.
~GOOD LORD, GIVE US THE GRACE TO FORGIVE
OURS.

Lord Jesus, from the cross you promised
paradise to a repentant criminal.

~Good Lord, make us long for paradise and
eternal bliss.

Lord Jesus, from the cross you confided
your Blessed Mother to your beloved disciple.

~Good Lord, make us children of Mary.

Lord Jesus, you cried out in agony
to your Father and died with a loud cry.

~Good Lord, have mercy on us, now and at
the hour of our death.

Lord Jesus, the Roman centurion
recognized you as the Son of God.

~Good Lord, may we always praise and
exalt you as our blessed Savior.

Lord Jesus, you were taken down from the cross
and laid in the arms of your sorrowful
Mother.

~Good Lord, entrust us to the care of your
Blessed Mother.

Lord Jesus, Joseph of Arimathea
wrapped your body in a linen shroud
and laid you in his rock-hewn tomb.

~Good Lord, grant us the gift of tears at
the memory of your suffering, death,
and burial.

Lord Jesus, the women who had followed you
   from Galilee watched as you were put to rest
   in the tomb.
~Good Lord, we await with joy your
   glorious resurrection on the third
   day

(Pause for special intentions.)

We adore you, O Christ, and we bless you,
~For by your holy cross you have redeemed
   the world.

Closing Prayer
Lord Jesus Christ,
you were fastened with nails
to the wood of the cross
and raised on high for all to see.
As the sun grew dark and the earth quaked,
you surrendered your spirit to your Father,
descended among the dead,
broke open the gates of hell,
and freed those bound in darkness.
As angel choirs rejoiced,
you were raised to life again on the third day,
destroying death by your own death
and canceling the power of sin.
By these mighty deeds on our behalf,
rescue us from our blindness and tepidity,

inspire us anew by your Holy Spirit,
and lead us into a life of prayer and service
worthy of your awesome sacrifice,
O Savior of the world,
living and reigning with the Father,
in the unity of the Holy Spirit,
one God, for ever and ever.
~AMEN.

May the glorious passion of our Lord Jesus Christ
✝ bring us to the joys of paradise.
~AMEN.

Devotion to the Seven Blood Sheddings of Jesus

Devotion to the precious Blood, the price of our salvation, is of apostolic origin, and those who meditate on the scriptural passages that describe the seven outpourings ground themselves in the love of God as it is expressed in the wounded Savior of the world. This devotion took on new forms in the nineteenth century, when several new orders of men and women were dedicated to the precious Blood. In North America, the Canadian founder, Mother Catherine Aurelia (1833–1905), established the Sisters Adorers of the Precious Blood, a contemplative order of nuns that has many houses in Canada and the United States.

The following meditation from the English visionary, Blessed Julian of Norwich (1343–ca. 1423), will assist us in our contemplation of the shed blood of Christ our Lord.

> I saw the body bleeding copiously in representation of the scourging, and it was thus. The fair skin was deeply broken into the tender flesh through the vicious blows delivered all over the lovely body. The hot blood ran out so plentifully that neither sin nor wounds could be seen, but everything seemed to be blood. And as it flowed down to where it should have fallen, it disappeared. Nonetheless, the bleeding continued for a time, until it could be plainly seen. And I saw it so plentiful that it seemed to me that it had in fact and in substance been happening there, the bed and everything all around it would have been soaked in blood.

Then it came into my mind that God has created bountiful waters of the earth for our use and bodily comfort, out of the tender love he has for us. But it is more pleasing to him that we accept for our total cure his blessed blood to wash us from our sins, for there is no drink that is made which it pleases him so well to give us. For it is most plentiful, as it is most precious, and that through the power of the blessed divinity. And it is of our own nature, and blessedly flows over us by the power of his precious love.[100]

This devotion may be spread over seven days or used as a single offering on one day.

1. Jesus Is Circumcised and Named on the Eighth Day

LEADER: Come, † Lord, and help your people,

ALL: BOUGHT WITH THE PRICE OF YOUR OWN BLOOD.

LEADER: You shall call his name Jesus,

ALL: FOR HE SHALL SAVE HIS PEOPLE FROM THEIR SINS.

HYMN

Alone, in depths of woe,
Upon that scornful tree
Hangs Christ, redeemer of the world,
In shame and agony.

His feet and hands outstretched
By hammered nails are torn;
In mocking, on his head is thrust
A crown of bitter thorn.

Come, kneel before the Lord:
He shed for us his blood;
He died the victim of pure love
To make us one with God.[101]

READING   **SHEDDING OF BLOOD**   **LUKE 2:21**

After eight days had passed [since his birth], it was
time to circumcise the child; and he was called
Jesus, the name given by the angel before he was
conceived in the womb.

RESPONSORY   **PSALM 8**   **THE HOLY NAME**

LEADER: You will bear a Son, Mary,

ALL: AND NAME HIM JESUS.

O Lord, our Lord,
how majestic is your name in all the earth!

ALL: YOU WILL BEAR A SON, MARY, AND NAME HIM
       JESUS.

Your glory is chanted above the heavens
by the mouth of babes and infants;
you have set up a defense against your foes,
to still the enemy and the avenger.

ALL: YOU WILL BEAR A SON, MARY, AND NAME HIM
       JESUS.

When I look at your heavens, the work of your
       fingers,
the moon and the stars which you have
       established;

Devotion to the Seven Blood Sheddings of Jesus **299**

what are human beings that you are mindful of
   them,
and mortals that you care for them?

All: You will bear a son, Mary, and name him
   Jesus.

You have made them little less than God,
and crowned them with glory and honor.
You have given them dominion over the works
   of your hands;
you have put all things under their feet,

All: You will bear a son, Mary, and name him
   Jesus.

all sheep and oxen,
and also the beasts of the field,
the birds of the air, and the fish of the sea,
whatever passes along the paths of the seas.

All: You will bear a son, Mary, and name him
   Jesus.

O Lord, our Lord,
how majestic is your name in all the earth!

All: You will bear a son, Mary, and name him
   Jesus.

To the One seated on the throne
and to the Lamb who was slain
be blessing and honor and glory and might
forever and ever! Amen.

All: You will bear a son, Mary, and name him
     Jesus.

Prayer
Lord Jesus,
on the eighth day after your birth,
you obeyed the law of circumcision,
became a child of Abraham,
and were named Jesus/Savior.
By this first shedding of your precious blood,
we offer ourselves to you
to ratify the new and eternal covenant
that you established on the cross,
O Savior of the world,
whom we praise, honor, and glorify,
now and for ever.
~Amen.

Blest † be the name of Jesus, now and for ever!
~Amen.

2. Jesus Agonizes in the Garden of Gethsemane

Come, † Lord, and help your people,
~Bought with the price of your own blood.
Jesus offered up prayers and supplications
~With loud cries and tears to God.

Hymn (see pages 298–299)

READING   **GETHSEMANE**

Jesus came out and went, as was his custom, to the
Mount of Olives; and the disciples followed him.
When he reached the place, he said to them, "Pray
that you may not come into the time of trial."
Then he withdrew from them about a stone's
throw, knelt down, and prayed, "Father, if you are
willing, remove this cup from me; yet, not my will
but yours be done." Then an angel from heaven
appeared to him and gave him strength. In his
anguish he prayed more earnestly, and his sweat
became like great drops of blood falling down on
the ground.

RESPONSORY   **PSALM 13**   **CHRIST RELIES
ON HIS FATHER**

ANTIPHON I am deeply grieved ~EVEN TO DEATH.

How long, O Lord? Will you forget me forever?
How long will you hide your face from me?
How long must I bear pain in my soul,
and have sorrow in my heart all the day?
How long shall my enemy be exalted over me?
~I AM DEEPLY GRIEVED EVEN TO DEATH.

Consider and answer me, O Lord my God;
lighten my eyes, lest I sleep the sleep of death;
lest my enemy say, "I have prevailed";
lest my foes rejoice because I am shaken.
~I AM DEEPLY GRIEVED EVEN TO DEATH.

But I trusted in your steadfast love;
my heart shall rejoice in your salvation.
I will sing to the Lord,
for the LORD has dealt richly with me.
~I AM deeply GRIEVED EVEN TO DEATH.

To the One seated on the throne
and to the Lamb who was slain
be blessing and honor and glory and might
forever and ever! Amen.
~I AM DEEPLY GRIEVED EVEN TO DEATH.

PRAYER
Lord Jesus, Man of Sorrows,
as you prayed in agony
in the Garden of Gethsemane,
you asked to be spared the cup of suffering
and yet submitted completely to the Father's will.
By this second shedding of your precious blood,
wash away all our sins of sloth and negligence
and keep us awake in your presence
as we await your coming in glory,
O Savior of the world,
whom we praise, honor, and glorify,
now and for ever.
~AMEN.

Blest † be the name of Jesus, now and for ever!
~AMEN.

3. Jesus Is Scourged at the Pillar

Come, † Lord, and help your people,

~Bought with the price of your own blood.

By his wounds we are healed;

~By his blood we are washed clean.

Hymn (see pages 298–299)

Reading **The Flogging** **Mark 15:12–15**

Pilate spoke to the crowd, "Then what do you wish me to do with the man you call the King of the Jews?" They shouted back, "Crucify him!" Pilate asked them, "Why, what evil has he done?" But they shouted all the more, "Crucify him!" So Pilate, wishing to satisfy the crowd, released Barabbas for them; and after flogging Jesus, he handed him over to be crucified.

Responsory **Psalm 16** **The Path of Life**

Antiphon We have confidence to enter the sanctuary ~by the blood of Jesus.

Preserve me, O God, for in you I take refuge.
I say to the Lord, "O Lord, you are my fortune, only you!"

~We have confidence to enter the sanctuary by the blood of Jesus.

The Lord is my chosen portion and my cup;
you hold my lot.

The boundary lines have fallen to me in pleasant
    places;
I have a goodly heritage.
~WE HAVE CONFIDENCE TO ENTER THE
    SANCTUARY BY THE BLOOD OF JESUS.

I bless the Lord who gives me counsel;
my heart also instructs me in the night.
I have set the Lord always before me;
the Lord is at my right hand;
I shall not be moved.
~WE HAVE CONFIDENCE TO ENTER THE
    SANCTUARY BY THE BLOOD OF JESUS.

Therefore my heart is glad, and my soul rejoices;
my body also dwells secure.
For you do not give me up to Sheol,
or let your godly one see the Pit.
~WE HAVE CONFIDENCE TO ENTER THE
    SANCTUARY BY THE BLOOD OF JESUS.

You show me the path of life;
in your presence there is the fullness of joy,
in your right hand are pleasures forevermore.
~WE HAVE CONFIDENCE TO ENTER THE
    SANCTUARY BY THE BLOOD OF JESUS.

To the One seated on the throne
and to the Lamb who was slain
be blessing and honor and glory and might
forever and ever! Amen.
~WE HAVE CONFIDENCE TO ENTER THE
    SANCTUARY BY THE BLOOD OF JESUS.

PRAYER

Lord Jesus, Man of Sorrows,
by the orders of Pontius Pilate
you were flogged like a slave
by cruel and pitiless soldiers.
By this third shedding of your precious blood,
wash away all our sins and misdeeds,
make us pure and righteous in your sight,
and ready to suffer in union with you,
O Savior of the world,
whom we praise, honor, and glorify,
now and for ever.
~AMEN.

Blest ✝ be the name of Jesus, now and for ever!
~AMEN.

4. Jesus Is Crowned with Thorns

Come, ✝ Lord, and help your people,
~BOUGHT WITH THE PRICE OF YOUR OWN BLOOD.
The blood of Jesus God's Son
~CLEANSES US FROM ALL SIN.

HYMN (SEE PAGES 298–299)

READING	THE CROWN OF THORNS	MARK 15:16–20

Then the soldiers led him into the courtyard of
the palace (that is, the governor's headquarters);
and they called together the whole cohort. And

they clothed him in a purple cloak; and after twisting some thorns into a crown, they put it on him. And they began saluting him, "Hail, King of the Jews!" They struck his head with a reed, spat upon him, and knelt down in homage to him. After mocking him, they stripped him of the purple cloak and put his own clothes on him.

RESPONSORY **PSALM 27:7–14** **GOD OF SALVATION**

ANTIPHON Do not forsake me, ~O GOD OF MY SALVATION!

Hear, O Lord, when I cry aloud,
be gracious to me and answer me!
"Come," my heart says, "seek the LORD's face."
Your face, Lord, do I seek.
~DO NOT FORSAKE ME, O GOD OF MY SALVATION!

Do not hide your face from me.
Do not turn your servant away in anger,
you who have been my help.
~DO NOT FORSAKE ME, O GOD OF MY SALVATION!

If my father and mother forsake me,
the Lord will take me up.
Teach me your way, O Lord;
and lead me on a level path
because of my enemies.
~DO NOT FORSAKE ME, O GOD OF MY SALVATION!

Do not give me up to the will of my adversaries;
for false witnesses have risen against me,
and they breathe out violence.
~Do not forsake me, O God of my salvation!

I believe that I shall see the goodness of the Lord
in the land of the living!
Wait for the Lord;
be strong, and let your heart take courage.
Wait for the Lord!
~Do not forsake me, O God of my salvation!

To the One seated on the throne
and to the Lamb who was slain
be blessing and honor and glory and might
forever and ever! Amen.
~Do not forsake me, O God of my salvation!

Prayer
Lord Jesus, Man of Sorrows,
arrayed in mock purple,
crowned with thorns,
and holding a scepter of reed,
you were mocked and humiliated
by the whole cohort of Pilate's soldiers.
By this fourth shedding of your precious blood,
may we acknowledge your full sovereignty over us
in every aspect of our life,
and be willing to be humiliated for your sake,
O Savior of the world,

whom we praise, honor, and glorify,
now and for ever.
~AMEN.

Blest † be the name of Jesus, now and for ever!
~AMEN.

5. Jesus Walks the Way of the Cross
Come, † Lord, and help your people,
~BOUGHT WITH THE PRICE OF YOUR OWN BLOOD.
This is the blood of the covenant
~THAT GOD HAS ORDAINED FOR US.

HYMN (SEE PAGES 298–299)

		HEBREWS
READING	OUR HIGH PRIEST	10:19–22

My friends, since we have confidence to enter
the sanctuary by the blood of Jesus, by the new
and living way that he opened for us through the
curtain (that is, through his flesh), and since we
have a great priest over the house of God, let us
approach with a true heart in full assurance of
faith, with our hearts sprinkled clean from an evil
conscience and our bodies washed with pure water.

	PSALM	
RESPONSORY	56:1–4, 8–13	SET FREE

ANTIPHON Blest be Jesus ~WHO FREED US FROM
   OUR SINS BY HIS BLOOD.

Be gracious to me, O God, for people trample on
      me;
all day long foes oppress me;
my enemies trample on me all day long,
for many fight against me.
~Blest be Jesus who freed us from our sins
by his blood.

O Most High, when I am afraid, I put my trust in
      you.
In God, whose word I praise,
in God I trust; I am not afraid.
What can flesh do to me?
~Blest be Jesus who freed us from our sins
by his blood.

You have witnessed my trembling,
stored my tears in your bottle.
Are they not in your book?
Then my enemies will retreat
in the day when I call.
This I know, that God is for me.
~Blest be Jesus who freed us from our sins
by his blood.

In God, whose word I praise,
in the Lord whose word I praise,
in God I trust; I am not afraid.
What can a mere mortal do to me?
~Blest be Jesus who freed us from our sins
by his blood.

I must perform my vows to you, O God;
I will render thank offerings to you.
For you have delivered my soul from death,
and my feet from falling,
so that I may walk before God
in the light of life.
~BLEST BE JESUS WHO FREED US FROM OUR SINS
BY HIS BLOOD.

To the One seated on the throne
and to the Lamb who was slain
be blessing and honor and glory and might
forever and ever! Amen.
~BLEST BE JESUS WHO FREED US FROM OUR SINS
BY HIS BLOOD.

PRAYER

Lord Jesus, Man of Sorrows,
carrying the cross on your shoulders,
you stumbled through the streets of Jerusalem
toward the Place of the Skull,
with only a handful of women to mourn your
        passing.
May this fifth shedding of your precious blood
give us the strength and courage to follow
in your bloodstained footsteps,
falling at one point, rising at another,
until we become true followers of your cross,
O Savior of the world,
whom we praise, honor, and glorify,

now and for ever.
~Amen.

Blest † be the name of Jesus, now and for ever!
~Amen.

6. Jesus Sheds His Blood on the Cross
Come, † Lord, and help your people,
~Bought with the price of your own blood.
Proclaim to the nations:
~The Lord reigns from the tree.

Hymn (see pages 298–299)

	The Way of	John
Reading	the Cross	9:16–19

They took Jesus; and carrying the cross by
himself, he went out to what is called The Place
of the Skull, which in Hebrew is called Golgotha.
There they crucified him, and with him two
others, one on either side, with Jesus between
them. Pilate also had an inscription written and
put on the cross. It read, "Jesus of Nazareth, the
King of the Jews."

	Psalm 22:1–2,	
Responsory	6–8, 14–18	Christ Crucified

Antiphon They have pierced my hands and my
feet ~and lay me in the dust of death.

My God, my God, why have you forsaken me?
Why are you so far from helping me,
from the words of my groaning?

O my God, I cry by day, but you do not answer;
and by night, but find no rest.
~THEY HAVE PIERCED MY HANDS AND MY FEET
AND LAY ME IN THE DUST OF DEATH.

But I am a worm, not human;
scorned by others, and despised by the people.
All who seek me mock at me,
they make mouths at me, they wag their heads
    and say:
"You committed your cause to the Lord:
let the Lord deliver you.
Let the Lord rescue you,
for the Lord delights in you!"
~THEY HAVE PIERCED MY HANDS AND MY FEET
AND LAY ME IN THE DUST OF DEATH.

I am poured out like water,
and all my bones are out of joint;
my heart is like wax,
melted within my breast;
my mouth is dried up like a potsherd,
and my tongue sticks to my jaws;
you lay me in the dust of death.
~THEY HAVE PIERCED MY HANDS AND MY FEET
AND LAY ME IN THE DUST OF DEATH.

Indeed, dogs surround me;
a company of evildoers encircles me;
my hands and feet are bound.
~THEY HAVE PIERCED MY HANDS AND MY FEET
AND LAY ME IN THE DUST OF DEATH.

Devotion to the Seven Blood Sheddings of Jesus **313**

I can count all my bones;
they stare and gloat over me;
they divide my garments among them
and cast lots for my clothing.
~THEY HAVE PIERCED MY HANDS AND MY FEET
AND LAY ME IN THE DUST OF DEATH.

To the One seated on the throne
and to the Lamb who was slain
be blessing and honor and glory and might
forever and ever! Amen.
~THEY HAVE PIERCED MY HANDS AND MY FEET
AND LAY ME IN THE DUST OF DEATH.

PRAYER
Lord Jesus Crucified,
as your sorrowful Mother and her friends stood
        nearby,
Roman soldiers drove spikes into your hands and
        feet
and fastened you to the rude cross of pain.
By this sixth shedding of your precious blood,
may we cherish the Five Wounds
that led to your death on the cross,
and be prepared to suffer for your sake
as we await our own death,
O Savior of the world,
whom we praise, honor, and glorify,
now and for ever.
~AMEN.

Blest † be the name of Jesus, now and for ever!
~AMEN.

7. Jesus' Heart Is Pierced by a Roman Spear

Come, † Lord, and help your people,
~BOUGHT WITH THE PRICE OF YOUR OWN BLOOD.
You were ransomed by the precious blood of
    Christ,
~LIKE THAT OF A LAMB WITHOUT DEFECT OR
    BLEMISH.

HYMN (SEE PAGES 298–299)

READING	BLOOD AND WATER	JOHN 19:32–34, 36–37

The soldiers came and broke the legs of the first criminal and of the other who had been crucified with him. But when they came to Jesus and saw that he was already dead, they did not break his legs. Instead, one of the soldiers pierced his side with a spear, and at once blood and water came out. These things occurred so that the scripture might be fulfilled, "None of his bones shall be broken." And again another passage of scripture says, "They will look on the one whom they have pierced."

RESPONSORY **PSALM 70** **SAVED BY BLOOD**

ANTIPHON The Lord has laid on him ~THE
    INIQUITY OF US ALL.

Be pleased, O God, to deliver me!
O Lord, make haste to help me!
Let them be put to shame and confusion
who seek my life!
~THE LORD HAS LAID ON HIM THE INIQUITY OF
    US ALL.

Let them be turned back and dishonored
who desire my pain!
Let them turn back because of their shame
who say, "Aha, Aha!"
~THE LORD HAS LAID ON HIM THE INIQUITY OF
    US ALL.

May all who seek you
rejoice and be glad in you!
May those who love your salvation
say evermore, "God is great!"
~THE LORD HAS LAID ON HIM THE INIQUITY OF
    US ALL.

But I am poor and needy;
hasten to me, O God!
You are my help and my deliverer;
O Lord, do not tarry!
~THE LORD HAS LAID ON HIM THE INIQUITY OF
    US ALL.

To the One seated on the throne
and to the Lamb who was slain
be blessing and honor and glory and might
forever and ever! Amen.

~The Lord has laid on him the iniquity of
us all.

PRAYER
Lord Jesus, Man of Sorrows,
when a Roman spear pierced your broken heart,
you embraced the cross to the bitter end
and poured out your lifeblood for the last time.
May this final shedding of your precious blood
be the cleansing of all our sins,
our growth in personal holiness,
and a blessing for all humanity,
O Savior of the world,
whom we praise, honor, and glorify,
now and for ever.
~Amen.

Blest † be the name of Jesus, now and forever!
~Amen.

Litany of the Precious Blood of Jesus

This litany may be used in conjunction with the "Seven Blood Sheddings" or as a separate devotion.

Lord, have mercy	~LORD, HAVE MERCY
Christ, have mercy	~CHRIST, HAVE MERCY
Lord, have mercy	~LORD, HAVE MERCY
God our Father in heaven	~HAVE MERCY ON US
God the Son, Redeemer of the world	~HAVE MERCY ON US
God the Holy Spirit	~HAVE MERCY ON US
Holy Trinity, one God	~HAVE MERCY ON US
Blood of Christ, only Son of the Father	~BE OUR SALVATION
Blood of Christ, incarnate Word	~BE OUR SALVATION
Blood of Christ, of the new and eternal covenant	~BE OUR SALVATION
Blood of Christ, that spilled to the ground	~BE OUR SALVATION
Blood of Christ, that flowed at the scourging	~BE OUR SALVATION
Blood of Christ, dripping from the thorns	~BE OUR SALVATION
Blood of Christ, shed on the cross	~BE OUR SALVATION
Blood of Christ, the price of our redemption	~BE OUR SALVATION
Blood of Christ, our only claim to pardon	~BE OUR SALVATION
Blood of Christ, our blessing cup	~BE OUR SALVATION
Blood of Christ, in which we are washed	~BE OUR SALVATION
Blood of Christ, torrent of mercy	~BE OUR SALVATION
Blood of Christ, that overcomes evil	~BE OUR SALVATION

Blood of Christ, strength
of the martyrs ~BE OUR SALVATION
Blood of Christ, endurance
of the saints ~BE OUR SALVATION
Blood of Christ, that makes
the barren fruitful ~BE OUR SALVATION
Blood of Christ, protection
of the threatened ~BE OUR SALVATION
Blood of Christ, comfort
of the weary ~BE OUR SALVATION
Blood of Christ, solace of
the mourner ~BE OUR SALVATION
Blood of Christ, hope of
the repentant ~BE OUR SALVATION
Blood of Christ, consolation
of the dying ~BE OUR SALVATION
Blood of Christ, our peace and
refreshment ~BE OUR SALVATION
Blood of Christ, our pledge of life ~BE OUR SALVATION
Blood of Christ, by which we pass
to glory ~BE OUR SALVATION
Blood of Christ, most worthy of
honor ~BE OUR SALVATION

(Pause for spontaneous prayer.)

Lamb of God, you take away
the sins of the world ~HAVE MERCY ON US
Lamb of God, you take away
the sins of the world ~HAVE MERCY ON US
Lamb of God, you take away
the sins of the world ~HAVE MERCY ON US

Lord, you redeemed us by your blood.
~YOU HAVE MADE US A KINGDOM TO SERVE OUR GOD.

Litany of the Precious Blood of Jesus **319**

Let us pray:

Father,
by the blood of your Son
you have set us free and saved us from death.
Continue your work of love within us,
that by constantly celebrating the mystery of our
    salvation
we may reach the eternal life it promises.
We ask this through Christ our Lord.
~AMEN.[102]

The Seven Gifts of the Holy Spirit

The seven gifts of the Holy Spirit are wisdom, understanding, counsel, fortitude, knowledge, piety, and fear of the Lord (Isaiah 11:2). The Holy Spirit, the Third Person of the Blessed Trinity, is the inner core of the Church's being who causes "the fruits of the Spirit" to come to maturity in us—"love, joy, peace, patience, kindness, generosity, faithfulness, gentleness, and self-control" (Galatians 5:22–23)—and who constantly gives us the gifts of the Spirit to enlighten and lead us to personal holiness and the total transformation of our personality.

The Latin Church possesses two outstanding hymns to the Holy Spirit—*Veni, Creator Spiritus* and *Veni, Sancte Spiritus*—that express a profound teaching on the gifts and also inspire us to strive for such gifts and blessings.

This devotion may be spread over seven days or used as a single offering on one day.

1. The Gift of Wisdom

LEADER: Come, † Holy Spirit, fill the hearts of your faithful,

ALL: ~AND KINDLE IN THEM THE FIRE OF YOUR LOVE.

LEADER: When you send forth your Spirit, they are created;

ALL: ~AND YOU RENEW THE FACE OF THE EARTH.

HYMN TO THE HOLY SPIRIT

O Holy Spirit, by whose breath
life rises vibrant out of death:

come to create, renew, inspire;
come, kindle in our hearts your fire.

You are the seeker's sure resource,
of burning love the living source,
protector in the midst of strife,
the giver and the Lord of life.

THE SPIRIT OF THE LORD

READING   **ISAIAH 11:1–3**

A shoot shall come out from the stump of Jesse,
and a branch shall grow out of his roots. The spirit
of the LORD shall rest on him, the spirit of wisdom
and understanding, the spirit of counsel and
might, the spirit of knowledge and the fear of the
LORD. His delight shall be in the fear of the LORD.

RESPONSE

LEADER: The earth will be full
ALL: ~OF THE KNOWLEDGE OF THE LORD.

PRAYER

God of infinite wisdom,
by your gracious gift
of Holy Wisdom, Jesus himself,
you enlighten your Church
and every living soul
with profound insight
into the mysteries of your kingdom.
Open our hearts to your Holy Spirit

who is the fire and light of our lives.
We ask this through Christ our Lord.
ALL: ~AMEN.

May the holy and life-giving Spirit
† inhabit our hearts, now and for ever.
~AMEN.

2. The Spirit of Understanding

Come, † Holy Spirit, fill the hearts of your
        faithful,
~AND KINDLE IN THEM THE FIRE OF YOUR LOVE.
When you send forth your Spirit, they are created;
~AND YOU RENEW THE FACE OF THE EARTH.

HYMN

In you God's energy is shown,
to us your varied gifts made known.
Teach us to speak, teach us to hear;
yours is the tongue and yours the ear.

Flood our dull senses with your light;
in mutual love our hearts unite.
Your power the whole creation fills;
confirm our weak, uncertain wills.

	THE PRAYER OF	I KINGS
READING	SOLOMON	3:9, 11–12

O LORD my God, give your servant an
understanding mind to govern your people, able to
discern between good and evil. God said to him,
"Because you have asked for yourself understanding

to discern what is right, I now do according to
your word. Indeed I give you a wise and discerning
mind; no one like you has been before you and no
one like you shall arise after you.

RESPONSE
God appeared to Solomon in a dream,
~AND GOD SAID, "ASK WHAT I SHOULD GIVE
YOU."

PRAYER
God of infinite understanding,
of your gracious gift of the Word of God,
Christ Jesus himself,
you grant understanding of the Holy Gospel
to your church and to every Christian
who seeks to know you better.
Open our hearts to your Spirit
that we may ask in prayer for understanding
and receive it as a gracious gift of your giving.
We ask this through Christ our Lord.
~AMEN.

May the holy and life-giving Spirit
† inhabit our hearts, now and for ever.
~AMEN.

3. The Spirit of Counsel
Come, † Holy Spirit, fill the hearts of your
faithful,
~AND KINDLE IN THEM THE FIRE OF YOUR LOVE.

When you send forth your Spirit, they are created;
~AND YOU RENEW THE FACE OF THE EARTH.

HYMN
From inner strife grant us release;
turn nations to the ways of peace.
To fuller life your people bring
that as one body we may sing:

Praise to the Father, Christ his Word,
and to the Spirit, God the Lord;
to them all honor, glory be
both now and for eternity. Amen.[103]

READING   THE SPIRIT   JOHN
OF TRUTH   16:13–15
Jesus said to his disciples, "When the Spirit of
truth comes, he will guide you into all the truth;
for he will not speak on his own, but will speak
whatever he hears, and he will declare to you
the things that are to come. He will glorify me,
because he will take what is mine and declare it
to you. All that the Father has is mine. For this
reason I said that he will take what is mine and
declare it to you."

RESPONSE
The Spirit of truth who comes from the Father,
~WILL TESTIFY ON MY BEHALF.

God of boundless good counsel,
of your gracious gift of Jesus our Teacher,
you grant us wise instruction and guidance
by his holy word and wondrous works.
Open our hearts to the Spirit of truth
that we may learn from the holy tradition
the guidance and warnings we need
to walk the straight and narrow path
that leads to eternal life.
We ask this through Christ our Lord.
~AMEN.

May the holy and life-giving Spirit
† inhabit our hearts, now and for ever.
~AMEN.

4. The Gift of Fortitude

Come, † Holy Spirit, fill the hearts of your
    faithful,
~AND KINDLE IN THEM THE FIRE OF YOUR LOVE.
When you send forth your Spirit, they are created;
~AND YOU RENEW THE FACE OF THE EARTH.

HYMN

Holy Spirit, font of light,
focus of God's glory bright,
shed on us a shining ray.

Father of the fatherless,
giver of gifts limitless,
come and touch our hearts today.

Source of strength and sure relief,
comforter in time of grief,
enter in and be our guest.

READING **THE ROAD TO LIFE** **MATTHEW 7:13–14**

Jesus said to his disciples, "Enter through the narrow gate; for the gate is wide and the road is easy that leads to destruction, and there are many who take it. For the gate is narrow and the road is hard that leads to life, and there are few who find it."

RESPONSE

Blessed are they who hunger and thirst for
    righteousness,
~FOR THEY WILL BE FILLED.

PRAYER

Holy, mighty, and immortal God,
you are the strength of all who seek you
and enable our quest to become our bliss.
Open our hearts to your Holy Spirit
that we may obtain the courage
to do what needs to be done
by the inspiration of your Word and Spirit.
We ask this through Christ our Lord.
~AMEN.

May the holy and life-giving Spirit
† inhabit our hearts, now and for ever.
~AMEN.

5. The Gift of Knowledge

Come, † Holy Spirit, fill the hearts of your
    faithful,
~AND KINDLE IN THEM THE FIRE OF YOUR LOVE.
When you send forth your Spirit, they are created;
~AND YOU RENEW THE FACE OF THE EARTH.

HYMN

On our journey grant us aid,
freshening breeze, and cooling shade,
in our labor inward rest.

Enter each aspiring heart,
occupy its inmost part,
with your dazzling purity.

All that gives to us our worth,
all that benefits the earth,
you bring to maturity.

READING	COME, HOLY SPIRIT	JOEL 2:28–29

I will pour out my spirit on all flesh; your sons
and your daughters shall prophesy, your old men
shall dream dreams, and your young men shall
see visions. Even on the male and female slaves, in
those days, I will pour out my spirit.

RESPONSE

I, the LORD, am your God,
~AND THERE IS NO OTHER.

Almighty and everlasting God,
giver of all gifts and dispenser of every blessing,
by and through Jesus Christ our Lord:
Grant us fuller knowledge of your holy will
that we may love and serve you in this world
and be happy with you in the next.
We ask this through Christ our Lord.
~AMEN.

May the holy and life-giving Spirit
† inhabit our hearts, now and for ever.
~AMEN.

6. The Gift of Piety

Come, † Holy Spirit, fill the hearts of your
faithful
~AND KINDLE IN THEM THE FIRE OF YOUR LOVE.
When you send forth your Spirit, they are created;
~AND YOU RENEW THE FACE OF THE EARTH.

HYMN

With your soft, refreshing rains,
break our drought, remove our stains;
bind up all our injuries.

Shake with rushing wind our will;
melt with fire our icy chill;
bring to light our perjuries.

PRACTICAL PIETY

Jesus said to his disciples, "Beware of practicing your piety before others in order to be seen by them; for then you have no reward from your Father in heaven."

RESPONSE

Where your treasure is,
~THERE YOUR HEART WILL BE ALSO.

PRAYER

God of loving concern for us,
by the gracious teaching of Jesus
you warn us to pray, fast, and give alms in secret
that we may please you in all sincerity.
Open us to the guidance of the Holy Spirit
that we may store up for ourselves
treasures in heaven, where thieves do not break in
    and steal.
We ask this through Christ our Lord.
~AMEN.

May the holy and life-giving Spirit
† inhabit our hearts, now and for ever.
~AMEN.

7. The Gift of the Fear of the Lord

Come, † Holy Spirit, fill the hearts of your
    faithful,
~AND KINDLE IN THEM THE FIRE OF YOUR LOVE.

When you send forth your Spirit, they are created;
~AND YOU RENEW THE FACE OF THE EARTH.

HYMN

As your promise we believe
make us ready to receive
gifts from your unbounded store.

Grant enabling energy,
courage in adversity,
joys that last for evermore.
Amen.[104]

	GIVER OF	ACTS
READING	**THE SPIRIT**	**2:32–33**

This Jesus God raised up, and of that all of us
are witnesses. Being therefore exalted at the right
hand of God, and having received from the Father
the promise of the Holy Spirit, he has poured out
this that you both see and hear.

RESPONSE

Repent and be baptized every one of you,
~AND YOU WILL RECEIVE THE GIFT OF THE HOLY
SPIRIT.

PRAYER

Great God and Savior Jesus Christ,
who died and rose and who will come again in
glory
to judge the living and the dead:
As we stand in awe before your gracious majesty,

in union with the great Mother of God, Mary
      most holy,
and the whole host of heaven,
be pleased to flood your Church
with the gifts and fruits of the Holy Spirit
that we may love and serve you
faithfully and fully, now and for ever.
~Amen.

May the holy and life-giving Spirit
✝ inhabit our hearts, now and for ever.
~Amen.

A Litany of the Holy Spirit

This litany may be used in conjunction with "The Seven Gifts of the Holy Spirit" or as a separate devotion.

For a fresh outpouring of the Holy Spirit on all
    here present,
  let us pray to the Lord.
~LORD, HEAR OUR PRAYER.

For the welfare of God's holy church, let us pray to
    the Lord.
~LORD, HEAR OUR PRAYER.

For the seven precious gifts of the Holy Spirit,
  let us pray to the Lord.
~LORD, HEAR OUR PRAYER.

For the virtues of faith, hope, and love, let us pray
    to the Lord.
~LORD, HEAR OUR PRAYER.

For new life, joy, and peace among us, let us pray
    to the Lord.
~LORD, HEAR OUR PRAYER.

For the unity and reconciliation of families and
    nations, let us pray to the Lord.
~LORD, HEAR OUR PRAYER.

For our beloved dead who have fallen asleep in
    Christ
(Here we state the names of our deceased.)
  let us pray to the Lord.
~LORD, HEAR OUR PRAYER.

For all our needs, temporal and spiritual
(Here we state our needs.)
let us pray to the Lord.
~LORD, HEAR OUR PRAYER.

For the prayers of the Virgin Mary and of all the
saints,
let us pray to the Lord.
~LORD, HEAR OUR PRAYER.

PRAYER

Be present, be present,
Holy Spirit of comfort and consolation,
and inspire and guide us into all truth,
as Jesus promised.
Be present to us in wind and fire
as you were to your friends at Pentecost
and give fresh life to our Gospel witness,
now and for ever.
~AMEN.

DOXOLOGY

Blessing and honor and thanksgiving and praise,
more than we can utter, more than we can
conceive,
be yours, O holy and glorious Trinity,
Father, Son, and Holy Spirit,
by all angels, by all human beings, and by all
creatures,
now and for ever.
~AMEN.[105]

Invocation to Mary

Mary, dear Mother, who gave God birth,
Help and care for us living here on earth.
    Govern, give us knowledge, and advise.
Since you're our mother too, maiden and wife,
Bathe away our sin; grant us good life
    And, in every need, help us to be wise.[106]

The Seven Joys of the Blessed Virgin Mary

The devotion to the seven joys of Mary grew up in the Capuchin Franciscan Order and took several forms. One is the "Rosary of the Seven Joys," comprising seven decades of Hail Marys. The following devotion is another way of venerating and participating in her seven joys.

This devotion may be spread over a week, commemorating one joy each day, or it may be prayed as a whole in a single day.

THE EVE/MARY PARALLEL

Mary is the flower of the field from whom arose the precious lily of the valley through whose birth the wounded nature that we inherited from our first parents is transformed and our sins blotted out. Eve mourned, Mary rejoiced. Eve bore tears in her womb, Mary bore joy, for Eve gave birth to sinners, Mary to the Innocent One. The mother of our race introduced punishment into the world, the Mother of our Lord brought salvation into the world. Eve was the author of sin, Mary the author of merit. By killing Eve was an obstacle to us, by giving life Mary was our helper. Eve wounded us, Mary healed us. Disobedience is replaced by obedience, faith compensates for unbelief. Mary's canticle puts an end to the lamentations of Eve.

St. Augustine of Hippo (354–430),
Homily 2 on the Annunciation[107]

First Joy

Gabriel Brings the Good News to Mary

LEADER: A virgin shall conceive and bear a son, alleluia!

ALL: ~AND SHE SHALL CALL HIS NAME EMMANUEL, ALLELUIA!

LEADER: You are the great Mother of God, Mary most holy!

ALL: ~YOU ARE WITHOUT EQUAL AMONG ALL WOMEN.

	THE	LUKE 1:26–28,
READING	**ANNUNCIATION**	**31–32 NAB**

In the sixth month, the angel Gabriel was sent from God to a town of Galilee called Nazareth, to a virgin betrothed to man named Joseph, of the house of David, and the virgin's name was Mary. And coming to her, he said, "Hail, favored one! The Lord is with you. You will conceive in your womb and bear a son, and you shall name him Jesus. He will be great and will be called Son of the Most High."

RESPONSE

LEADER: Mary kept all these things, alleluia!

ALL: ~REFLECTING ON THEM IN HER HEART, ALLELUIA!

REJOICE, holy Mary, Mother of God,
because of the great bliss you experienced

at the angel's greeting
when God's only Son assumed flesh
in your immaculate womb.
I greet you as Gabriel did,
"Hail, Mary, full of grace. The Lord is with you!"
and beg the overshadowing Spirit to rest on me
and bring forth Christ in my whole person
by the help of your unceasing prayers.
ALL: ~AMEN.

Blest be † the Virgin Mother of Christ our Lord.
ALL: ~AMEN.

Second Joy
The Birth of the Christ Child

The Virgin gave birth to the Son of God, alleluia!
~AND CALLED HIS NAME JESUS, ALLELUIA!
You are the great Mother of God, Mary most holy!
~YOU ARE WITHOUT EQUAL AMONG ALL WOMEN.

READING	THE NATIVITY	LUKE 2:15–17 NAB

When the angels went away from them to heaven,
the shepherds said to one another, "Let us go,
then, to Bethlehem to see this thing that has taken
place, which the Lord has made known to us." So
they went in haste and found Mary and Joseph,
and the infant lying in the manger. When they
saw this, they made known the message that had
been told them about this child.

RESPONSE

Jesus lies in the manger, alleluia!

~But reigns in the heavens, alleluia!

REJOICE, holy Mary, Mother of God,
because of the bliss you experienced
when you brought forth Jesus
in the stable of Bethlehem,
as the angel choirs sang:
"Glory to God in the highest
and peace to God's people on earth."
With the humble shepherds of Bethlehem,
may we hasten to the Child lying in the manger
and reflect with you on all these events,
O glorious and blessed Virgin.

~Amen.

May the Virgin Mary mild
† bless us with her holy Child.

~Amen.

Third Joy — The Wise Men Worship the Christ Child

The Magi adore the divine Child, alleluia!

~Who is enthroned on Mary's lap, alleluia!

You are the great Mother of God, Mary most holy!

~You are without equal among all women.

READING   **ADORATION OF THE MAGI**   **MATTHEW 2:1–2 NAB**

When Jesus was born in Bethlehem of Judea, in
the days of King Herod, behold, magi from the

east arrived in Jerusalem, saying, "Where is the
newborn king of the Jews? We saw his star at its
rising and have come to do him homage."

Gold for a King, incense for a God,
~AND MYRRH FOR A DEAD SAVIOR.

REJOICE, holy Mary, Mother of God,
because of the great bliss you experienced
when the Magi presented their mystical gifts
of gold, frankincense, and myrrh
to the Christ Child to do him homage.
May the star of Bethlehem illumine our hearts
    and minds
that we who know Jesus now by faith
may be brought to the vision of his glory
in the heavenly home reserved for us.
~AMEN.

May the Blessed Virgin Mary
✝ intercede for us with Christ our Lord.
~AMEN.

Fourth Joy

**Jesus Is Presented
in the Temple**

The Virgin presents Jesus to his Father, alleluia!
~WITH JOY AND THANKSGIVING, ALLELUIA!
You are the great Mother of God, Mary most holy!
~YOU ARE WITHOUT EQUAL AMONG ALL WOMEN.

There was a man in Jerusalem whose name was Simeon. This man was righteous and devout, awaiting the consolation of Israel, and the holy Spirit was upon him. It had been revealed to him by the holy Spirit that he should not see death before he had seen the Messiah of the Lord. He came in the Spirit into the temple; and when the parents brought in the child Jesus to perform the custom of the law in regard to him, he took him into his arms and blessed God.

RESPONSE

The child's father and mother were amazed, alleluia!

~BY WHAT WAS SAID ABOUT HIM, ALLELUIA!

REJOICE, holy Mary, Mother of God,
because of the great bliss you experienced
when you presented Jesus in the temple
forty days after his birth.
With old Simeon and the prophet Anna,
we recognize the Christ Child and praise God
with all who are looking for the redemption of
Israel.
May Christ, the light of revelation to the nations
and the glory of his people Israel,
be our light and our salvation, now and for ever.
~AMEN.

By the prayers of Mary the Virgin and Joseph her
    spouse,
may the Light of the world † be our salvation.
~Amen.

Fifth Joy   The Resurrection of Christ

Rejoice and be glad, O Virgin Mary, alleluia!
~For the Lord has truly risen, alleluia!
You are the great Mother of God, Mary most holy!
~You are without equal among all women.

Reading   **He Is Risen!**   **Mark 16:1–4 NAB**

When the sabbath was over, Mary Magdalene,
Mary, the mother of James, and Salome bought
spices so that they might go and anoint him.
Very early when the sun had risen, on the first
day of the week, they came to the tomb. They
were saying to one another, "Who will roll back
the stone for us from the entrance to the tomb?"
When they looked up, they saw that the stone had
been rolled back; it was very large.

Response

You seek Jesus of Nazareth, the crucified, alleluia!
~He has been raised; he is not here,
    alleluia!

REJOICE, holy Mary, Mother of God,
because of the great bliss you experienced
when you received the good news

of Christ's glorious resurrection from the dead.
May your radiant and dazzling Son
have us die and rise with him
as we renew the vows of our Baptism
and embrace the new and Spirit-filled life
in this world and in the next.
~Amen.

Through the prayers of the Virgin Mary
may we † enjoy the happiness of eternal life.
~Amen.

Sixth Joy   Christ Ascends into Heaven
Rejoice and be glad, O Virgin Mary, alleluia!
~For your son has ascended into heaven,
    alleluia!
You are the great Mother of God, Mary most holy!
~You are without equal among all women.

	The	Mark
Reading	Ascension	16:19–20 NAB

So then the Lord Jesus, after he spoke to them,
was taken up into heaven and took his seat at
the right hand of God. But they went forth and
preached everywhere, while the Lord worked
with them and confirmed the word through
accompanying signs.

Response
I know that my Redeemer lives,
~And in my flesh I shall see God.

REJOICE, holy Mary, Mother of God,
because of the great bliss you experienced
as your Son ascended into heaven's glory
with the sound of trumpets and shouts of joy.
He who was taken down from the cross
and was laid in your lap
now reigns in the heights of heaven
and will come again in glory
to judge the living and the dead.
~AMEN.

May the devout prayers of Mary the Virgin
† bring us to the joys of paradise.
~AMEN.

Seventh Joy
Mary Is Assumed into Heaven

Rejoice and be glad, O Virgin Mary, alleluia!
~FOR YOUR SON ASSUMED YOU INTO HEAVEN,
    ALLELUIA!
You are the great Mother of God, Mary most holy!
~YOU ARE WITHOUT EQUAL AMONG ALL WOMEN.

POEM
Hark! She is call'd. The parting hour is come.
Take thy farewell, poor world! Heav'n must go
        home
A piece of heav'nly earth, purer and brighter
Than the chaste stars, whose choice lamps come
        to light her

While through the crystal orbs, clearer than they,
She climbs and makes a far more milky way.
She's called. Hark how the dear immortal dove
Sighs to his silver mate, "Rise up, my love!
Rise up, my fair, my spotless one!
The winter's past, the rain is gone."

Richard Crashaw (1613–1649)

READING **THE WOMAN** **REVELATION 12:1, 5 NAB**

A great sign appeared in the sky, a woman clothed with the sun, with the moon under her feet, and on her head a crown of twelve stars. She gave birth to a son, a male child, destined to rule all the nations with an iron rod. Her child was caught up to God and his throne.

RESPONSE

Death came through Eve, alleluia!
~BUT LIFE THROUGH MARY, ALLELUIA!

REJOICE, holy Mary, Mother of God,
because of the great bliss you experienced
when Jesus, the life and light of the world,
exalted you above the choirs of angels,
setting a crown of twelve stars on your head
and putting the moon under your feet.
Queen of heaven,
flaming like the sun in the midst of all the saints,

accept these seven salutations in your honor
and have us reign with Christ Jesus for ever and
ever.
~Amen.

May the risen Lord of glory, the Son of Mary,
✝ bless us and keep us, now and for ever.
~Amen.

The Seven Sorrows of the Blessed Virgin Mary

Not only did our Christian forebears venerate the cross of Christ, they also learned to honor the sorrows of his Blessed Mother. She accompanied him in prayer and contemplation throughout his life and during the long hours of his bitter passion and death on Good Friday. Whenever we feel that the troubles and afflictions of life are wearing us down, we are called to consider Jesus' way of the cross and the seven sorrows of Mary.

The Servants of Mary, a religious order founded in the thirteenth century, concentrates on the seven sorrows of our Blessed Mother by preaching and promoting a Rosary of the seven sorrows and the stations of the seven sorrows in their churches and shrines. These praiseworthy popular devotions draw us to contemplate Jesus and Mary in the singular tragedy of their intertwined lives.

This devotion may be spread over a week, commemorating one sorrow each day, or it may be prayed as a whole in a single day.

First Sorrow

The Prophecy of Old Simeon

LEADER: Blessed † be the great Mother of God, Mary most holy,

ALL: ~WHO HEARD THE FEARFUL PROPHECY OF SIMEON.

HYMN   **STABAT MATER DOLOROSA**

At the cross her station keeping
stood the mournful Mother weeping,

close to Jesus to the last.

Through her heart, his sorrow sharing,
at his bitter anguish bearing,
now at length the sword has passed.

Oh, how sad and sore distressed
was that mother highly blessed
of the sole begotten One!

	THE SWORD	**LUKE 2:22,**
READING	**OF DIVISION**	**25–26, 34–35**

Forty days after his birth, Mary and Joseph
brought Jesus up to Jerusalem to present him
to the Lord. Now there was a man in Jerusalem
whose name was Simeon; this man was righteous
and devout, looking forward to the consolation of
Israel, and the Holy Spirit rested on him. It had
been revealed to him by the Holy Spirit that he
would not see death before he had seen the Lord's
Messiah. Then Simeon blessed them and said to
his mother Mary, "This child is destined for the
falling and the rising of many in Israel, and to
be a sign that will be opposed so that the inner
thoughts of many will be revealed—and a sword
will pierce your own soul too."

RESPONSE
LEADER: Blessed are they who mourn
ALL: ~FOR THEY WILL BE COMFORTED.

THE CANTICLE OF THE VIRGIN MARY LUKE 1:46–55

ANTIPHON Mary's canticle PUTS AN END
TO THE LAMENTATIONS OF EVE.

My soul ✝ proclaims the greatness of the Lord,
my spirit rejoices in God my Savior,
for you, Lord, have looked with favor on your
        lowly servant.

From this day all generations will call me blessed:
    you, the Almighty, have done great things for
        me
    and holy is your name.
    You have mercy on those who fear you,
    from generation to generation.

You have shown strength with your arm
and scattered the proud in their conceit,
casting down the mighty from their thrones
and lifting up the lowly.
You have filled the hungry with good things
and sent the rich away empty.

You have come to the aid of your servant Israel,
to remember the promise of mercy,
the promise made to our forebears,
to Abraham and his children forever.

Glory to the Father, and to the Son,
and to the Holy Spirit:
as it was in the beginning, is now,
and will be forever. Amen.

Antiphon Mary's canticle puts an end to the lamentations of Eve.

Litany of Mary's Seven Sorrows

Leader: By the first sword of sorrow predicted by old Simeon at your presentation of Jesus in the temple:

All: ~Mother of Sorrows, pray for us.

By the second sword of sorrow experienced during your flight into Egypt and the slaughter of the Holy Innocents:

~Mother of Sorrows, pray for us.

By the third sword of sorrow occasioned by the loss of your Child Jesus in the temple:

~Mother of Sorrows, pray for us.

By the fourth sword of sorrow at the meeting with your Son on the bloodstained way of the cross:

~Mother of Sorrows, pray for us.

By the fifth sword of sorrow of your broken heart as you stood at the foot of the cross with Mary of Magdala and the beloved disciple:

~Mother of Sorrows, pray for us.

By the sixth sword of sorrow as the body of Jesus was taken down from the cross and laid in your arms:

~Mother of Sorrows, pray for us.

By the seventh sword of sorrow that pierced your
soul at the burial of your Son in the rock-
hewn tomb:
~MOTHER OF SORROWS, PRAY FOR US.

PRAYER
Gracious Lady, Mother of God,
by the first sword of sorrow that pierced your heart
when holy Simeon predicted your life of affliction,
implore your blessed Son to give us courage
to bear the troubles and trials of this life.
Let me stand by your side,
the close companion of your sorrow,
as you and your Son face your harsh destiny together.
Lady of Mercy, soften our hard hearts,
give us true contrition for our sins,
and bless all those who do us good
for your name's sake.
ALL: ~AMEN.

LEADER: By the intercession of Our Lady of
Sorrows,
may the Lord Jesus † conduct us to our heavenly
home.
ALL: ~AMEN.

Second Sorrow   The Flight into Egypt

Blessed † be the great Mother of God, Mary most
holy,
~WHO FLED INTO EXILE TO ESCAPE CRUEL
HEROD.

HYMN

Christ above in torment hangs,
she beneath beholds the pangs
of her dying, glorious Son.

Is there one who would not weep,
whelmed in miseries so deep,
Christ's dear mother to behold?

Can the human heart refrain
from partaking in her pain,
in that mother's pain untold?

READING   EXILE IN EGYPT   MATTHEW 2:13–15

Now after the wise men had left, an angel of the
Lord appeared to Joseph in a dream and said,
"Get up, take the child and his mother, and flee to
Egypt, and remain there until I tell you; for Herod
is about to search for the child, to destroy him."
Then Joseph got up, took the child and his mother
by night, and went to Egypt, and remained there
until the death of Herod.

RESPONSE

Precious in the sight of the Lord
~IS THE DEATH OF THE SAINTS.

The Canticle of the Virgin Mary (see page 349)

Antiphon A voice was heard in Ramah,
WAILING AND LOUD LAMENTATION,
RACHEL WEEPING FOR HER CHILDREN.

Litany of Mary's Seven Sorrows (see pages 350–351)

Prayer
Lady of Compassion, Mother of God,
by the second sword of sorrow that pierced your
     heart
when you and Joseph were forced to flee into
     Egypt
to save your Son from cruel Herod's slaughter,
let me stand by your side,
the close companion of your sorrow.
By the blood of the Holy Innocents
and the tears of their despairing mothers,
look with compassion on the refugees
who flee before the Herods of our time.
Lady of Mercy, mother of the persecuted and
     exiled,
by your loving prayers
may God pull tyrants from their thrones
and lift up the poor and lowly to praise his holy
     Name,
now and for ever.
~AMEN.

By the intercession of Our Lady of Sorrows,
may the Lord Jesus † conduct us to our heavenly
home.

~AMEN.

The Loss of the Child

Third Sorrow   **Jesus in the Temple**

Blessed † be the great Mother of God, Mary most
holy,

~WHO SUFFERED GREAT ANXIETY FOR THREE
DAYS.

HYMN

Bruised, derided, cursed, defiled,
she beheld her tender Child,
all with bloody scourges rent.

For the sins of his own nation
saw him hang in desolation
till his spirit forth he sent.

O sweet Mother! font of love,
touch my spirit from above,
make my heart with yours accord.

READING   **JESUS IN HIS FATHER'S HOUSE**   **LUKE 2:41–43, 46–49**

Now every year his parents went to Jerusalem
for the festival of the Passover. And when he was
twelve years old, they went up as usual for the
festival. When the festival was ended and they
started to return, the boy Jesus stayed behind
in Jerusalem, but his parents did not know it.

After three days they found him in the temple, sitting among the teachers, listening to them and asking them questions. And all who heard him were amazed at his understanding and his answers. When his parents saw him they were astonished; and his mother said to him, "Child, why have you treated us like this? Look, your father and I have been searching for you in great anxiety." He said to them, "Why were you searching for me? Did you not know that I must be in my Father's house?"

RESPONSE

His mother treasured all these things
~IN HER HEART.

THE CANTICLE OF THE VIRGIN MARY (SEE PAGE 349)

ANTIPHON When they did not find him, THEY RETURNED TO JERUSALEM TO SEARCH FOR HIM.

LITANY OF MARY'S SEVEN SORROWS (SEE PAGES 350–351)

PRAYER

Gracious Lady, Mother of God,
by the third sword of sorrow that pierced your
    heart
when your Son was lost to you for three days,
let me stand by your side,
the close companion of your sorrow,

as you and Joseph were baffled by his wisdom
and by the forebodings of his destiny.
Lady of Mercy,
help us to grasp the claims that Jesus has on us
and acknowledge his lordship over our lives,
as we too increase in wisdom and in years,
and by God's grace, in divine and human favor.
~Amen.

By the intercession of Our Lady of Sorrows,
may the Lord Jesus † conduct us to our heavenly
    home.
~Amen.

Fourth Sorrow   The Way of the Cross
Blessed † be the great Mother of God, Mary most
    holy,
~Who lamented Jesus on the way to
    Golgotha.

Hymn
Make me feel as you have felt;
make my soul to glow and melt
with the love of Christ, my Lord.

Holy Mother, pierce me through,
in my heart each wound renew
of my Savior crucified.

Let me share with you his pain,
who for all our sins was slain,
who for me in torments died.

As they led him away, they seized a man, Simon
of Cyrene, and they laid the cross on him, and
made him carry it behind Jesus. A great number
of the people followed him, and among them
were women who were beating their breasts and
wailing for him. But Jesus turned to them and
said, "Daughters of Jerusalem, do not weep for me,
but weep for yourselves and for your children. For
if they do this when the wood is green, what will
happen when it is dry?"

RESPONSE
For these things I weep;
~MY EYES FLOW WITH TEARS.

THE CANTICLE OF THE VIRGIN MARY (SEE PAGE 349)

ANTIPHON Look and see IF THERE IS ANY SORROW
         LIKE MY SORROW.

**LITANY OF MARY'S SEVEN SORROWS (SEE PAGES
350–351)**

PRAYER
Compassionate Lady, Mother of God,
by the fourth sword of sorrow that pierced your
        heart,
you wept and wailed with the women of
        Jerusalem,
as you took his warning to heart:

"If they do this when the wood is green,
what will happen when it is dry?"
As you trailed the bloodstained streets of
     Jerusalem,
your breaking heart was martyred with his,
Mother and Son in agony together.
Lady of mercy, let me stand by your side,
the close companion of your sorrow,
as your exhausted Son stumbled and fell again and
     again.
Increase our devotion to Jesus crucified
as we bear our own cross daily for his sake
and await in hope for the joy of his return in glory,
to judge the living and the dead.
~Amen.

By the intercession of Our Lady of Sorrows,
may the Lord Jesus † conduct us to our heavenly
     home.
~Amen.

Sorrow's Mother

In shade of death's sad tree
    stood doleful she.
    Ah she! Now by none other
Name to be known, alas, but sorrow's mother.
    Before her eyes
    Hers and the whole world's joys
Hanging all torn she sees, and, in His woes
    And pains, her pangs and throes:

Each wound of his, from every part,
All more at home in her one heart.

Richard Crashaw (1613–1649)

The Fifth Sorrow   Mary at the Cross

Blessed † be the great Mother of God, Mary most
    holy,
~WHO STOOD NEAR THE FOOT OF THE CROSS.

HYMN

Let me mingle tears with you,
mourning him who mourned for me,
all the days that I may live.

By the cross with you today,
there with you to weep and pray,
is all I ask of you to give.

Virgin of all virgins blest!
listen to my fond request:
let me share your grief divine.

READING   CALVARY   JOHN 19:25–27

Standing near the cross of Jesus were his mother,
and his mother's sister, Mary the wife of Clopas,
and Mary Magdalene. When Jesus saw his mother
and the disciple whom he loved standing beside
her, he said to his mother, "Woman, here is your
son." Then he said to the disciple, "Here is your
mother." And from that hour the disciple took her
into his own home.

Response

The soldier's lance opened the side of our Savior
~And pierced the heart of his Mother.

The Canticle of the Virgin Mary (see page 349)

Antiphon Come, let us climb the mountain of the
Lord and see if there is any sorrow like
my sorrow.

Litany of Mary's Seven Sorrows (see pages 350–351)

Prayer

Mary, Mother of Compassion,
as the fifth sword of sorrow pierced your heart
at the bitter agony and death of your blessed Son,
let me stand by your side,
the close companion of your sorrow,
as you watch the final moments
of the Savior of the world.
Mother of Sorrows,
as we contemplate his five precious wounds
and the priceless blood of our redemption,
may we who meditate on your sufferings
reap the happy fruit of your Son's passion and
death.
~Amen.

By the intercession of Our Lady of Sorrows,
may the Lord Jesus † conduct us to our heavenly
   home.
~Amen.

The Sixth Sorrow
The Descent from the Cross

Blessed † be the great Mother of God, Mary most
   holy,
~Who held her dead Son in her arms.

Hymn

Let me to my latest breath,
in my body bear the death
of that dying Son of yours.

Wounded with his every wound,
steep my soul till it has swooned
in his very blood away.

Be to me, O Virgin, nigh,
lest in flames I burn and die,
in his awful judgment day.

Reading
Dead in Mary's Arms
Lamentations 2:13

What can I say for you, to what compare you, O
daughter Jerusalem? To what can I liken you, that
I may comfort you, O virgin daughter Zion? For
vast as the sea is your ruin; who can heal you?

RESPONSE

Jesus is now crowned with glory and honor
~BECAUSE OF THE DEATH HE SUFFERED.

THE CANTICLE OF THE VIRGIN MARY (SEE PAGE 349)

ANTIPHON Blest are those who weep now
FOR THEY SHALL LAUGH.

LITANY OF MARY'S SEVEN SORROWS (SEE PAGES 350–351)

PRAYER

Lady of Sorrows, Mother of God,
by the sixth sword of sorrow that pierced your heart
as your dear Son was taken down from the cross
and deposited in your arms,
let me stand at your side,
the close companion of your sorrow,
as you mingle your tears with the blood
of the Savior of the world.
Lady of Mercy,
as you suffer the pangs of martyrdom
at the sight of his broken and wounded body,
prepare us for the joys of paradise,
the fruit of his blessed passion and death.
~AMEN.

By the intercession of Our Lady of Sorrows,
may the Lord Jesus † conduct us to our heavenly
    home.
~AMEN.

The Seventh Sorrow

The Burial of Jesus

Blessed ✝ be the great Mother of God, Mary most
    holy,

~WHO SAW THE TOMB AND HOW HIS BODY WAS LAID.

HYMN

At the cross her station keeping
stood the mournful Mother weeping,
close to Jesus to the last.

Christ, when you shall call me hence,
be your mother my defense,
be your cross my victory.

While my body here decays,
may my soul your goodness praise,
safe in heaven eternally. Amen.[108]

READING   THE TOMB   LUKE 23:52–56

Joseph of Arimathea went to Pilate and asked for
the body of Jesus. Then he took it down, wrapped
it in a linen cloth, and laid it in a rock-hewn tomb
where no one had ever been laid. It was the day
of Preparation, and the sabbath was beginning.
The women who had come with him from Galilee
followed, and they saw the tomb and how his
body was laid. Then they returned, and prepared
spices and ointments. On the sabbath they rested
according to the commandment.

RESPONSE

Queen of Martyrs, at the burial of your divine
    Son,

~PRAY FOR US IN OUR HOUR OF NEED.

THE CANTICLE OF THE VIRGIN MARY (SEE PAGE 349)

ANTIPHON She weeps bitterly in the night,
WITH TEARS ON HER CHEEKS.

LITANY OF MARY'S SEVEN SORROWS (SEE PAGES 350–351)

PRAYER

Lady of Tears, Mother of God,
by the seventh sword that pierced your heart,
as your Son was wrapped in a linen shroud
and laid in noble Joseph's rock-hewn tomb,
let me stand at your side,
the close companion of your sorrow,
as you weep with the other women from Galilee.
Lady of Mercy,
who alone kept faith for three days
as Jesus lay in the tomb,
may we rejoice with you
in the glorious resurrection of your dear Son,
the Savior of the world,
who lives and reigns with the Father,
in the unity of the Holy Spirit,
one God, for ever and ever.
~AMEN.

By the intercession of Our Lady of Sorrows,
may the Lord Jesus ✝ conduct us to our heavenly
home.
~Amen.

Antiphon and Prayer

We adore your cross, O Lord,
And we praise and glorify your holy
resurrection,
for by the wood of the cross, joy came into
the whole world.

Jesus is the Lamb of God
~Who takes away the sin of the world.

Let us pray:

Lord Jesus Crucified,
by your submission to the Father's will
and your bitter suffering and death on the cross,
you radically redeemed the whole human race.
May you be praised, adored, and loved
at all times and in all places
for your perfect love for sinful humanity
and gather us all together with Mary your mother
at the foot of your Father's throne,
for ever and ever.
~Amen.

Litany of the Blessed Virgin Mary

This is a much extended litany to the Virgin Mary as she comes to us in all her grace-filled moments presented in the Gospels. She is the first of all God's creatures, the first one to believe in her Son, the faith-filled one who stuck with Jesus through all his life, passion, and death.

Holy Mother of God, Mary most holy,
   blest are you above all women:

ALL: ~HEAR US AND HELP US, WE HUMBLY PRAY.
   (Repeat each time.)

By your grace-filled conception for the sake of the coming Messiah:

By Gabriel's dangerous and glorious message to you in your humble home of Nazareth:

By your fear and trembling before God's choice of you and by your obedient acceptance of God's will:

By the incarnation of the Word of God in your virginal womb:

By your marriage to Joseph the Carpenter of Nazareth:

By your nine months of pregnant waiting for the birth of the promised Messiah:

By your solicitous visit to Zachary and Elizabeth and by the welcome John extended from the womb:

By your astonishing Magnificat of rejoicing and
prophecy:

By your birth-giving to the Son of God in
Bethlehem of Judea:

By the visit of the humble shepherds of Bethlehem
to see your newborn Son:

By your presence at the circumcision and naming
of Jesus on the eighth day:

By the visit of the wise men from the East and
their adoration of the Christ child on your
lap:

By your presentation of Jesus in the temple on the
fortieth day after his birth:

By the welcome reception of Jesus as the light of
revelation to the nations and the glory of
your people Israel:

By Simeon's prophecy of the passion of Jesus-
Messiah and of your own sorrows also:

By your flight into Egypt as Herod massacred the
innocent children of Bethlehem:

By your years of exile in Egypt and your return to
Nazareth at the death of Herod:

By your Passover pilgrimage each year with the
Christ Child to Jerusalem:

By your anxiety and loss as Jesus chose to be at
his Father's house and about his Father's
business when he was twelve years old:

By the silent and hidden years of Jesus, the young
man of Nazareth:

By his steady visits to the synagogue at Nazareth
and his study of the Torah, the Prophets, and
the Psalms:

By his parting from you to take up his public life
and the preaching of the reign of God:

By his baptism by John in the Jordan, by the Spirit
descending from heaven, and the voice of
the Father:

By his rejection by his own hometown of Nazareth
and his residence in Capharnaum by the sea:

By the woman who cried out: "Blessed is the
womb that bore you and the breasts that
nursed you!"

By your slipping into the background as Jesus
emerged as healer, exorcist, and itinerant
preacher:

By your presence with the other women from
Galilee as Jesus was tried, convicted, and
executed:

By your standing near the foot of the cross as your
Son died in agony and dereliction:

By the final leave-taking of the sorrowful Mother
and the dying Son:

By Jesus' descent from the cross and his burial in
noble Joseph's tomb:

By your undying faith in Jesus' glorification by his
Father:

By the joyful news of his glorious resurrection and
his many appearances for forty days:

By your presence with Jesus' disciples in the upper
room, awaiting the promised Holy Spirit:

By the coming of the Holy Spirit in wind and fire
on the day of Pentecost:

By the remaining years of your earthly life at the
heart of the Church:

By your assumption, body and soul, into heaven
and your coronation as the Queen of all
saints:

By your appearances to St. Juan Diego at Tepeyac,
St. Bernadette Soubirous at Lourdes, and the
three children at Fatima:

Pray for us, holy Mother of God,
~THAT WE MAY BECOME WORTHY OF THE
PROMISES OF CHRIST.

Let us pray:
Gracious God and Father,
in Mary, the firstborn of redemption,
you have given us a Mother most tender.
Open our hearts to the joy of the Spirit,
and grant that by imitating the Virgin
we too may learn to magnify you

through the great work accomplished in Christ
your Son.
He lives and reigns with you and the Holy Spirit,
one God, for ever and ever.
~AMEN.

Obsecro Te: A Prayer of Petition to the Blessed Virgin Mary

This prayer derives from a large number of medieval Books of Hours in both Latin and Middle English. This expanded version bases its addresses and petitions on the most obvious events in the life of the Blessed Virgin Mary. Her work on our behalf makes her not only the Mother of Jesus but our mother as well.

Holy, glorious, and blessed Virgin Mary,
with great affection I address you,
daughter of the Most High,
mother of God's only Son,
and bride of the Holy Spirit.
You are more worthy of honor than the many-
eyed cherubim
and far more glorious than the six-winged
seraphim
who sing the hymn of victory to our triune God.

Fountain of mercy and consolation,
source of piety and every joy,
be the mother of orphans,
the comforter of the afflicted,
a path for those who have gone astray,
and a refuge for all who put their hope in you.

By that holy gladness
when, at the message of the angel Gabriel,
you conceived the Son of God in your womb:

By that gracious acceptance and humility
by which you replied to Gabriel:
"Here am I, the servant of the Lord;
let it be with me according to your word."

By the overshadowing of the Holy Spirit,
who accomplished in you
the divine mystery of the Word made flesh:

By the mystic joy you experienced
when you gave birth to Jesus,
in Bethlehem of Judea, the city of David,
as the angel choirs sang, "Glory to God in the
      highest!"

By the overwhelming joy you felt
when you presented your newborn Son
to the awestricken shepherds of Bethlehem,
and the adoring wise men from the East
with their mystic gifts of gold, frankincense, and
      myrrh:

By the great and holy joys you experienced
when you and Joseph brought Jesus to the temple
and old Simeon and Anna, filled with the Holy
      Spirit,
acknowledged him as Messiah and Lord.

By the fear and desolation you underwent
when the tyrant Herod drove you into exile in
      Egypt
and murdered the Holy Innocents of Bethlehem
in his jealous and envious rage:

By your contemplative experience
of the quiet years in Nazareth of Galilee,
in the daily company of the Son of the Most High,
as he grew in wisdom and years,
and in divine and human favor:

By the profound experience of loss and separation
you experienced when your dear Son parted from
    you
to undergo his baptism by John in the Jordan,
and to begin his public ministry in Galilee:

By the sharp grief and deep compassion
you experienced when you saw your Jesus
stumbling along the way of the cross,
raised and hanging on the cross of pain,
and crying out to his Father as he died:

By the infinite pain you felt when a Roman spear
pierced the broken heart of the Man of Sorrows,
and blood and water poured forth:

By the sword of sorrow that pierced your heart
as Joseph of Arimathea removed his body from
    the cross,
wrapped it in a linen shroud, and laid it in his
    own new tomb:

By your unshaken faith in your dead Jesus
as you cherished the promises and prophecies
of his rising on the third day:

By your keen joy in his dazzling resurrection
that vanquished death and hell,

brought life to those in the grave,
and made all things new:

By your delighted experience of his risen life
and the many convincing proofs he offered
to his chosen friends during forty days:

By his wonderful ascension into heaven
as he took his place at the right hand of the Father,
where he reigns in glory, now and for ever:

By your radiant encounter with the Holy Spirit of
    Pentecost
that clothed the apostles with power from on high
and empowered them to preach the Good News
throughout the whole world:

By your glorious assumption into heaven,
and your coronation as Queen of all the saints in
    glory:

Gracious Lady of Mercy,
please come with all God's shining saints
to assist and support me in my every need.

Stand by me in each hour and moment of my life
and obtain for me from your beloved Son Jesus
every blessing and growth in holiness,
all peace and prosperity, all joy and gladness.

In the company of all the saints and angels,
watch over my immortal soul,
rule and protect my mortal body,
suggest holy thoughts to me,
beg pardon for my sins of the past,

help me amend my present life,
and prepare me for what is to come.

Above all, pray that I may entrust myself entirely
to the Good News proclaimed by your Son,
hope in his sure and loving promises,
and have sincere love for my neighbor.
Help me to lead an honorable and Christian life,
shield me from any form of mortal sin,
and defend me by your maternal prayers,
at the hour of my death.

By your unwearied intercession, O Mary,
may God graciously hear and receive this prayer
and bring me, by the merits of Christ my Savior,
to everlasting life in our heavenly home. Amen.[109]

Notes

1. Directory on Popular Piety and the Liturgy (Vatican City, December 2001), #6.
2. Directory on Popular Piety and the Liturgy (Vatican City, December 2001), #7, 9, 15.
3. Directory on Popular Piety and the Liturgy (Vatican City, December 2001), #16.
4. St. Augustine of Hippo Regius (354–430), *Sermons to the People*, #185, trans. William Griffin (New York: Image Books, 2002), 60.
5. St. Catherine of Siena (1347–1380), *The Dialogue*, chapter 15, trans. Suzane Nofke, OP (New York: Paulist Press, 1980), 53.
6. *O gloriosa femina*, attributed to Venantius Fortunatus (530–609), trans. John Mason Neale (1818–1866), alt.
7. St. Nicetas of Remesiana (ca. 335–ca. 414), *Te Deum laudamus*, ELLC.
8. December 20, *The Roman Missal*.
9. The Roman Breviary, January 13. Translated by William G. Storey.
10. St. Patrick's *Lorica*, trans. Cecil Frances Alexander (1818–1895).
11. ELLC.
12. ELLC.
13. Translated by William G. Storey.
14. Paraphrase of Psalm 72 by James Montgomery (1771–1854).
15. TEV.
16. The Roman Breviary, July 1, first lesson of the third nocturn. Translated by William G. Storey.

17. Cecil Frances Alexander (1818–1895), *The Hymnal 1982 According to the Use of the Episcopal Church* (New York: Church Publishing Inc., 1985), #167, alt.
18. English Prymer, fifteenth century, translated by William G. Storey.
19. Thomas Kelly (1769–1855) *The Hymnal 1982 According to the Use of the Episcopal Church* (New York: Church Publishing Inc., 1985), #483.
20. *Sub tuum praesidium*, late second century, in *A Book Of Prayers* (Washington, DC: ICEL, 1982), 35.
21. *Regina coeli*, twelfth century, translated by William G. Storey.
22. St. John of Damascus (ca. 675–ca. 749), "Ode I" in *Passion and Resurrection*, trans. Monks of New Skete (Cambridge, NY: New Skete, 1995), 227–228.
23. Other Gospel accounts for succeeding Sundays: Mark 16:9–20; Matthew 28:1–10, 16–20; Luke 24:1–12, 13–35, 36–53; John 20:1–10, 11–18, 19–31; 21:1–14.
24. St. Nicetas of Remesiana (ca. 335–ca. 414), *Te Deum laudamus*, ELLC.
25. Peter Abelard (1079–1142), *Advenit veritas, umbra praeteriit*, in Alan Gaunt, *The Hymn Texts of Alan Gaunt* (London: Stainer and Bell, 1991), #110, 138–39.
26. James Quinn, SJ, *Praise for All Seasons* (Pittsburgh: Selah, 1994), 18.
27. Latin, fifth century, translated by John Mason Neale (1851) and others.
28. *Regina coeli*, twelfth century, translated by William G. Storey.
29. Archbishop Stephen Langton of Canterbury (ca. 1150/55–1228) *Veni, sancte Spiritus*, trans. John Webster Grant (1919–2006), *The Hymn Book of the Anglican Church of Canada and the United Church of Canada* (Toronto: Cooper & Beatty, 1971), #248.
30. St. Nicetas of Remesiana (ca. 335–ca. 414), *Te Deum laudamus*, ELLC.
31. From the Byzantine Liturgy, translated by William G. Storey.

32. James Quinn, SJ, *Praise for All Seasons* (Pittsburgh: Selah, 1994), 22.
33. Stanbrook Abbey Hymnal © 1974 and 1995, Callow End, Worcester WR2 4TD.
34. *Veni, Creator Spiritus*, attributed to Rabanus Maurus (ca. 780–856), trans. John Webster Grant (1919–2006), in *Common Praise: Anglican Church of Canada* (Toronto: Anglican Book Centre, 1998), #638.
35. *Phos hilaron*, late second century, translated from the Greek by William G. Storey.
36. Richard F. Littledale (1833–1890).
37. James Quinn, SJ, *Praise for All Seasons*, (Pittsburgh: Selah, 1994), 71.
38. Sarum Prymer, 1524, translated by William G. Storey.
39. George Herbert (1593–1633).
40. *In paradisum*, in James Quinn, SJ, *Praise for All Seasons*, (Pittsburgh: Selah, 1994), 68.
41. William W. How (1823–1897), verses 1–3.
42. St. Nicetas of Remesiana (ca. 335–ca. 414), *Te Deum laudamus*, ELLC.
43. November 1, *The Roman Missal*.
44. William W. How (1823–1897), verses 4–7.
45. November 1, alternate Collect, *The Roman Missal*, 1973.
46. James Quinn, SJ, *Praise for All Seasons* (Pittsburgh: Selah, 1994), 93.
47. Stanbrook Abbey Hymnal © 1974 and 1995, Callow End, Worcester WR2 4TD.
48. *Phos hilaron*, late second century, translated from the Greek by William G. Storey.
49. *O salutaris hostia*, St. Thomas Aquinas, OP (1225–1274), in James Quinn, SJ, *Praise for All Seasons* (Pittsburgh: Selah, 1994), 73.
50. St. Nicetas of Remesiana (ca. 335–ca. 414), *Te Deum laudamus*, ELLC.
51. Corpus Christi, *The Roman Missal*.

52. James Quinn, SJ, *Praise for All Seasons* (Pittsburgh: Selah, 1994), 68.

53. Corpus Christi, alternate Collect, *The Roman Missal*, 1973.

54. *Failte rombat*, in James Quinn, SJ, *Praise for All Seasons* (Pittsburgh: Selah, 1994), 56.

55. Corpus Christi, *The Roman Missal*.

56. *Pange lingua gloriosi*, St. Thomas Aquinas, OP (1225–1274), in James Quinn, SJ, *Praise for All Seasons* (Pittsburgh: Selah, 1994), 59.

57. Corpus Christi, *The Roman Missal*.

58. *Tantum ergo sacramentum*, St. Thomas Aquinas, OP (1225–1274), in James Quinn, SJ, *Praise for All Seasons* (Pittsburgh: Selah, 1994), 73.

59. Stanbrook Abbey Hymnal © 1974 and 1995, Callow End, Worcester WR2 4TD.

60. Attributed to Thomas à Kempis (ca. 1380–1471), translated by John Mason Neale (1851).

61. Text adapted from Edward Caswall (1814–1878), from *Saevo dolorum turbine*, Roman Breviary (Bologna, 1827); this version © Panel of Monastic Musicians, Mount Saint Bernard Abbey, Coalville, Leicester LE67 5UL, UK.

62. John Rippon, *A Selection of Hymns* (Chillicothe: J. Hellings, 1815), #477, alt. by William G. Storey.

63. Peter Abelard (1079–1142), *Solus ad victimam procedis, Domine*, in Alan Gaunt, *The Hymn Texts of Alan Gaunt* (London: Stainer and Bell, 1991), #94, 121–22.

64. St. Augustine of Hippo Regius (354–430), *Sermons to the People*, #186, trans. William Griffin (New York: Image Books, 2002), 66.

65. *Quem terra, pontus sidera*, Venantius Fortunatus (ca. 530–609), trans. John Mason Neale (1818–1866), alt.

66. *Te Matrem laudamus*, adapted from several medieval manuscripts and translated by William G. Storey.

67. St. Augustine of Hippo Regius (354–430), *Sermons to the People*, #204, trans. William Griffin (New York: Image Books, 2002), 194.

68. *Alma Redemptoris Mater*, in James Quinn, SJ, *Praise for All Seasons* (Pittsburgh: Selah, 1994), 97.

69. January 1, *The Roman Missal*.

70. December 25, Mass at Dawn, *The Roman Missal*.

71. Julian of Norwich (1343–ca. 1423), *Showings*, chap. 10 (short text), trans. Edmund Colledge, OSA and James Walsh, SJ (New York: Paulist Press, 1978), 142.

72. James Quinn, SJ, *Praise for All Seasons* (Pittsburgh: Selah, 1994), 16.

73. Julian of Norwich (1343–ca. 1423), *Showings*, chap. 13 (short text), trans. Edmund Colledge, OSA and James Walsh, SJ (New York: Paulist Press, 1978), 146.

74. James Quinn, SJ, *Praise for All Seasons* (Pittsburgh: Selah, 1994), 18.

75. Common of the Blessed Virgin, IV. In Easter Time, *The Roman Missal*.

76. Pope John Paul II, *Rosarium Virginis Mariae*, (October 16, 2002), #23.

77. *Salve Regina*, eleventh century, in James Quinn, SJ, *Praise for All Seasons* (Pittsburgh: Selah, 1994), 96.

78. August 15, alternate Collect, The Mass during the Day, *The Roman Missal*, 1973.

79. *Pange lingua gloriosi*, St. Thomas Aquinas, OP (1225–1274), in James Quinn, SJ, *Praise for All Seasons* (Pittsburgh: Selah, 1994), 59.

80. St. Cyril of Jerusalem (ca. 315–386), *Mystagogical Catecheses*, Sermon 4, 1–2, 6, in Edward Yarnold, SJ, *The Awe-Inspiring Rites of Initiation*, (Collegeville, MN: Liturgical Press, 1994), 86–87.

81. This litany is a composite drawn from several nineteenth and twentieth century sources. The closing prayer is from Corpus Christi, *The Roman Missal*.

82. *Pange lingua gloriosi*, St. Thomas Aquinas, OP (1225–1274), in James Quinn, SJ, *Praise for All Seasons* (Pittsburgh: Selah, 1994), 59.

83. St. Ambrose of Milan (ca. 339–397), *Sermons on the Sacraments*, Sermon 4, 13–14, in Edward Yarnold, SJ,

    The Awe-Inspiring Rites of Initiation (Collegeville, MN: Liturgical Press, 1994), 132–33.

84. St. Thomas Aquinas, OP, *Verbum supernum*, in James Quinn, SJ, *Praise for All Seasons* (Pittsburgh: Selah, 1994), 59.

85. Translated by William G. Storey.

86. St. Thomas Aquinas, OP, *Sacris sollemnis*, in James Quinn, SJ, *Praise for All Seasons* (Pittsburgh: Selah, 1994), 60.

87. St. Cyril of Jerusalem, *Mystagogical Catecheses* 4, 9, in Edward Yarnold, SJ, *The Awe-Inspiring Rites of Initiation* (Collegeville, MN: Liturgical Press, 1994).

88. Reginald Heber (1783–1826), alt.

89. St. Cyril of Jerusalem, *Mystagogical Treatise*, Sermon 5, 21, in Edward Yarnold, SJ, *The Awe-Inspiring Rites of Initiation* (Collegeville, MN: Liturgical Press, 1994), 96.

90. St. Thomas Aquinas, OP, *Lauda Sion Salvatorem*, in James Quinn, SJ, *Praise for All Seasons* (Pittsburgh: Selah, 1994), 67.

91. St. John Chrysostom (ca. 347–407), *Baptismal Homily* 2, 27, in Edward Yarnold, SJ, *The Awe-Inspiring Rites of Initiation* (Collegeville, MN: Liturgical Press, 1994), 162–63.

92. James Quinn, SJ, *Praise for All Seasons* (Pittsburgh: Selah, 1994), 61.

93. Theodore of Mopsuestia (ca. 350–428), *Baptismal Homilies*, Homily 4, 15, in Edward Yarnold, SJ, *The Awe-Inspiring Rites of Initiation* (Collegeville, MN: Liturgical Press, 1994), 209.

94. Philippians 2:9–11

95. Anonymous, *Jesu, dulcis memoria*, twelfth century, translated by Edward Caswall, alt.

96. In its present form, this litany was approved by Pope Leo XIII (1810–1903); *A Book of Prayers* (Washington, DC: ICEL, 1982), 21–23.

97. George Every, et al., *The Time of the Spirit* (Crestwood, NY: St. Vladimir's Seminary Press, 1984), 155.

98. Julian of Norwich (1343–ca. 1423), *Showings*, chap. 3, trans. Edmund Colledge, OSA and James Walsh, SJ (New York: Paulist Press, 1978), 129–30.

99. Italian, eighteenth century, translated by Edward Caswall (1814–1878), alt., in *The Hymnal 1982*, #479.

100. Julian of Norwich, *Showings* chap. 12 (long text), trans. Edmund Colledge, OSA and James Walsh, SJ (New York: Paulist Press, 1978), 199–200.

101. Adapted from Edward Caswall (1814–1878), from *Saevo dolorum turbine*, Roman Breviary (Bologna, 1827).

102. This litany was approved for the universal Church by Pope John XXIII on February 24, 1960; *Book of Prayers*, 26–27.

103. *Veni, Creator Spiritus*, attributed to Rabanus Maurus (ca. 780–856), trans. John Webster Grant (1919–2006), in *Common Praise: Anglican Church of Canada* (Toronto: Anglican Book Centre, 1998), #638. Used with permission of John Webster Grant.

104. Archbishop Stephen Langton of Canterbury (ca. 1150/55–1228) *Veni, sancte Spiritus*, trans. John Webster Grant (1919–2006), *The Hymn Book of the Anglican Church of Canada and the United Church of Canada* (Toronto: Anglican Book Centre, 1998), #248. Used with permission of John Webster Grant.

105. Written by William G. Storey.

106. Anonymous, fourteenth century, Middle English, translated by Dolores Warwick Frese, professor of English, University of Notre Dame. Used with permission.

107. Translated by William G. Storey.

108. Jacapone da Todi, OFM (ca. 1230–1306), *Stabat Mater dolorosa*. Translated by Edward Caswall (1814–1878).

109. Translated and expanded by William G. Storey.

Acknowledgments (continued)

The Litany of the Holy Name of Jesus and the Litany of the Precious Blood are taken from *A Book of Prayers* 1982, International Commission on English in the Liturgy Corporation (ICEL); six Collect prayers from the English translation of *The Roman Missal*, © 2010 by ICEL; three alternate Collect prayers from the English translation of *The Roman Missal* © 1973 by ICEL; and one prayer from the *Book of Mary*, ICEL. All rights reserved.

Three quotations from William Griffin, *Augustine of Hippo, Sermons to the People*. New York: Image Books, 2002.

Two hymns by Alan Gaunt from *The Hymn Texts of Alan Gaunt*. London: Stainer & Bell Ltd, 1991. Permission given by Hope Publ. Co., Carol Stream, IL.

Two translations from medieval Latin by Professor John Webster Grant: *Veni Creator Spiritus* and *Veni Sancte Spiritus*. With the permission of the author.

Six selections from Edward Yarnold, SJ, *The Awe-Inspiring Rites of Initiation*. Collegeville, MN: The Liturgical Press, 2nd edition, 1994.

Three hymns from the *Stanbrook Abbey Hymnal*, 1974 and 1979.

One passage from George Every et al., *The Time of the Spirit*. Crestwood, NY: St. Vladimir Seminary Press, 1984.

Ode 1 from *The Great Canon of St. John of Damascus in Passion and Resurrection*. Cambridge, NY: New Skete, 1995.

Two Hymns from *The Hymnal 1982*. New York: Church Publ. Inc., 1985.

One hymn from SCM-Canterbury Press Ltd., on behalf of the Panel of Monastic Musicians. Norwich England.

A translation of an anonymous fourteenth-century Middle English poet by Dolores Warwick Frese, Professor of English, The University of Notre Dame. Used by permission.

Three passages are taken from the *Directory on Popular Piety and the Liturgy.* Vatican City, December 2001.

Four excerpts from Julian of Norwich, *Showings*, from the Classics of Western Spirituality translated from the Middle English by Edmund Colledge, OSA and James Walsh, SJ © 1978. And an excerpt from *Catherine of Siena: The Dialogue*, from the Classics of Western Spirituality, translation and introduction by Suzanne Nofke, OP. Paulist Press Inc., New York/Mahwah, NJ. Used with permission. www.paulistpress.com

Prayers without other attribution can be considered to be composed or translated by the author.

About the Author

William G. Storey was professor emeritus of Liturgy and Church History at the University of Notre Dame. He compiled, edited, and authored some of the best-loved prayer books of our time, most notably *Lord, Hear Our Prayer*; *Hail Mary: A Marian Book of Hours*; *An Everyday Book of Hours*; *A Seasonal Book of Hours*; and *Mother of the Americas*.